BULLWINKEL

The true story of Vivian Bullwinkel, a young Army
Nursing Sister, who was the sole survivor of a
World War Two massacre by the Japanese

by

NORMAN G. MANNERS

HESPERIAN
PRESS

2000
HESPERIAN PRESS
P.O. BOX 317
VICTORIA PARK 6979
65 OATS STREET
CARLISLE 6101
WESTERN AUSTRALIA.

ISBN 0 85905 265 6

Revised memorial edition
October 2000.
© N.G. Manners 1999

Front Cover Portrait
The oil painting of Sister Vivian Bullwinkel is by Victorian artist Shirley Bourne, the original of which is displayed in the Australian War Memorial, Canberra.

Jacket Design & maps
Brett Manners

Hesperian books are available direct from the publisher. For a full catalogue of Hesperian books on Australiana, natural history, military history, exploration, Aboriginal ethnography, bush verse and gold prospecting, please forward a self-addressed, stamped business size envelope (220 x 110) to the above address.

All Hesperian books are printed on quality paper and will not discolour with age. They are section sewn in signatures, the pages will not drop out and the binding will not crack. This book is made to last.

To the nurses of this world who give

unstintingly in war and peace.

There is no nobler profession.

CONTENTS

ACKNOWLEDGEMENTS

My appreciation is extended to the staff of the National Archives, Singapore, who went out of their way to assist me in obtaining photographs taken during the period leading up to the fall of Singapore. Also to the local tour operators for helping me explore the various battle grounds and hospitals of the 8th Australian Division.

To Max Baker, long-time friend and former fellow officer, my gratitude for the hours spent proof-reading the manuscript.

The people named in this biography existed and the main events occurred as recorded. The author has taken some liberties with certain conversations.

They are however, in harmony with the times and events.

THE AUTHOR

With a background of commercial radio and television programming and production, Norman Manners also served in the Australian Army Reserve in both the Armoured Corps and Command Headquarters for some 16 years before retiring as a Captain.

He met Vivian Statham in 1977 and later accompanied her to Bangka Island, the scene of the massacre, and the battlefields of Singapore before writing this book.

A Western Australian, he lives in Perth.

MAPS

ILLUSTRATIONS

CAREFREE DAYS

Mr MacKinnon the Headmaster of the Broken Hill and Districts High School leaned forward in his chair.

"Wondering why you are here eh, Vivian?" said the Headmaster, "well I shan't keep you in suspense. Effective immediately you are appointed Captain of Burke House."

Vivian was dumbfounded as he went on to explain what a great honour it was, one they reserved for students with outstanding results in sport as she had in basketball and tennis, winning Blue for both.

Eventually she found her tongue and blurted out a "thank you Sir".

"And," Mister MacKinnon said "the coach of the Roman Catholic basketball team mentioned he was going to invite you to play with them this season."

Trembling with excitement, all she wanted to do was run from the room and tell her friends and parents of her good fortune.

The clanging school bell gave her the excuse and with a quick "Excuse me Sir" she hurried from the office with her heart thumping and head in a whirl.

Waiting outside the Headmaster's door in the corridor was Vivian's best friend, Zelda Treloar. After hearing the news Zelda squealed in delight and slipping her arm through that of Vivian's they headed off towards Argent Street and their homes.

Vivian burst through the front door to find her mother preparing the evening meal.

Elated, she related the story of being told to report to the headmaster and of the news that followed.

Eva was genuinely thrilled for her daughter for it reflected the esteem in which the school held her. The appointment as House Captain was a reward for the effort she had put into her studies as well as her dedication to sport. However, this other thing about the basketball offer could present a problem as far as her husband was concerned.

Vivian was quick to pick up her mother's change of mood. When she asked what was wrong there was a vague reply to the effect ' there was nothing wrong at all.'

Not to be dissuaded Vivian pressed for an answer, knowing it had something to do with the offer from the Catholic team.

"Your father will explain, my dear, when he comes home." was all Eva would say and despite Vivian's pleadings she made no further comment on the matter.

1

Bewildered and knowing the discussion was at an end Vivian went off to change out of her uniform and await the arrival of her father and the explanation she so badly wanted.

****

George Albert Bullwinkel was 53 years old.

He had arrived in New South Wales as an 18 year old seeking work as a book-keeper. He worked on Mutooroo station for 13 years before moving to Broken Hill as clerk/timekeeper with the De Bavay Amalgamated Zinc Company.

At the age of 35 he married Eva Kate Shegog, the daughter of a Senior Police Constable stationed at Kapunda, South Australia. There were two children by the marriage, Vivian and John William.

In 1923 the De Bavay mine was forced to close and many were thrown out of work, including George Bullwinkel. Well known and respected in local Masonic circles, George was quickly placed as a store's clerk at the South mine.

During this period a deep rift developed in the town between Protestants and Roman Catholics.

George, fiercely Masonic, had been installed as Vice-President and Director on the Board of the Broken Hill Masonic Club and also held office with the Ancient Order of Foresters. His sympathies were solidly Protestant.

Vivian waited for the usual greetings to be exchanged and for her father to settle into his favourite chair before approaching him with the news of her appointment.

Seeing the obvious joy and pride with which it was received encouraged her to immediately carry on and tell him of the offer she had received to play with the Catholic school team.

His reaction was quick and decisive.

"I am afraid that is impossible."

Although half expecting it, his rejection still came as a shock to her.

"But why, Father, what possible reason could there be for not allowing me to play for the districts top team?"

She watched him draw his pipe and tobacco pouch from his vest pocket and carefully begin to fill the bowl.

"Saint Joseph's is a Roman Catholic High School, Vivian, run by the Sisters of Mercy, we happen to be a Protestant family and the two do not mix."

Vivian had heard talk of the division but she thought it only applied to the adults.

"Are you are saying I cannot play basketball because they are Catholic?"

"That is what I am saying, Daughter."

"I can't believe you mean that."

"The fact is, Vivian, I am a senior office-holder in the Masonic Order in this town and there would be very serious ramifications for us should you associate with a Roman Catholic team."

Her father paused to place the pipe in his mouth and light it, expelling a thin plume of bluish smoke before continuing.

" Broken Hill is almost half Catholic and half Protestant. We do not mix with one another and we do not intermarry. They have their customs and we have ours. That's the way it has always been and will continue to be and you will not change it. Now, instead of filling your head with all this nonsense about basketball I suggest you start planning what you are going to do when you leave school…remember, there is a depression on and jobs are hard to get."

Vivian shot an appealing glance towards her mother and immediately saw there was no hope of support. She was alone in this.

With shoulders squared in defiance, Vivian gave her father a withering look and strode from the room.

On turning seventeen, Vivian graduated from school and slipped into holiday mode remaining at home and making a few casual inquiries of several local store owners as to the possibility of employment, without any luck.

Eva decided it was time to speak to Vivian about her future employment.

One afternoon, when they were alone, she raised the subject of the family's financial position.

Vivian was well aware of the need to contribute to the family income. The problem was she didn't know what she wanted to do except, perhaps, become a sports mistress at a school.

"Nursing is a very respectable, honourable and rewarding profession that offers security," counselled Eva, "it will stand you well for all of your life because it's essential to the good health of the nation."

Vivian was not completely convinced she would like nursing. It required her to be around sick people all the time rather than being on the sporting field.

In the end she promised her mother she would give the matter serious consideration and left it at that. By the time she had reached her bedroom door Vivian had put any thought of a nursing career out of her mind.

She did not know that her mother had already secured the papers for her application.

Then Vivian's friend Zelda, announced that she would be applying to become a probationary nurse in training at the hospital.

Although still not totally convinced nursing was for her, Vivian obtained the papers from her mother, filled them in and sent them off with Eva's words ringing in her ears. "You will make a wonderful nurse, my darling, you wait and see."

HOSPITALS AND MATRONS

In March 1934 Vivian, Zelda and five other local girls, enrolled as 'Probationer-in-Training' at the Broken Hill and Districts Hospital.

Vivian's first visit to the surgical ward was something of an ordeal.

Walking reluctantly down the central isle between the two facing rows of beds, she kept her eyes fixed straight ahead lest eye contact should prompt a question from one of the patients.

Nearing the end of the ward she began to breathe a little easier and was about to congratulate herself on surviving her first visit when a voice uttered that fateful word.

"Nurse."

" Oh no," she thought, "not me. Perhaps if I ignore the fellow and keep walking he would stop calling out?"

"Nurse."

Trapped! and not another nurse in sight. She would have to ask what he wanted. Slowly she turned to see a young man lying in bed with his hand raised and a look of appeal on his face.

Walking briskly to his bedside Vivian asked in the clipped tones adopted by the senior nurses, what he wanted, to be told he wanted a bottle.

"A bottle? A bottle of what?" she asked herself. "What would he want with a bottle?"

Confused by this unexpected request she asked the patient why he wanted such a thing and was told he simply wanted to use it.

Completely mystified she nodded at the now bewildered young man, turned and strode regally from the ward with the intention of reporting the matter to the Ward Sister.

There was a roar of laughter from the senior nurse when told of the patient's request and Vivian's confusion as to why he would want a bottle. Leading the way to the pan room the Ward Sister handed her a metal container and carefully explained how the utensil was used together with the method of disposal of the contents and washing and storage of the pan for future occasions.

Although red in the face and acutely embarrassed Vivian returned to the ward and handed the young man his bottle before retiring with great dignity.

Matron Hunter terrified the trainee nurses, giving no quarter to those who did not meet the high standards she set.

Matron assigned Vivian to the male surgical ward, instructing her to report to the Sister-in-Charge, Irene Drummond.

Sister Drummond was considered old by the young trainee's standards, having almost reached the age of twenty-eight.

Strict and never one to suffer fools lightly, Sister Drummond's professional competence commanded the respect of the medical and nursing staff of the hospital while the soft, motherly side to her nature endeared her to the young trainees.

Vivian, on meeting Sister Drummond, immediately warmed to the no-nonsense but charming woman and felt that it was an acceptance mutually shared. And so she settled down happily to master the day to day demands of the surgical ward under the watchful eye of her superior who ran it with determined efficiency.

The harsh programme of work and study left very little time for relaxation and only on the rarest of occasions was Vivian able to indulge in a set, or two, of her beloved tennis.

Night duty involved a stretch of 12 hours, with lectures during the day, study to be crammed in and at some point sleep, before reporting to the ward for another long, lonely night's vigil.

During these hours of darkness Vivian learned the basics of cooking by preparing snacks, such as fried, scrambled, poached or boiled eggs, for the night staff. Her fellow workers voted her attempts disastrous

****

It was a warm September night in 1934 and Vivian sat alone in the darkened ward.

Hearing footsteps she got out of her chair and went out into the corridor to see who it was and was confronted by the Senior Night Sister.

"Nurse, would you come with me?" she said in lowered tones and led her into a nearby vacant room.

Vivian thought it was strange for the Senior Sister to carry on so for she was normally very abrupt in her manner.

Switching on the light the senior turned to face Vivian. It was then she saw the sombre look on her face and a feeling of dread, of something terribly wrong, gripped her.

The Sister's words were calm and precise yet Vivian caught only a few.

"It's your father.....a massive heart attack... he was brought here only a little while ago.....Doctor Ramsay Smith did all he could.....he is gone, Vivian...I'm terribly sorry."

The numbness spread through her body leaving her strangely detached and tranquil, as if her mind was shielding her from the pain and grief she should be feeling.

From a long way off Vivian heard the Senior Sister telling her to go home to her mother and not to worry about the rest of her shift. Automatically she obeyed the voice and walked out of the hospital and into the hot night air.

George Bullwinkel was 55 when he died of a heart attack. The family, shattered by his loss both emotionally and financially, took stock of their position. Eva received a pay-out from the mine of eight hundred and seventy seven pounds and ten shillings, a sum that would not last long unless

5

supplemented by another income. It was now Vivian's responsibility to provide for the three of them.

Determined to support the family, Vivian threw herself into her studies with a new enthusiasm and following her graduation as a certificated nurse stayed on to complete a twelve months course in midwifery.

The years were lean financially and life very hard at 'The Hill.' Eva, Vivian and John decided that it would be easier for the family to split up and follow their independent desires.

Eva chose to move to Sydney, John, elected to stay and Vivian, with her two girl friends Zelda Treloar and Connie Samson, sought nursing appointments in Hamilton, Victoria.

Kiaora was an exclusive private hospital which catered for the more well-to-do of the district. The three girls, now double certificated, had no problems in being appointed to the nursing staff.

The workload and life style was very different to that experienced at 'The Hill.' The hospital's exclusivity meant relatively few patients allowing the nursing staff time for tennis, the cinema and local dances.

While listening to the wireless Vivian, Zelda and Connie heard the Prime Minister, Robert Gordon Menzies, announce, on the 3rd of September, 1939, that a state of war existed between Great Britain and Nazi Germany and consequently Australia too was at war.

They agreed there was nothing they could do about service at this time and they would wait until the government called for volunteers from amongst the nursing profession, for the armed forces.

****

The following year Vivian, Zelda and Connie moved to Guildford Private Hospital in Camberwell, outside Melbourne.

The hours, coupled with a restrictive social life, became irksome for Vivian and Connie and they joined the staff of Jessie McPherson Private Wing at Queen Victoria Hospital, central Melbourne and were welcomed by Senior Sister Olive Paschke.

Melbourne, with its nightlife of cabarets, picture theatres, stage shows, nightclubs and dances, captivated Vivian. In her time off she enjoyed visits to the museum, the art gallery, horse racing meetings, boating on the River Yarra and steam train excursions through the rolling, picturesque countryside of Gippsland.

Historic, majestic, with buildings that reflected the splendour of the Victorian era, Melbourne was the most thrilling city of them all for Vivian. Fulfilled and enjoying every moment of a new found life, the girl from Broken Hill decided this is what she wanted, this is where she would stay.

Part of her enthusiasm could also be attributed to the satisfaction she found in working in the Jessie McPherson Private Wing and Vivian believed she had, at last, found her niche.

During this settling in period the war in Europe took a back seat in Vivian's mind until Connie called her to a window overlooking the main street.

Below, young men, resplendent in the dark blue uniform of the Royal Australian Air Force, marched four abreast down the middle of the road, arms swinging, to a military band at the head of the column.

Many of the hospital staff crowded the windows and the verandahs to cheer.

Connie, her eyes sparkling with excitement, announced she wasn't going to wait any longer but would lodge her application to join the women's services the next day.

Vivian, watching the ranks of blue as they passed, knew Connie was right.

"There's a recruiting office in William Street," she heard herself say. "we can nip down there tomorrow."

A month dragged by with no word from the Army and in a fit of pique they decided to apply to the Air Force.

Weeks later the Air Force told them to report for medical examinations following which Connie was accepted and Vivian rejected, for flat feet.

****

1941 began with news of the capture of the Libyan town of Bardia by Australian and British troops. It also saw the departure of Connie for Laverton and of Senior Sister Olive Paschke, together with a number of her colleagues, for active duty with the Australian Army Nursing Service.

Vivian was to wait a further 3 months before told by the Army to report to the Quarter Master's store at the Recruiting Depot for her initial issue.

The government allotted nursing sisters a clothing allowance of 20 Australian pounds for service within the country, paid upon entering camp, with a further 20 pounds for overseas duty, payable upon departure.

This meant enlisted members had to initially bear the cost of their uniforms.

Vivian calculated she was up for over 8 pounds what with 7 pounds 7 shillings for her uniform and great coat, 12 shillings and 11 pence for gloves and then there were stockings, blouse, tie and a hat.

Not having the funds she pleaded with the issuing officer to allow her to pay when she received the Army allowance. To her surprise he agreed.

Vivian Bullwinkel in 1922, aged seven taken in Kapunda, South Australia with her police Sub-Inspector grandfather William Lyle Shegog.
(V. Bullwinkel collection)

Vivian, left, with fellow trainee nurse Gwen McMahon,
at the Broken Hill & Districts Hospital
(V. Bullwinkel collection)

A social night at the Broken Hill & Districts Hospital, 1935.
Four student nurses, centre, wear uniforms from the past while those either end show the uniform of the day.
Vivian Bullwinkel is on the far right and Zelda Treloar is third from the left.
(V. Bullwinkel collection)

WAR NURSE

On the 15th of May 1941, Vivian took a phone call from the Army, instructing her to report at 1430 hours on the following Monday and to be prepared to board a train at 1900 hours for the Military Training Camp at Puckapunyal.

Puckapunyal was set amongst the rolling hills of countryside Victoria. A furnace in summer, the temperature could also drop to below zero in winter, bursting water pipes and freezing the ground. Accommodation had been hastily thrown up to cater for the thousands mobilised into the army.

The huts were wood-framed, timber-clad, topped with corrugated iron roofs. They held the heat in during summer and allowed the wind to whistle through cracks in the walls. Hundreds of these temporary structures, sited in disciplined rows, radiated out over the valley with large ablution blocks scattered amongst them.

At the epicentre of these lines of huts stood the separate mess halls for Other Ranks, Non- Commissioned Officers and the Officers, while standing slightly apart was the cinema, which also served as a conference hall and Church.

The contingent of nurses, which included Staff Nurse Vivian Bullwinkel, who held the nominal rank of Lieutenant, were hardly noticed amongst the larger formations that were arriving daily.

They were allocated barracks sub-divided into a series of twin rooms. Each unit contained two cyclone-wire beds, each with a palliasse stuffed with straw, two very thin blankets and a pillow and a dresser for clothes and personal items.

Ward duties and other aspects of training, they were informed, would commence the next day.

On her second night in Puckapunyal Vivian, penned a letter to her mother.

Dear Mum,

Well, here endeth my second night in camp. The first being spent on a very hard bed, really I never thought anything could be so hard having been used to them for the last seven years, as I thought, and the cold, well I'm sure I'm in the very centre of the South Pole, it couldn't be any colder. Our quarters are of wood and iron, not badly fitted out, nothing to growl about really – a bit cramped for room – am sharing it with a lass I have not seen yet. Then there is the mess room where we drink our tea and coffee after meals, a fairly large room with a heater in the centre.

Then there is the dinning room attached to that and there is no relaxation after meals you sit-up with cape and veil all complete.

My morning in the wards was of-course very different to what I have been used to, but it brought back training days at Broken Hill. I am in the medical ward at present. At 11.00am every morning there is an inspection when the Commanding Medical Officer, Matron and a couple of Sergeants do a round of the wards. He appears after much blowing of whistles on the Sergeants part and all the staff drops whatever they are doing and stand to attention.

As for the patients, they have been sitting up not daring to move for at least fifteen minutes for fear of wrinkling their quilts. And now I am on night duty and in the same ward fortunately there is another lass on with me who is specialling a sick man – how long I am on for I have no idea. 'Mine not to reason why'

I think I will like it very much when I get used to the red tape and routine of the place.

There are about twenty five girls here and they all appear very nice and one of them I knew at Jessie Mac's – it was not the girl who was told to equip with me and she was furious that I was called up before her. It's so nice to be out in the wide open spaces and to see a few green trees – it's so nice and fresh – will probably put on weight and then my suit and uniforms wont fit which will be a pity because they look quite nice. The girls gave me a dinner and then went to a show last Friday night and we had quite a nice time—then the staff of Jessie Mac's gave me the loveliest writing case from which I am writing now. It really is the loveliest thing and I'm very thrilled with it.

Well, I must stop now and commence some work.

Lots of love.
Viv.

Four months were to pass before three Staff Nurses received their postings in the Middle East and on their departure five trainees marched in to Puckapunyal. During that same month all of the male orderlies moved out.

Ten staff nurses had their leave and time off entitlements cancelled. Several days after that they were allocated overseas service numbers and transferred to the Lady Dugan Hostel just outside central Melbourne.

Vivian was one of those ten and was allocated VX 61330.

****

The owners of the Lady Dugan Hostel had presented the building to the A.A.N.S. for the duration of the war. It was a beautiful piece of early colonial architecture with timbered balconies and rustic stonework, surrounded by manicured lawns and picturesque garden beds.

The numerous bedrooms were decorated in pastel shades with matching drapes and table lamps. The lounge boasted a baby grand piano and period furniture from the early days of the settlement. Around its papered walls were hung magnificently-framed paintings depicting early Australian scenes.

In this delightful environment 56 Staff Nurses had been assembled before embarkation for overseas. Rumours were rife, with the majority confident they were going to the Middle East. A few, however, suspected it could be the Far East where Australia had recently stationed several battalions in Malaya and Singapore.

EMBARKATION

On the day Vivian arrived at the Lady Dugan Hostel, elements of the newly raised 2/13th Australian General Hospital, camped at Caulfield Race Course, were preparing to load supplies and equipment aboard a hospital ship berthed at Station Pier.

This was disrupted when the wharf-labourers decided to strike. Major A.R.Home, the Officer Commanding, sent 8 men, under Sergeant Ogburn and Corporal Arthurson, to organise the loading.

The established strength of the 2/13th, at the time, was 18 Officers, a Chaplain, 44 Staff Nurses, 3 masseuses, 20 Warrant Officers and Sergeants and 126 Other Ranks. This gave the unit the capability to run a hospital of 600 beds.

Their quarters at Caulfield were far from comfortable. Straw-filled palliasses were placed on the floor of the smelly and very draughty horse stalls and apart from the regulation two-blanket issue they had only their great-coats to ward off the chill of the night.

They slept fitfully until dawn when Regimental Sergeant Major Sesom Gabb's bellowed invitation to join him in a brisk walk could not be refused or ignored.

With stiff joints protesting every movement they would fall-in to be marched off through the main gate and into the streets of Caulfield accompanied by the forceful voice of the R.S.M berating them with references to their slovenly marching.

With the loading of the ship completed by the unit they awaited the arrival of the remaining Staff Nurses in the warmth and comfort of their sea cabins.

It was still dark when the young women at the Lady Dugan Hostel rose and assembled in the main room, their chattering dying when Matron entered.

She told them to be ready for transportation to the dock at 0900 hours. Their ultimate destination was unknown.

Debussing, the new arrivals gaped at the ship berthed alongside the wharf.

She was His Majesty's Hospital Ship *Wanganella* of 9,500 tons.

The women slung the heavy kit-bags over their shoulders and climbed the companionway in single file.

As Vivian stepped aboard she heard a voice greet her and saw it was Doctor Crabbe whom she had worked with at the Broken Hill Hospital.

Crabbe remarked that it was like 'old home week' for the Matron in Charge was Irene Drummond, another from 'The Hill.'

They were briefly addressed by the Matron in Chief A.A.N.S., Miss Fields, who concluded by wishing them 'Godspeed and good luck,'

Later that night *HMHS Wanganella* slipped out of Port Phillip Bay, passed silently through the heads at Queenscliff and headed out into Bass Straight where she came onto a course that would take her to Fremantle.

****

The first day was idyllic with bright sunshine and a flat sea. The unit's main activity was to become familiar with the orders of the day issued by the Second-in-Command, Major Crankshaw. For example, members were not permitted to throw message bottles overboard as they might give their position away to German raiders or U-Boats.

Perhaps the most unpopular order was that all ranks were restricted to one shower a day because of the shortage of water.

The good news was that bottled beer would be issued on the starboard side of the promenade deck from 1100 to 1130, 1600 to 1800 and 1900 to 2100 hours. The bad news was that N.C.O's and O.R's were restricted to one bottle per day.

Boat drill would be conducted daily at various times and lectures would be held in the Men's Mess from 0900 to 1400 hours.

On the fifth day the Captain altered course and took the ship to latitude forty degrees, south of the commercial shipping lanes where there was less likelihood of meeting a German U- Boat.

As they moved deeper into the Southern Ocean the weather began to deteriorate, the wind whipping up a big, rolling sea that sent great walls of water cascading over the ship's bow.

The pounding continued unabated and several lifeboats were damaged.

The heavy weather kept most of the passengers below decks, for another two days before the Captain altered course, bringing *Wanganella* onto a North-West heading and into calmer waters.

The brilliant white hospital ship, as it steamed into Gage Roads, Fremantle contrasted dramatically with that of two huge grey shapes lying at anchor.

Every Doctor, Staff Nurse and Orderly turned out to wonder at the towering hulls of the world's two great ocean liners, the *Queen Mary* and her sister ship *Queen Elizabeth,* their decks crowded with Australian soldiers.

The troops cheered and cooeed the nurses as *Wanganella* passed and the women, laughing and smiling at this enthusiastic reception, waved back until the distance between the ships increased and they entered the inner harbour.

As they slowly steamed up harbour they heard a new chorus of voices rolling across the water toward them. Lying alongside Victoria Quay was the long grey shape of a warship. Her main armament of eight-inch guns, mounted in stepped turrets, faced forward and aft while smaller calibre anti-aircraft guns bristled along her decks.

A County-Class cruiser, she flew the Australian ensign and her decks were crammed with cheering, waving, whistling, hooting Aussie sailors.

"It's the *Canberra,*" shouted a voice from aboard *Wanganella* and the men and women of the 2/13th A.G.H yelled back as loudly as their voices would permit. Their enthusiastic response was not only in appreciation of the reception given them by their fellow-countrymen but also for the pride they felt for the Senior Service.

The stay in Fremantle was brief. They only stopped to take on board the Western Australian contingent headed by Major Bruce Hunt, a distinguished veteran of the First World War who would show heroism again.

Also joining was Major Nairn, the Medical Registrar, Captain Finch, Sisters Bales and Bates, Staff Nurses Gertrude McManus, Minnie Hodgson, Iole Harper, Alma Beard, Sarah Baldwin-Wiseman and Privates Burke, Logan and Vickers-Bush.

The unit now totalled 216 all ranks, their full establishment, and on 9 September, 1941, *Wanganella* headed out into a glassy Indian Ocean.

The same day Major Home, the O.C., assembled the 2/13th and told them; "We're going to Singapore."

A loud moan of disappointment rippled through the assembled men and women.

Vivian could not understand why they were being sent to an area where there was no war when they must be desperately needed in the Middle East.

Major Home stressed, "You are needed in Singapore. We have a lot of very sick Australian soldiers there suffering from malaria and other tropical illnesses.

Already the 2/10th A.G.H. has set up a hospital in the town of Malacca, in southern Malaya and the 2/13th will take over Saint Patrick's Boys' School in Singapore.

Despite the fact there isn't a war going on in the Far East," Home said in closing, "we have a big job ahead of us and a duty to do, so let's do it well."

Disappointment faded as the unit concentrated on lectures, mainly with tropical medicine, boat-drills and lazing about until they reached the Equator.

On approaching 'the line' Vivian and the other members of the unit learned of the time- honoured tradition of initiating all those who had not crossed it before. This applied to the majority of the 2/13th and so the Sisters of the 21st, who were stationed on *Wanganella* and had therefore completed many crossings decided there would be a mass initiation.

Transforming themselves into denizens of the deep with the aid of mosquito netting, cotton wool and lobster shells, the Sisters of the 21st prepared an evil brew with which to coat their luckless victims before dunking them in the ship's swimming pool.

Onlookers and participants alike shared in the fun and Vivian, after a clean-up, joined Staff Sisters Mounsey and Lawson, both from the 21st, in their cabin, for a sherry. The party quickly grew in numbers eventually transferring to the Wardroom where the ship's officers were hosting a farewell function in their honour, for the next day they would dock in Singapore.

It was hot and sticky and the morning air was heavy with humidity as the *Wanganella* glided by small, jungle-grown islands to the inner harbour of Singapore. Sampans and junks scurried around, their crews sheltering from the already ferocious sun under large conical hats and umbrellas. A heavy, sweet aroma, a mixture of spices dominated by sandalwood, wafted on a faint breeze and for Vivian, standing transfixed at the ship's railing, it was cloying, dominating, and above all fascinating. It was the essence of Singapore and she loved it.

****

Major Home announced that Staff Nurses Brewer, Bridge, Bullwinkel, Clancy, Glover, Gunton, Harris, Kerr, Rayner and Tait were to be detached for duty with the 2/10th at Malacca. Transport for those people would not be ready until later that night.

The small group of women watched bleakly from the upper deck as the last of the trucks and ambulances drove off the wharf leaving them with several medicos and a skeleton ship's crew. Some of the nurses were crying while others looked forlornly at the point where the last vehicle had disappeared with their friends. Without exception they all felt abandoned and depressed. It was then they were approached by Doctor Manson.

Manson, who was looked upon by the nurses of the 2/13th as a fatherly figure, was a gentle man, always available to offer advice or assistance where it was needed.

He called the girls together, expressed his sympathy and concluded with the reminder. "Remember you are in the Army so you come under its discipline."

Finally he reminded them that they were Australian Army Nursing Sisters, and not emotional little schoolgirls.

Smiling at them as they brushed away their tears, Doctor Manson told them they would be laughing about the matter in a few days and would eventually return to the 2/13th.

Later that night the detached party of nurses left the ship by ambulance with orders to report to the Railway Transport Officer, Captain Abramovich, at the railway station.

The ride was short despite an air-raid drill which resulted in the lights of the city being extinguished slowing the ambulance considerably.

Arriving at the station they pushed their way through a mass of people to eventually locate the R.T.O.

Captain Abramovich, who appeared a little flustered by their lateness, nevertheless greeted them courteously and enquired if they were 'all present?' whereupon he was immediately assured by the girls that they were.

"But there are only eight of you and my documents say there should be ten." he said.

The perplexed nurses began to check each other.

"Gunton and Brewer" said a startled Vivian to the R.T.O.

Abramovich immediately signalled a Military Policeman and ordered him to take several men, retrace the route taken by the ambulance and to find the two missing women.

As the M.P.'s hurried off he stressed to the worried nurses the importance of remaining where they were and not to move away from the platform in the half-light of the Air Raid drill.

As he spoke the 'all clear' sounded and the station's lights came on. The R.T.O. hurried off to find a telephone while the Australian women settled down to await the outcome of the search.

The two missing staff nurses, Gunton and Brewer were eventually discovered, by the searching military police, sitting in the music room of *Wanganella* singing.

When asked to explain they said they were only following the orders they had been given which were to await the arrival of a Captain Abramovich.

As he hustled them aboard the waiting train Abramovich warned them about staying together. He also briefed them on the overnight journey to Lampin where they would be met with transport by the Australian 2/15th Field Artillery. Following breakfast at Lampin they would be taken on to Malacca.

Bidding them a good trip the Captain thankfully waved the train away.

With a loud venting of steam and a blast from its whistle, the engine pulled the long line of carriages out of the station, across the Causeway and into the jungle of Malaya.

****

It was four o'clock in the morning when they reached Lampin. Met by Captain O'Donnell of the 2/15th the tired but cheerful women were ushered to a group of utilities parked near the platform.

They grinned at each other when they saw that cane chairs had been placed in the back of each vehicle, obviously provided by the unit for their comfort, a gesture they thought very sweet.

Clambering over the tail-gates the party settled down for the short drive to the Regiment's lines where they were offered the facilities of the Commanding Officer's quarters to freshen up, before enjoying lashings of bacon and eggs washed down with tea in the Officer's Mess'.

During breakfast Captain O'Donnell related how, the previous day, he had called for volunteers to accompany him, at three in the morning, to pick up a party arriving from Singapore.

There were no takers. However, when he disclosed it was a party of Australian Army Nursing Sisters the Regiment volunteered to a man and the Mess had been raided for its chairs to ensure a comfortable journey for the girls.

After expressing their appreciation to the men of the Field Artillery the group re-boarded the utilities for the final leg of their journey.

When they came out of the Mess hut they saw that the chairs were still sitting in the back of the vehicles but with one modification. Lashed firmly to the side of each utility was a very large umbrella, which effectively shaded the seats offering its passengers protection from the fierce tropical sun. To the women, as they climbed once more over the tail-gates, it demonstrated the thoughtfulness of their fellow Australians.

In high spirits and seated in comfort the girls settled back to watch the jungle and the occasional village with its smiling, waving children slip by.

Eventually the tangle of greenery gave way to vast rubber-tree plantations.

Planted in orderly rows the trees went on endlessly, mile after mile, until the repetitious green blur, combining with the heat of the day had its effect and most of the girls dozed off.

The hospital at Malacca was a two-story structure located north of the city on a hill overlooking the Straits.

The Sumatran coast could be seen from the verandah and there were sweeping views of the busy waterway and the many freighters taking the shortest route from Singapore to the Andaman Sea and the Bay of Bengal.

The 2/10th A.G.H. had been in residence at the hospital for nine months and the staff had settled into an efficient work routine and organised leisure time.

They serviced the medical needs of a number of Australian infantry battalions stationed in the area, the principal enemy being malaria, followed by skin diseases, broken bones, sprains and all the minor injuries expected from a large number of troops.

Matron Paschke greeted the 10 nurses warmly, especially Vivian whom she remembered from the Jessie McPherson Wing, before sending them to bed to recover from their long journey, saying there would be plenty of time tomorrow for a familiarisation tour of the hospital.

The heat, accompanied by cloying humidity, was excessive in Malacca and it had a debilitating effect upon Vivian. She passed a comment about it to one of the 2/10th girls and was told that Malacca was renowned for being one of the hottest spots in the world and certainly the hottest on the Malayan peninsular.

Her informant was Betty Jeffrey, who also suggested it was time for her to meet the Sister in Charge, Nesta James, whom she described as a diminutive dynamo.

Sister James briefed Vivian on the facilities of the hospital, which was designed to accommodate 200 patients with the capability of expanding to 1,600 in an emergency.

Later in the day there was a tour of the wards and a meeting with the Deputy Assistant Director Medical Services Malaya, Lieutenant-Colonel J.G. Glyn-White.

Following a brief welcoming speech he urged the visiting nurses to explore Malacca and its historic buildings and to get to know the locals and their customs. He stressed the importance of learning about the types of disease and their treatment while at the hospital because they were expected to pass on that knowledge to their colleagues in the 2/13th on their return to Singapore.

Vivian was assigned to Ward C11, joining Sister Clarice Halligan whom she knew from Puckapunyal days.

Another Sister she met up with was Mary Marsden, who she had worked with during her time at Jessie Mac's.

Following a short stay in Ward C11 Vivian was moved to the blood bank, administered by Doctor Osborne, and began to learn about the extraction, storage and transfusion of whole blood.

She also learnt that Doctor Osborne would be responsible for the setting up of a similar bank at the 2/13th and would therefore be returning to Singapore with them. This necessitated Vivian learning everything as quickly as possible.

Her instructors were Sisters Flo Trotter from Queensland and Jenny Greer from New South Wales. Because of the urgency involved the two 2/10th nurses spent long hours teaching Vivian the technique and in a matter of weeks she was duly certified as being fully conversant with and capable of carrying out the procedure.

Pleased with Vivian's achievement, Matron Paschke assembled the girls from the 2/13th and in congratulating them on their work, told them they were ready and therefore would leave the following Monday to rejoin their unit.

Matron chatted with Vivian for some time, exchanging reminiscences of their days together at Jessie Mac's. Before wishing her good luck in the future Matron expressed a wish that their paths would cross again in Malaya. Vivian thanked her and with Matron's permission left to join the others.

On Monday the 5th of October 1941 Vivian and the other 2/13th girls set out from the hospital in motor transport headed for Lampin, to connect with their train.

Arriving eventually in Singapore following an uncomfortably hot and boring journey they were told their luggage had been inadvertently left in Lampin. Furious, they rounded on Sergeant Buck, the driver who had arrived late to pick them up with the excuse he had been caught in the 'five o'clock rickshaw rush' Buck was told in no uncertain terms that he had better, 'get them back pronto.'

The Sergeant took off promising to sort something out and returned within minutes to inform the Sisters that their luggage would be delivered to their rooms that very night.

Placated, they entered the ambulance for the short trip to East Coast Road, Katong and Saint Patrick's Boys' School where Matron Drummond was waiting to greet them.

****

Irene Drummond, born in Sydney, was educated in Adelaide and Broken Hill before deciding on a nursing career. Returning to Adelaide she commenced training at Miss Lawrence's Private Hospital. On graduating she completed an obstetrics course at the Queen Victoria Maternity Hospital, Adelaide, and accepted a position with the Angaston Hospital also in South Australia.

In 1933 Drummond decided to return to Broken Hill where she spent the next ten years at the District Hospital and in that time rose to the position of Acting Matron. Called up for service with the A.A.N.S. in January 1941 and posted to the 2/4th Casualty Clearing Station, she embarked aboard the *Queen Mary* in February bound for Singapore. A short term with the 2/4th C.C.S. at Kluang was followed by a promotion and a posting to the 2/13th A.G.H. Singapore as Matron.

Drummond found the return of her ten Sisters from Malacca most satisfying, for now the unit was complete. She was also pleased with the knowledge they had acquired during their attachment to the 2/10th and with an instruction to 'take some rest' she left them to their own devices.

The accommodation in the three-storey school could be described as 'comfortable' despite having to share.

Although the quarters and food were acceptable the rejoining nurses discovered Singapore could not be compared with their days at the 2/10th in Malacca. Not only did they have a heavier workload at St. Pat's; there was the inconvenience of constant Air-Raid and gas- attack drills which involved the shifting of patients and interrupted the daily routine.

Free time was restricted to alternate nights with leave commencing at 1400 hours and concluding at midnight. It was during these periods that Vivian and the others were invited to Dining-in Nights held in the Officers' Messes of various Australian units, including the 2/29th, who were waiting to move to new barracks, currently under construction, at Segamat in northern Johore.

Another popular venue with the Sisters was the renowned Singapore Club, which enrolled all Australian Officers as Honorary Members. It boasted all the finest leisure facilities including darts, billiards, cards, dancing to a live orchestra and the best in fine dining and wining.

Once the expatriates of Singapore discovered the 2/13th however, they opened up some of the city's most prestigious homes to the girls to enjoy a little bit of good old family life again.

Mrs. Dodd, the wife of a wealthy planter, offered to take eight nurses a day into her opulent home for tennis, swimming, or simply to relax on the terrace overlooking two levels of magnificent gardens and be served drinks by white-coated stewards.

Peg Hanson had an 'open house' for the 2/13th. Well-connected and appearing to know everyone in Singapore who was influential, she and her businessman husband Richard shared a deep knowledge and understanding of Malaya and its people, which Vivian found fascinating.

During one of Vivian's visits to the Hanson's home, in company with Sister Nancy Harris, Peg invited them to join both Richard and herself for dinner aboard a ship in the harbour.

The ship's engineer was an old friend and he had arranged the dinner. Peg said an extra two would not be inconvenient and the officers would bless her for gracing the table with two attractive young Australian nurses.

On the appointed night the three women, in formal evening wear, were escorted to their sampan by Richard Hanson and they set off to look for a ship anchored in middle harbour.

When she asked Richard the name of the ship he told her it was the *Vyner Brooke*.

Climbing the companion-way they were introduced by Richard to two of the ship's officers, Jimmy Miller, the Engineer and John Thomas, the Second Officer.

Apologising for the absence of both the Captain and First Officer, who were ashore on business, Miller and Thomas then led their guests to the ship's dining room.

Jimmy Miller, young, British and charming told them the *Vyner Brooke* was owned by the White Rajah, Sir Charles Vyner Brooke who, with his two sons, ruled Sarawak. The ship was an island trader.

It was getting late and approaching their midnight curfew at the hospital when Vivian and Nancy, accompanied by the Hansons, took their leave and climbed into their sampan for the trip back to the island.

****

In late October, 1941, it was announced the 2/4th C.C.S would move to a mental hospital in Tampoi, a suburb of Johore Bahru, just across the Causeway from Singapore.

The building had been virtually given to the Australian Government by His Majesty the Sultan of Johore, for a sum of twenty-five thousand pounds.

The only condition put by the Sultan was that the mental patients were to remain. However, they and their attendants could be moved to a separate wing away from the proposed military hospital. The Australian Headquarters' plan was to have the 2/4th C.C.S. convert the facilities to suit the 2/13th as an A.G.H., before moving further north to where the bulk of Australia's troops were located. This complemented the 2/4th's primary war time task which was to set up as close as possible to the fighting, without endangering the lives of the staff or their patients, to receive battle casualties as soon as possible after they had been wounded.

The Sister in Charge, Kathleen Kinsella, together with Staff Nurses Hilda Dorsch, Bessie Wilmott, Peggy Farmaner, Wilhelmina Raymont, Dorothy Gardam and Mavis Hannah, packed themselves and their equipment into a small convoy of trucks and ambulances and left for Tampoi.

Several weeks later Vivian was ordered, together with Maisie and four doctors, to move to Tampoi as the 2/13th's advance party. The 2/4th had reported there were 257 sick soldiers, mainly suffering from malaria, in the few wards they had opened and they were not coping.

The asylum at Tampoi was set in extensive grounds separated from the jungle by a twenty-foot high wall, with a single, very narrow gateway as its only entrance.

Several duckboard paths radiated from the main reinforced concrete building. Approximately eight feet wide, the pathways, fitted with overhead canopies and offering pedestrians some shelter from tropical downpours, wound their way through the estate passing a number of wood and atap roof structures.

These were wards capable of accommodating up to fifty patients and their dispersal, although inconvenient for the medical staff, was in fact perfect in times of war for they would not present enemy aircraft with one large target.

In a far corner of the grounds stood a large building and this they chose to accommodate the mental patients.

On the arrival of the advance party and the relief of the 2/4th C.C.S. Vivian was appointed Sister in Charge of Ward C-1 which held the malarial cases. She was appalled to find there were no sinks, running water or electricity in the ward.

The lack of facilities made their task extremely difficult and frustrating and was compounded by frequent rainstorms, which flattened the tents they were living in, soaking personal equipment and clothing.

With relief they welcomed the main body of the 2/13th on the twenty-third. Immediately the staff set about equipping wards and theatres, recruiting local labour for the construction of staff quarters and the installing of water taps, electricity and telephones. It was even better when work began on the unit's cookhouse.

A nearby unit of the Royal Australian Engineers sent a party to the hospital to breach the wall in several places so staff and patients could be quickly evacuated into the jungle should air raids occur.

Working 16-hour days, the medical staff, nursing Sisters and orderlies had the place ready to function as a General Hospital, with an 1,100 bed capability, by the 25th of November, which at the time was a record.

Leave was immediately granted to those who had formed the advance party and, grateful for the break, Vivian packed a small bag and arranged for a lift into Singapore with the intention of staying at Saint Pat's. Dropped at the front entrance Vivian found the hospital almost deserted with only a handful of medical staff and a few recuperating patients. Popping her bag into a vacant room she decided to catch a rickshaw into the centre of town and do some sightseeing.

Walking down the long ground floor corridor leading to the entrance she passed a young Australian Army Lieutenant walking in the opposite direction.

She nodded and smiled noting how intently he scrutinised her as they passed. She heard his footsteps stop then his voice.

"Sister Bullwinkel?"

She turned and saw a rugged, handsome face that was familiar to her. 'Where? When?' she asked herself and then he came to her rescue, no doubt after seeing the confused expression on her face.

"Jim Austin, we met in Puckapunyal." he said quickly.

It was then she remembered the dining-in-nights with his unit.

"Of-course," she bubbled, "you were with the 2/15th Field Artillery."

"That's right and still am." he said cheerfully and walked up to her.

"I didn't see you when we went through Lampin?"

"No, I wasn't there." he said without further explanation.

Vivian's trained eyes had been closely examining Austin while they spoke. She noted his face was drawn and pallid with dark circles under lustreless eyes and he was perspiring more than he should have been. 'Jim Austin,' she thought, 'has obviously been very ill and is now recuperating and no doubt that was the reason for him being at Saint Pat's.'

"Are you alright?" she asked.

"Yes quite, thank you, I picked up a bit of a bug in the jungle."

"And you're an out-patient here?"

"Yes," he said pausing and appeared to reflect on something before going on. "I did ask after you."

Vivian felt he sounded a little unsure of himself and rather hesitant, but then, 'that could be the fever.' she told herself.

"Look, I was wondering if you would like to go out to dinner?"

Now she knew why he had hesitated.

"If you feel up to it I would be delighted." she said with a short laugh.

"Right then," his voice was a little brighter now, " what about tonight, say the ANZAC Club at 1700 hours?"

"1700 it is." she said giving him a big smile.

"Right, well that's great, look I'm sorry but I had...er, better get moving."

He shook her hand, smiled and slowly walked back down the passageway.

Vivian looked at his receding back and thought. 'What a nice young man.' then heading for the door she forgot about the young officer as her excitement grew at the prospect of spending the day discovering Singapore.

Vivian met Jim Austin at the ANZAC Club that night and after a round of drinks they moved on to the Adelphi Hotel for dinner. Here they met several Officers and nurses including Sister Beryl Woodbridge of the 2/10th. The Australian officers were from the 2/30th who had recently moved to Jemaluang in central Malaya, astride the strategic crossroads of the North/South Coast and East/West Roads.

Following a round of drinks they decided to have dinner at the Airport Hotel, then the party called for taxis and headed for Raffles.

At the main entrance to the foyer Vivian noted two Military Policemen on either side of the door. Raffles was 'out of bounds' to all ranks except officers. Proceeding through the foyer the party entered the opulent ballroom. The floor was inlaid with squares of brown glass from which shafts of coloured light were reflected from floodlights in the ceiling. The windows were framed with richly-embroidered curtains and the over-all lighting was soft and luxuriant. At the far end of the huge room was a raised platform on which sat Dan Hopkins and six other dinner-suited musicians. They were playing Lily of Laguna and the dance-floor was filled with women dressed in flowing evening gowns. Their male partners wore uniforms representing nearly every service in the British Empire.

Vivian had a wonderful night and just before midnight Jim Austin dropped her off at the main entrance to St. Pat's.

Promising he would visit her at Tampoi as soon as it was possible the young Lieutenant said goodnight and told the driver to proceed.

On her return to Tampoi Vivian found a letter from her brother.

Before she left Australia John had phoned to say he had joined the airforce and was off to do his pilot training. Later he phoned her at Jessie Mac's with the news of his graduation and presentation of wings, after that there had been silence. Neither knew where the other was and with a pounding heart she tore open the envelope and looked at the return address at the top of the page. It was England.

Aus. No 407780
Sgt. Bullwinkel. J.W.
R.A.A.F.
c/o R.A.F. Records Office
Gloucester. England.
30/11/41

Dear Old Viv.

Greetings my sister and how in the world are you and where on the face of this universe are you? Somewhere hot so I was told, but there are lots of places that are hot. At times I wish I were there just to feel the old sun on me. As you can see I have realised one dream and landed myself plumb into England.

First of all, I have seen all our relations except Peggy who lives far away out of London. She has, as indeed the rest have, invited me to their place when on leave.

All the London people are quite broad-minded believe you me. Uncle Dudley, Captain Bullwinkel to you, said. 'Well my boy, you are quite welcome here at our place for as long as you like, but we are middle-aged and believe me I would go to London and have a good time.' Which advice I took as Tom was with me and as they all had small houses they couldn't put us both up.

Old Gran is a dear and wouldn't move from her house during the blitz. Her face is quite young and her brain is nimble. She is badly crippled with rheumatism though.

Had six days leave of which about four and a half were spent in London and did we have a good time. Met a couple of nurses and we took them everywhere we could and of course spent quite some cash but we certainly enjoyed spending it.

I have not received any mail from Australia as yet and I expect I won't get any until after the New Year so I don't know what's going on at home.

All the family hopes to see you over here before the end of this show. All enquired after you and wanted to know all about you.

By gosh the two nurses, who come from the country, are jolly nice girls. Just like the girls of Broken Hill District Hospital when you were there. They're so easy to get on with and speak to. They made our London stay quite enjoyable what with dances and dinners and luncheons.

By the way did you get my Christmas present? I should say you'd get it about February or March even though I posted it about October First in Canada. It was a pair of silk pyjamas and boy did we have fun buying them. Am afraid we had the poor shop assistant blushing most of the time.

Whilst in London we saw only a few of the historical and interesting places. We are leaving the rest for another time. Saw the Changing of the Guard at the Palace but without all the colour it was nothing to speak about. Glanced hastily through Westminster Abbey where we saw the last resting-places of the great. Being a gaping tourist we had to be able to say that we saw the Tower of London so dashed along there. Am afraid the ancient history of it left me cold. Madame Tassaud's interested us for about an hour one day. Some of the figures are exceptionally well done whilst others, particularly Mister Menzies, is very poor.

The actual damage done to London during the blitz is rather small when compared to the size of the city and the number of bombs that must have fallen. London is so huge that as Churchill said, 'It would take twenty years to raze the place by bombing.'

Saw a couple of stage shows the first was 'Black Vanities' with Flanagan and Allen of radio fame. This is really like a Sydney Tivoli show with the corresponding hot spots. The other one was a real good play, 'No Time for Comedy' with Rex Harrison and Diana Wynard. I saw the film version but consider the play much better. Have been separated from Tom (Worley, if you don't know) and miss him quite a lot. Was posted, on my return from London, to a training unit in Wales and have been flying Spitfire aircraft. Believe you me they're the goods. The country really appeals to me more than the cities and on my way here the country we passed through certainly came up to my expectations. The lovely green fields, gentle undulating hills and little streams lined with trees, with little hamlets tucked away in the hills, is truly gorgeous. I suppose you are in the middle of sand desert, or else in the middle of the jungle with all its accompanying discomfort. Cheer up kiddo and, believe you me, I sometimes wish I were there.

We are at present stationed miles from anywhere and in the middle of mud. Still our quarters are quite nice and the Mess jolly good. Plenty of food and beer so really when we get settled down properly we should be fairly comfortable. Since being in England I have put on half a stone so that shows just how much food shortage there is. There is practically none.

Our trip across the Atlantic was quite uneventful, didn't see a hostile craft the whole time.

Well old dear am afraid I'll have to leave off. Drop me a line at the address on this letter and it will be forwarded on to me some time.

All the very best.

Love John.

Vivian slowly folded John's letter and slipped it into the pocket of her uniform. At least, she assured herself, he was not on operations and was safe, well, as much as he could be learning to fly a Spitfire.

Only three nurses stood night duty, which meant each had to look after two wards. Vivian was allocated C 1 and C 2 with orderlies Ernie Ward and Jim Carmody to assist her.

Vivian found the patients were sleeping soundly.

Kicking off her shoes she put her feet up onto a chair and sighed. Aching feet was one aspect of the profession they all complained about.

Across the water the lights of Singapore blazed in the night.

The more she saw of the Lion City the more she was captivated by it and she became impatient for the week to end so she might spend another two days roaming its streets and making new discoveries.

Out of the corner of her eye she saw a brief flash of colour and she turned and looked down at the timbered floor.

In the gold light was the prettiest snake she had ever seen. Its glistening body was a rich royal blue, its tail and head a brilliant orange. The colours were so vivid they mesmerised her as it slowly slithered across the floor toward the light source.

'How beautiful.' she thought and began to rise with the thought of getting a broom to sweep it off the verandah and back into the jungle when the amah appeared.

The thick stick in her hand blurred as she brought it down across the reptile's back in one sharp, powerful blow. The short, thin body contorted into a mass of moving coils as the woman struck again before calmly sliding the stick under the serpentine body and flicked it into the night.

Vivian, who was no stranger to snakes for the bush around the 'Hill' held many, was upset that such a beautiful creature should be killed and said as much to the amah.

"That was the most deadliest of all the snakes in the Malayan jungle," replied the petite woman, "If you had been bitten by it you would have died even before Doctor Hunt could have got here from his quarters."

The thought of being so close to a sudden and terrifying death brought Vivian back to reality and she thanked her for what she had done. The little woman simply bowed and said she would now bring the tea.

When it arrived shortly after Vivian noticed the slight shaking of her hand as she raised the pot.

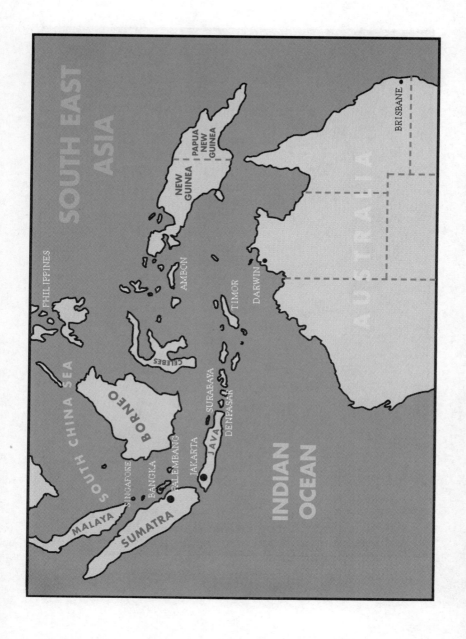

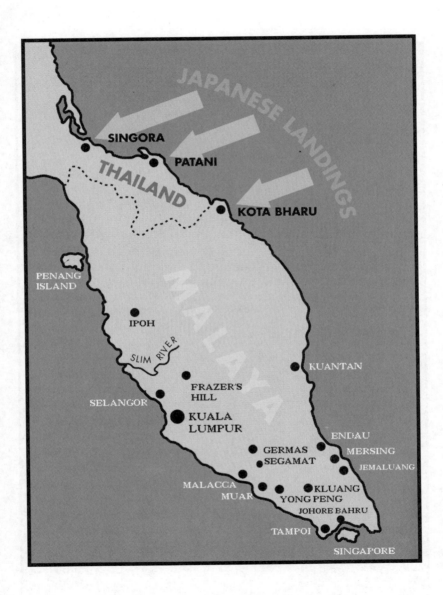

WAR IN THE FAR EAST

The distant voices grew louder and Vivian struggled to throw off the effects of sleep.

There were feet running, people shouting, an explosion of some sort. It was 3.17 a.m.

The explosions were coming frequently as she joined the rush to the opposite side of the hospital which overlooked the strait and Singapore.

Spotting Blanche Hempstead and Valerie Smith standing at the railing she pushed her way through the excited crowd of hospital workers to join them.

"What's going on?" she asked.

"They're bombing bloody Singapore." answered Blanche calmly.

"Who is?"

"I think it's the Japs, see the red dots on the planes?" said Val pointing to the sky above the island.

Following the direction in which she was indicating Vivian could see searchlight beams panning the full-moon sky. Some held in their incandescent shafts the silver bodies of aircraft around which were blossoming puffs of smoke from bursting anti-aircraft shells.

Lines of red tracer rose from the island and curved skyward toward the planes.

The bombs sent palls of black smoke billowing from the giant godowns along the docks, fuelled by countless tons of stored rubber.

The headline on the front page of Singapore's *Morning Tribune* on the 8th of December said it succinctly.

MALAYA AT WAR

The following is a communique from the Headquarters of the Far Eastern Command.

At 1.30 a.m on Monday morning some five merchant ships, escorted by warships, approached the mouth of the river north of Kota Baharu and landings from them began to be carried out, which were supported by covering fire from war vessels.

Fire was at once opened by our troops and later severe fighting developed on the shore, particularly in the neighbourhood of the Kota Baharu aerodrome. In this confused and difficult fighting some famous Indian units are reported to have distinguished themselves.

Later ten more merchant vessels were located some ten miles farther south. Bombers of the Royal Air Force carried out moonlight attacks on the vessels off-shore and by daylight at least two large enemy ships had been hit and set on fire.

At daybreak several bomber and torpedo bomber squadrons took off to continue the attack, the results of which are not yet known.

So far three of our aircraft have not yet returned from these operations. By eight o'clock in the morning all the remaining enemy ships appear to be retiring northwards, leaving some landing craft and troops ashore who are being mopped up by our land forces.

Air raids were carried out by Japanese aircraft as follows:

At about 3.15 a.m. a formation of Japanese aircraft attacked targets in the Singapore area, but no damage was done to military installations. Some damage to property and casualties are reported from bombs which were dropped on Singapore Town.

Daylight attacks were made against aerodromes in northern Malaya but reports so far indicate that little damage was done.

Vivian folded the paper and shaking her head, put it down, for she knew the report had played down the real situation having heard the truth from locals employed at the hospital. Evidently Raffles Square, the hub of the shopping district, had sustained some damage with an Indian stationery store levelled. Robinson & Company, the diamond merchants, had received a direct hit as had Guthrie's Building in Battery Road. She had been told that some 60 people had been killed and possibly 133 injured.

Matron Drummond confirmed they were at war with Japan and 103 of their patients were to be evacuated to the 2/10th in Malacca, with a further 67 to go to the Base Convalescence Depot.

This, Matron said, would let them increase their bed capacity at Tampoi to 1,200 in anticipation of the casualties to be expected once Australian troops were committed to the fighting in the north. Nursing staff were to wear steel helmets at all times, slit trenches would be dug outside each ward and the hospital would observe a nightly brown-out.

****

In the days that followed the hospital staff worked around the clock to ready and open new wards. Doctors, Staff Nurses and Orderlies worked side by side ripping iron bars from windows, erecting mosquito netting above beds and humping heavy equipment from distant storerooms. Operating theatres had to be fitted out, resuscitation and surgical wards equipped and literally tons of instruments, drugs, bedding, crockery and cutlery received, sorted and placed in position.

Their efforts were interrupted frequently by air raid sirens which would send them on the run to the patient wards to help the sick into the slit trenches. Those too ill to be moved were placed under beds and provided with steel helmets. Only then would the staff take cover.

They listened intently, when time permitted, to the daily wireless communiqués from Far East Command.

"It is as yet too early to forecast what the Japanese main plan is...." the announcer's voice was controlled and solemn. ".... but there are indications that following the collapse of resistance in Thailand and the heavy scale enemy air effort from bases in Indo China he is prepared to engage considerable forces in an endeavour to gain control of north Malaya.

This move was foreseen to be a likely one, and the dispositions of our forces before the outbreak of war was designed to meet it.

The Japanese engaged a considerable number of aircraft in their endeavour to obtain a measure of air superiority so as to cover their landing in southern Thailand and continue their efforts to gain control of Kota Baharu.

Air reconnaissance on Monday established that twenty-five further transports were proceeding down the coast of Thailand escorted by war ships, apparently preparing to land additional troops in the Singora and Kota Baharu areas. So far there is no information as regards further support for these forces, and the condition on the ground in the Singora area is such that advances, if attempted, will probably have to be restricted to the few roads available. Air raid warnings which have sounded in Kuala Lumpur and Singapore frequently in the last twenty-four hours are the result of reconnaissance planes slipping through.

No reports have been received of any bombs being dropped since early on Monday morning.

The following communiqué has just been released by Far East Command.

In Kedah our troops are in contact with the enemy near the Thai frontier where local patrol encounters took place. In the Kuantan area troops still hold the original frontier."

Despite her weariness Vivian forced herself to take time to write to her mother.

VX 61330
2/13th A.G.H.
A.I.F. Malaya.
11-12-41

Dear Mum,

As the boys say we are no longer the Militia of Malaya but the AIF.

They are all terribly excited and you have no idea how hard it is to keep them in hospital.

We have been confined to barracks now for a fortnight and naturally all looking forward to a change in scenery which, at the moment, does not appear to be in sight and of course our tin hats and respirators are our constant companions. We are now living in brown-outs of a night time which does not encourage late hours and believe it or not yours truly has been in bed by 9.30p.m. for the last week which is truly amazing and I find myself more tired than ever.

I don't think any of us will ever forget the last air raid, we were all woken by the anti aircraft guns and so congregated outside making up our minds whether it was the real thing or just a practice. Then we saw the planes approaching and they flew over us in the searchlights and all remarked what a pretty sight it was. Nothing else to see so all retired once again and some twenty minutes later heard the all clear signal and it wasn't until 10 a.m. next morning when we were about to have another air raid that we realised we were at war. So all that day we played at air raids which really was a jolly nuisance as we had to drag our verandah patients inside and put tin hats on our sick boys who muttered 'A fellow would be ill when the fun starts.'

I don't suppose it's much use telling you not to worry but really we are quite safe and all as happy as sandbugs. We are opening up new wards in anticipation and in our off-time duty we have all been madly working in an effort to equip a mobile theatre as soon as possible.

The quarters are just a hive of industry. This morning we had a spot of bad luck—the autoclave in the theatre blew up sending it right through the roof, scattering bricks everywhere and flames flying. I think everyone thought the Japs had arrived. Unfortunately one of our boys was badly burnt about the face and arms.

When you send the next parcel would you include that floral linen frock of mine - that is if it is not in use – the pink and blue flowers in rows – if I remember rightly – we are allowed to wear them about the quarters and as we are in a brown-out we don't have to dress for dinner, so if you wouldn't mind?

Jim Austin is much better and I was seeing quite a bit of him before all the leave was stopped and as his camp is only a couple of miles away, notes arrive periodically per ambulance driver. He expects to join one of the artillery units at a moments notice.

Well I must away and do a spot of sewing. Matron Drummond wishes to be remembered to you. Lots of love.

Viv.

P.S. The boy that was burnt yesterday died this morning and the entire unit is very upset.

Placing the letter in an envelope Vivian felt pleased that she had kept the news light and bright for the last thing she wanted was to set her mother worrying. The less she knew about the bombing and the Jap landings up north, the better.

Footsore and heavy-eyed she climbed into bed and instantly fell asleep.

The next morning the hospital was stunned by the news that Japanese planes, had sunk the battleship *HMS Prince of Wales* and the battlecruiser *Repulse*, sent by Prime Minister Winston Churchill to ensure the safety of Singapore.

Caught without air cover off Kuantan, in the Gulf Of Thailand, the two capital ships went down with the loss of over 800 men.

The news of the fighting in the north was sketchy with broadcasts reporting battles at Grik and Kelantan and the enemy taking heavy casualties.

The hospital staff at Tampoi could only prepare and be ready to receive wounded.

The atmosphere at Tampoi remained optimistic during December despite the news of the 11th Indian Division's withdrawal from Jitra following the annihilation of the Dogra Battalion at Kota Bharu. Enemy fighter planes strafed the streets of Ipoh, which was well down the Malay peninsular, and there were reports of a major retreat by the British and Malay forces.

Determined not to be dejected by the news they went ahead with the ward dinners inviting Major-General Bennett, Colonel Glyn-White and the officers of nearby units to join them for an 'at home' in their mess on Christmas night.

It was at this time Vivian was told by Sister Hurley, the Sister in Charge, she was to be re-assigned to Major Bruce Hunt's ward.

Her patients were mostly malaria cases and so she quickly slipped into the routine, which carried her over the Christmas period. During the lead-up to New Year Jim Austin came to see her.

Looking wonderfully healthy, so different from the person she had previously seen in Singapore, he smiled broadly as she stepped out onto the verandah.

There was a light-hearted exchange of greetings before Jim told her his regiment was on standby and would shortly move north.

Although saddened by the news, Vivian knew it was inevitable that the Australians would have to face the Japanese and when that happened they would start receiving wounded at Tampoi. She had thought about this a lot lately and wondered how she was going to react to the devastating wounds she no doubt would be exposed to very soon.

'What a heart-wrenching thing war is.' she thought. 'you are always saying goodbye to people sometimes, unknowing, for the last time.'

Looking at Jim Vivian wondered if this could be one of those occasions.

"Where are you off to?" she asked.

"I can't tell you." said Jim before going on to explain the situation.

It would appear the whole front was fluid with the Japanese outflanking and surrounding units, cutting them off, then systematically destroying them.

He had also heard British and Indian troops comment about the fact that the Japs were not taking prisoners. Claims that they wore glasses and couldn't see in the dark were, they said, a whole load of codswallop.

As far as the British front-line troops were concerned the Jap was a highly-skilled jungle fighter who was very adept at night infiltration.

Jim said Major-General Gordon Bennett had been given a line across Malaya to hold and was going to commit the Australians to a part of that line, despite their lack of jungle warfare training.

Having told her everything he could Jim fell silent and for a moment they both reflected on what had been said. Eventually it was up to Vivian to spark off a new conversation so she asked if she could write to him now and then.

He said he was agreeable but not hopeful they would be delivered.

"Well at least we can have a drink now." she said laughing and led him off to the Mess.

Several hours later they said goodbye to one another and Vivian watched as Jim Austin stepped from the porch and disappeared down the path.

The relentless advance by the Japanese was brought home to the 2/13th A.G.H. on New Year's Day when a truck arrived with 20 nurses from the 2/10th.

They said they were the advance party and that the 2/10th had received orders to evacuate Malacca and set up an A.G.H. at Oldham Hall, a former boy's school, on the island of Singapore.

They spoke of a Japanese woman, who broadcast regularly to the British forces in Malaya, saying she was very colourful but barbed with her words so the troops had nicknamed her 'Tokyo Rose.'

It was amazing, they said, what she knew even calling the 2/10th by name and advising them to be out of Malacca within 24 hours in which case they would not bomb the hospital.

They also brought word that the Japanese were at the Slim River, a scant ten miles from Frazer's Hill. Spear-heading the advance were the Imperial Guards, the troops who had over- run the Garrison at Hong Kong where, if rumours were correct, they had gone on a drunken killing and raping spree.

In preparation for the move south the 2/10th A.G.H. sent 76 patients to the 2/13th before moving 800 tons of equipment.

Oldham Hall, off Orchard Road, had been abandoned and was a depressing sight.

Torn textbooks were scattered throughout the rooms and broken furniture littered the grounds and the interior of the building, showing the work of looters.

After completing their tour of inspection many of the Sisters doubted that the mess could be converted into a hospital.

Matron Paschke quickly created a clean, operative 200-bed hospital and within a few days began to accept patients. Surgical instruments were boiled in billies on portable spirit stoves.

Quickly running out of space the unit requisitioned a number of bungalows surrounding the hospital and these were set aside for the specific use of the staff. The entire operation was a tribute to the energy and dedication of the 2/10th and their Matron.

On the 14th of January news reached Tampoi that the Australians had been committed to the fighting and the 2/30th Battalion had set up an ambush at Gemencheh, not far from Segamat.

From reports received the Australians caught the Japanese coming down the road and inflicted heavy casualties upon the enemy. However, it was not without cost to the Battalion. The attached Field Ambulance Unit quickly treated the wounded under fire before passing them to the Casualty Clearing Station who stabilised each man, then sent them on to the A.G.H. at Tampoi.

Warned of the situation, the 2/13th awaited their arrival.

Doctor Bruce Hunt gave instructions to dispense with normal routine and simply record the casualties' names and numbers as they arrived. This would let him get to the wounded more quickly. Once in the ward, Hunt emphasised, the staff must get them cleaned up, into bed, fed and bedded down for the night adding that, "They most probably have not slept in days."

Several hours passed before the ambulances began arriving in the early afternoon.

Springing into action the orderlies ran to the back of the mud-caked vehicles and gently slid the stretchers, with their battle wounded, out of the ambulances and carried them briskly to the Admission Building.

Here they lowered the stretchers to the floor before returning for more as another string of ambulances arrived.

Working frantically yet methodically the Nursing Sisters removed mud and gore-soaked bandages from the young men as Doctor Hunt moved swiftly from one soldier to the next, assessing the wounds of each man carefully before giving his instructions to waiting orderlies.

In the wards, jungle-fouled uniforms were cut swiftly but tenderly from mud-caked bodies by the Staff Nurses before each soldier was sponged, dressed in clean pyjamas and helped into a bed made up with crisp white sheets.

Finally they were hand-fed before lights out.

The flow of casualties continued throughout the early evening and the rows of wounded lying on the Admission Room floor began to mount up. Yet there was no crying out or even a moan as the badly wounded young men waited patiently, controlling their pain, knowing that their fellow Australians were going as fast as they dared and would be with them soon.

In the operating theatre doctors spared themselves only a moment to straighten painful backs before returning to their work while in the wards the Sisters, ignoring their exhaustion, carried on with grim determination.

Their energy source was Matron Drummond who, with rock like dependability, continued to do the rounds of the hospital encouraging, helping, giving advice and talking to patients.

Her leadership shone with an incandescence that touched them all and they looked, with pride, upon this short, chubby cheeked woman from Ashfield, Sydney.

By the earlier hours of the next morning the tide of incoming wounded dwindled to a trickle then stopped. Bruce Hunt, thoroughly exhausted, as were the others, spoke briefly to his staff thanking them for what he called "A magnificent effort that had saved the lives of many fellow Australians." He urged those who were not on duty to: "Get some sleep for the happenings of this day could well be frequently repeated in the days to come."

As they dispersed, some to sleep, some to continue to watch over their patients, word came that Kuala Lumpur had fallen.

Australian wounded continued to flow into the A.G.H. at Tampoi together with a growing number of typhus cases. The medical staff had little knowledge of this deadly disease, which had similar symptoms to that of cerebral malaria. The patient would suffer periods of deep coma alternating with bouts of uncontrollable raving and the only treatment that could be prescribed was intense nursing care.

Each day the Sisters listened to their patients tell grisly stories of fast-advancing Japanese troops refusing to take prisoners. Instead they either shot or bayoneted them to death.

One eye-witness told of some fifty wounded soldiers who were doused in petrol then set alight and left to burn. He had to live with their screams as well as his own wounds.

Many of the wounded at Tampoi were from the 2/29th Infantry Battalion, a Victorian unit, the 2/15th Field Regiment (Artillery) and the 4th Anti-Tank Regiment. These units had set up defensive positions on the Muar Road approximately one and a half miles north of Bakri on the Malay Peninsula. Their orders, from Major-General Gordon Bennett, were to hold for no less than seven days, regardless of cost, so that the entire British force north of Yong Peng could withdraw to the south. They held for longer than required and inflicted heavy casualties on the enemy.

During this battle of the Muar Road the 2/29th lost their revered Commanding Officer, Lieutenant-Colonel J. C. Robertson. The Regimental Medical Officer, Captain Vic Brand, distinguished himself by continuing with his treatment of the wounded even with hand-to- hand fighting around his small makeshift aid post.

Eventually the 2/29th and attached units had to retreat south and it was at this time Nancy Harris heard Tokyo Rose mention the 2/13th during one of her broadcasts.

Tokyo Rose sent a cheerio to the 2/13th Australian General Hospital at Tampoi, with a message to "Evacuate their patients before the 26th of January as the buildings and facilities would be needed by the victorious Imperial Japanese Army." She stressed, " it was imperative they did this before the 26th."

Independently of Tokyo Rose, the Commanding Officer of the unit, Lieutenant-Colonel Pigdon, decided to transfer 200 patients to the 2/10th on Singapore island, otherwise very soon they would run out of beds.

He took the problem to a meeting with the Commanding Officer of the 2/10th A.G.H., Lieutenant-Colonel Douglas White, and their chief, Colonel Glyn-White the Deputy Assistant Director Medical Services. It was soon decided that the 2/13th would move to Singapore and would relocate to Saint Patrick's Boys' School in three days.

The move to Singapore began on the 23rd of January with 40 patients and 31 staff being transported to Oldham Hall and the 2/10th with a further 198 patients going to No 2 Convalescence Depot. Later in the day a further 108 staff transferred to Oldham Hall as a fleet of trucks ferried eleven hundred hospital beds and hundreds of tons of equipment to Saint Patrick's Boys' School.

In the midst of moving, a group of medical reinforcements arrived from Australia. Led by Major Eddey they included Staff Nurses Forsyth, Gordon and Mulvihill, plus 29 men. Given a warm welcome by the exhausted staff the new arrivals stowed their gear then pitched in and helped effect the move to Singapore.

On the 25th Vivian was told to take the next ambulance leaving for Saint Pat's.

Reporting to Sister Hurley she was directed to a stately residence, several houses down from the hospital, which had been given to them by an Englishman for staff accommodation.

Dumping her baggage in a corner she climbed into a bed, as previously instructed by Sister Hurley and slept the sleep of the exhausted, not stirring at the sound of a siren and the explosions that followed.

The continuing influx of battle casualties to St. Pat's forced the hospital to expand to 700 beds and when that was taken up the wounded were accommodated in the chapel and surrounding houses. The chapel, with Sister Jenny Ashton in charge and Vivian as her assistant, was filled in one morning.

One casualty, a young lad, had taken a burst of fire from a Jap machine-gun and was severely wounded in the chest.

As they lifted him onto the operating table he asked the surgeon if he could have a smoke.

The doctor finally relented believing there was little hope of the boy surviving. Given a cigarette the young soldier inhaled deeply and an astounded theatre staff watched, mesmerised, as several wisps of smoke curled upwards from the bullet holes in his chest.

As the majority of incoming casualties required surgery the operating theatre was in use twenty-four hours a day with doctors and nurses working in shifts.

The bombing was increasing in intensity.

A lone bomber came over Katong and released five bombs. One exploded in the nearby sea, two landed in open land, the fourth exploded near the Officer's Mess next to Saint Pat's and the fifth crashed through the roof of the hospital exploding with devastating force in a ward.

Vivian, who was off duty and asleep at the time, woke immediately and raced toward the hospital as the screams of the wounded echoed down the street.

The bomb had plunged through the roof of the only ward which was not occupied at the time.

The outer wall had been blown out, the roof sagged with ruptured pipes spurting water over shattered beds and furniture. In the ward next door, patients were being pacified by the duty Sisters. They were holding the young boys in their arms, rocking them to and fro as they whispered words of encouragement. It had been a miracle; no one had been hurt.

On the 28th of January Lieutenant-General Arthur Percival, the British General Officer Commanding Malaya, conceded he could no longer defend southern Malaya and ordered the withdrawal of all troops to Singapore.

The sad cavalcade of dejected troops began crossing the Causeway. They poured into the island in thousands until finally, on January 31, a pathetically small but proud band of survivors crossed over. It was the rear guard, the Argyle and Sutherland Highlanders, who had stubbornly fought the Japanese all the way down the Malay Penninsula and still showing their defiance they marched onto the Causeway to the skirl of the pipes.

Seconds later the engineers blew several large gaps in the land bridge thus denying its use to the Japanese.

General Yamashita, the Tiger of Malaya, had taken Malaya in less than eight weeks: now only Fortress Singapore remained to be conquered.

Sister Jenny Ashton found Vivian attending to the needs of her patients in the Chapel and told her there was a young officer outside wanting to see her.

Finishing her task Vivian handed over to the senior before heading for the door.

Unshaven, and with a mud-splattered steel helmet on his head, Jim Austin appeared to be near collapse from exhaustion.

"Hello." he said with a tired smile, "I've been seconded to Australian Headquarters here on the island."

Vivian, who had not heard from him since his departure from Tampoi, was happy to see that he was all right and now in comparative safety with the rest of them.

They talked for sometime each filling in the gaps between Tampoi and the present until finally Jim said he had to go because there was a lot on.

Vivian asked if he thought the Japs would invade the island.

He nodded slowly saying it was inevitable but assured her the 8th Division would fight them all the way. With a quick farewell and 'God Bless' he hurried off without even a backward glance, his thoughts already back on the war.

The bombing increased noticeably with added Japanese artillery and mortar fire from batteries located at Johore Bahru. The shells were landing mainly in the Geylang area and along the shoreline where the huge naval oil storage tanks were located. Debris sprawled across streets, slowing traffic while fires raged out of control and generating great billowing palls of smoke that were joined by dense black clouds from the oil fires. They hung over Singapore, turning bright daylight into a bronze haze of half-light.

There were virtually no air raid shelters for the civilian population apart from a few six-foot long concrete pipes placed end to end at a number of road junctions.

The Singaporeans, if caught out of doors, preferred to jump into the deep monsoon drains on either side of the streets. These foul-smelling ditches held a foot or so of black water in summer and harboured a variety of revolting creatures including deadly water snakes, yet they provided excellent cover from the Jap's ultimate anti-personnel bomb the 'Grass Cutter.'

This most feared weapon, upon impact, would send hundreds of pieces of white-hot steel scything through the air at body height to shred any human being within its deadly range.

The shops had boarded up their windows and many traders built walls of sandbags to protect their customers from flying bomb fragments and blast. At the famous Cold Stores people sat unconcernedly at the bar sipping on ice cream sodas while the British went about their weekly shopping as if the Japanese did not exist.

The atmosphere was one of British invincibility for they believed in Fortress Singapore.

Hadn't the authorities stored large emergency stocks of tinned meat, rice, flour and other staple items in the city's two cinemas, the Capitol and the

Pavilion, as well as in dumps located all over the island? Besides there were the big naval guns and 100,000 soldiers to defend the island....Singapore would never fall.

Meanwhile the Japanese shut down the flow of drinking water from Johore's Pontian Ketchil Reservoir to Singapore's Bukit Brown, the latter at the time holding enough supplies for up to eight weeks. There was no other source of water for the island's population and troops.

At a meeting on Sunday February 8th Colonel A.P. Derham, the 8th Division's Assistant Director Medical Services, pleaded with Major-General Gordon Bennett to evacuate the Australian Army Nurses while there was still time.

Bennett did not agree, saying this could harm the morale of troops and civilians.

The Assistant Adjutant and Quarter-Master General, Colonel J.R. Broadbent, respectfully reminded his Commander of what had happened to the British nurses at St. Stephen's College in Hong Kong when the victorious Japanese bayoneted the doctors and the patients and then raped the nurses over a twenty-four hour period before putting them all to the bayonet.

Broadbent added that the same troops, the Imperial Guards, were standing across the strait at that very moment and preparing to assault Singapore.

In the indecisive silence that followed, a British officer spoke up saying he agreed with what the General had said and the nurses must stay. He went on to suggest that if, at the last moment, all looked lost, they could shoot the Australian nurses.

Derham, both shocked and disgusted by this suggestion, protested forcibly and pressed for permission to evacuate but Bennett would not accede and finally, in the face of further argument, the General was forced into making it an order.

With Bennett's permission Derham withdrew and was followed out of the room by Broadbent.

The A.A&Q.M.G. expressed his sympathy for the turn in events offering his further support for the evacuation of the nurses.

Derham, with a wry smile informed him that "There was more than one way of skinning a cat." and went on to tell Broadbent that "he intended giving Glyn-White an order to evacuate as many wounded soldiers as possible."

" And I will be sending Nursing Sisters along with them to continue their treatments." he said.

Broadbent smiled and after calling him a "wily old fox," shook hands with Derham and wished him ,"Good luck."

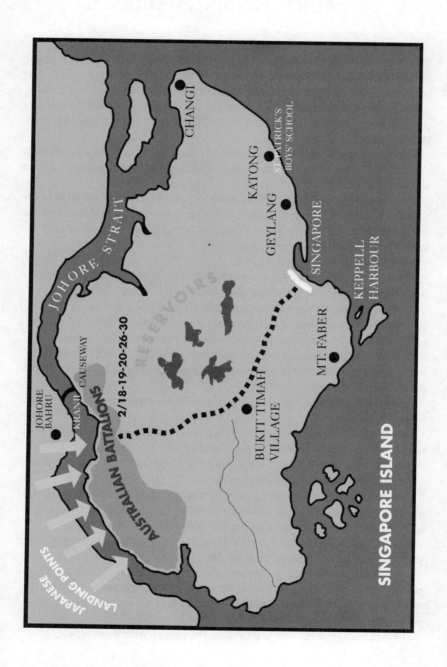

SINGAPORE ISLAND

JAPANESE LANDING POINTS

AUSTRALIAN BATTALIONS

2/18-19-20-26-30

JOHORE STRAIT

JOHORE BAHRU

KRANJI CAUSEWAY

RESERVOIRS

BUKIT TIMAH VILLAGE

MT. FABER

CHANGI

KATONG

ST PATRICK'S BOYS' SCHOOL

GEYLANG

SINGAPORE

KEPPELL HARBOUR

FORTRESS SINGAPORE

The Australian 22nd Brigade, hopelessly under-strength through battle casualties, began digging in on a sector of the northwest coast which was considered the most likely landing place for the Japanese water-borne assault.

While they prepared their positions the 22nd had to contend with heavy shelling which veterans of the First World War likened to the pounding on the Western Front..

Hours later, the barrage stopped abruptly then lifted to concentrate on the countryside behind the Australian lines in the hope of catching supply trucks and service dumps.

The Australians, crouched in their water-logged holes along the edge of the mangrove swamp, listened intently, eyes straining in the blackness of the night. Time ticked slowly by as clouds of mosquitos swarmed around the soldier's heads, probing for exposed flesh.

It was approaching eleven o'clock.

The forward positions of the Australian 2/20th Battalion were the first to hear a steady rhythmic splashing of paddles.

Men groped along the earthen ledge in front of their fox-holes for hand grenades and spare clips of rifle ammunition and brought themselves into a firing position, levelling their weapons in the direction of the sounds.

Slowly, dim dark shapes materialised from out of the low, soft mist clinging to the surface of the water and the waiting Aussies could make out rubber dinghies crowded with Japanese.

They squinted down their weapons' sights, drew breath and held it as their fingers tightened.

The harsh, thumping bark of a Vickers heavy machine-gun shattered the silence, momentarily preceding the storm of small arms fire that followed, sweeping the approaching boats, shredding rubber, dumping dead and wounded into the black, swampy water.

The ear-splitting din, punctuated by the crash of grenades, continued unabated as boat after boat loomed up out of the darkness to head for the shore only to be cut to pieces by the storm of steel.

The killing was ferocious as the fanatical Japanese, indifferent to their shocking casualties, pressed their attack.

Sixteen battalions had been sent against two Australian battalions and although they slaughtered the first two waves of Japanese assault troops, they were powerless to prevent a determined third wave from gaining a foothold on the shore.

The Australians went forward to meet the enemy with the bayonet.

Hand-to-hand they fought with grim determination in the foul-smelling blackness of the mangrove.

With a bridgehead established the Japanese stormed ashore in overpowering numbers and for the defenders, there could be but one outcome.

Withdrawing, the survivors of the two battalions took up new positions along the Jurong Line, a line of defence drawn across the centre of the island just north of the city. The Japanese now occupied the western third.

At 0900 hours the next morning the following communique was issued by Far East Command:

> Enemy landings from boats on the northwest of Singapore Island took place between Sungei Kranji and Pasir Liba between eleven o'clock last night and one o'clock this morning.
>
> The landing was preceded by a heavy enemy artillery bombardment of our forward positions in this area and from daybreak was supported by a considerable number of fighter and bomber aircraft. Our forward troops were pushed back in some places and there has been some enemy infiltration eastwards.
>
> Offensive action is being taken to mop up the enemy. The results of this action have not yet been received.
>
> Elsewhere on the island the enemy is continuing to dive bomb and shell our forward positions. Hurricane fighters of the Royal Air Force supporting our troops, successfully intercepted enemy raiders destroying three and probably three others and damaging thirteen.

****

Father Lionel Marsden, a Marist Priest and Chaplain to the 2/13th A.G.H., had no time to think about the latest communique and its grim news. He was in a hurry to get to the hospital, having been told of the arrival of a large batch of wounded.

It was his habit to administer the Last Sacraments to the Catholic boys before they were moved to the Resuscitation Ward and ignoring the incoming artillery and mortar shells he hurried into the grounds of St. Pat's and the receiving room.

The bloodied young men lay on stretchers covering every square foot of floor as the Priest moved among them.

Quickly checking the identity discs around their necks Marsden came across one that caused him to sharply draw breath as he read the engraved detail on the small piece of metal.

Brennan 2/30 Battalion R.C.

It was a common enough name but the face of the semi-conscious man was also very familiar to him.

Drawing closer he whispered into the man's ear.

"Come from Blacktown?"

"Yes." croaked the soldier.

"Did you go to Christian Brothers' Lewisham?"

"Yes."

"I thought so...I'm Lionel Marsden, we went to school together, same class."

The soldier's eyes opened slowly and there was a gleam of recognition.

"I'm a Chaplain." Marsden explained.

Brennan smiled, then his eyelids began to droop and Marsden quickly asked if he would like to be given the Sacraments. Bringing his ear closer to his classmate's lips to hear his weak reply he heard the whispered "Yes."

Inching his way through the stretchers, having left the dying Brennan, Marsden noticed a young man, who was unconscious and clutched a set of Rosary beads. Crouching over the wounded boy he delivered Conditional Absolution and Extreme Unction and was preparing to move on when the soldier's eyes fluttered open. Marsden assured him he had nothing to fear for he had received Absolution.

Perplexed by this the soldier told him he was not a Catholic, which prompted the surprised Priest to ask why he was clutching the Rosary.

It appeared the young soldier was given the Rosary by his Catholic wife and realising how busy the Priest must be under the circumstances he apologised for wasting his time.

Marsden brushed the apology aside, saying he could never waste his time or the Lord's.

The young man replied. "Father, I think I am going to die and just now.... I was wondering.... if you would let me become a Catholic, like my wife, before that happens?"

Father Marsden went down on his knees beside the wounded boy's stretcher and began.

Orders were received from Colonel Glyn-White for the 2/13th to transport 80 patients to the ship *Wah Sui* for evacuation. All Australian Army Nursing Service personnel, apart from 12 who were to remain at Saint Patrick's with the wounded, were also to go.

Red Cross armbands would be issued and were to be worn at all times on the upper left arm.

On the same day these orders were received Matron Drummond had news of a friend, a senior officer with one of the battalions, who had been badly wounded and, not wishing to hold up his men who were in a perilous position, shot himself. With her friend's sacrifice still fresh in her mind Drummond, on receipt of Glyn-White's order, decided to stay. The hardest task was to choose who was to stay with her.

"Harris, McGlade, Tait, Kerr, Wilton, Oram, Ashton, Casson, Hempstead, Short and Bullwinkel."

Vivian was listening for her name and was not surprised when Matron called it out. Some how she knew it would be on her list because of the affinity between their families and herself or, the ease in which they worked together. For whatever reason Vivian was content to be there with the wounded.

At 1500 hours there was an amendment to the previous order:

All Nursing Sisters were to be evacuated immediately, only the medical staff and Orderlies were to remain.

1630 hours. A further amendment: Those personnel being evacuated will now depart at 1100 hours the next day, Wednesday 10th February, 1942.

On the morning of the 10th the Sisters were assembled and told the orders had again changed and only 30 would be leaving. Vivian's name was not on the list and by now many who had been chosen were refusing to go on the grounds they were needed by the wounded.

St. Pat's was now so overcrowded that orderlies were forced to lay stretcher casualties on the lawns surrounding the building. Here, out in the open, many were wounded for a second time by falling artillery and mortar shrapnel.

The Sisters maintained there would not be enough personnel left to attend to bandaging, dispensing of medications, medical assistance and the essential care of all these men.

The protest snowballed to a point where not one of the Sisters was going to leave. This forced the Commanding Officer of the unit to order them to go, reminding the 30 women that they had a duty of care for those patients who were being sent out with them. Put in these terms the Sisters caved in and agreed to accompany the outgoing patients.

Vivian stood with Jenny Ashton, Jessie Simons and Veronica Clancy, waving the convoy of ambulances, with their sobbing friends aboard, goodbye and when they had disappeared through the gate turned and walked toward the Chapel Ward.

The short, thumping bursts of machine-gun fire intermingling with the cracking of rifles and what they took to be, the crump of grenades exploding, could be clearly heard by the four.

The fighting was only a few blocks away.

What they were not aware of was the Singapore Volunteer Force, weakened by heavy casualties, had withdrawn from their positions at Changi.

There were now no defending troops between Saint Patrick's Boys' School and the Japanese Imperial Guards, the conquerors of Hong Kong.

THE *EMPIRE STAR*

Captain Capon leaned on the bridge railing fascinated by the incredible scene he was witnessing.

He had sailed the Motor Vessel *Empire Star* many times from Australia to Singapore loaded with frozen meat.

It was a habit of his, whenever his ship was being unloaded, to stand on this very spot and absorb the spicy aromas as they wafted across the waters, to feel the island's humidity press around him as he watched the frantic activity on the harbour.

It was unlike any other port in the world and it was akin to a second home for Capon.

Tonight he stood watching as the godowns burned with flames of such intensity, they illuminated the waters of the great harbour, bathing the few ships left in a yellowish light.

Vivid flashes from amongst the flaming ruins of the dockyards marked where artillery shells continued to land, their explosions rolling over the *Empire Star* like a thunder clap.

Already the ship was packed with evacuees and they were awaiting the arrival of some 80 odd Australian wounded together with their nurses. As soon as they were on board he could get underway for Batavia.

His ship was a sitting duck for bombers in the half-light from the fires and it would be ten times worse in the morning.

As Captain Capon readied his ship for departure Margaret Anderson and Vera Torney, together with the other selected sisters of the 2/13th, were making a dash for St. Andrew's Cathedral to pick up the girls from the 2/10th who were going with them.

Reaching their destination they got out to the sound of air-raid sirens and, looking frantically around for cover, they saw the Adelphi Hotel and decided its cellar would be a good spot to wait out the raid.

Running as fast as they could and encouraged by deafening near-by explosions, the Sisters reached the safety of the hotel and flung themselves down the stairs leading to the basement.

Here they waited until the all clear sounded before gathering up the Sisters from the 2/10th and continued with all haste to the docks and their escape ship the *Empire Star.*

Arriving on the wharf they were quickly issued tins of bully beef and biscuits, the wounded Diggers were taken on board and finally the Sisters were allocated an empty cargo hold in which to rest.

It was bare, hot, and smelt of old meat, but thankfully it was open to the night sky and they settled down with an assorted crew of British nurses, Army and Air Force personnel and a few civilians. A few minutes later the throb of the ship's engines and the clatter of the anchor chain told them the Captain was wasting no time in putting to sea. Ahead lay their own minefields, enemy warships and the Japanese Air Force.

****

It was a hot, humid day as the *Empire Star* cut through the calm waters of the Durian Strait, south of Batam Island.

So far their passage had been uneventful, with the Captain hugging the coast of numerous small islands in an effort to hide from enemy aircraft.

Later that morning a lookout spotted a flight of aircraft approaching and knowing they could only be Japanese Capon gave the order to man the guns and prepare for evasive action.

Margaret and Vera, feeling trapped in the hold, decided to go topside and offer their services in case the ship was hit and they took casualties.

Reaching the deck they saw groups of servicemen lining the rails, firing their rifles at low flying planes. The anti-aircraft guns began to bark and the ship heeled over as it turned to avoid the bombs.

Both Sisters were finding it difficult to remain on their feet due to the gyrations of the ship and the huge geysers alongside that dumped water on the deck.

A brilliant flash of light and a blast of hot air swept across the deck picking them up and flinging the women savagely against the superstructure. An ear-splitting roar that overwhelmed the sounds of battle followed.

The *Empire Star* had been hit by a bomb on the starboard side leaving a huge gaping hole in the deck, the edges of which curled up and backward like the open jaws of a monstrous shark.

As Margaret and Vera arrived at the scene the ship's crews had already broken out the hoses and were pouring water down the throat of the hole in a desperate bid to quash the fires.

Many dead and wounded lay in pools of blood on the deck and seeing them the two Sisters ran to the nearest and began searching for signs of life. Where they found it they began basic first aid.

Despite brilliant conning, the *Empire Star* took two more hits and the crews battled with the fires as smoke billowed from the wounded vessel marking them well for the enemy.

The situation was grave for the 2000 souls aboard. If the ship were to sink the survivors would find themselves in shark-infested waters with little hope of rescue.

In the nurses' hold the women started a singalong to boost the children's morale and distract the civilians' thoughts from the battle above. On deck Margaret and Vera worked side by side attending the wounded, trying to buy time until they could be moved below to the sick bay.

Some one yelled "Look out!" and as Margaret and Vera looked up they saw a Japanese aircraft, almost level with the deck, heading for the ship, its nacelle-mounted guns winking with red flashes.

Instinctively, the two women threw themselves across the bodies of the people they were attending as bullets whined and ricocheted off the decking and superstructure.

With its motor screaming the aircraft pulled up and roared over the ship at mast height climbing rapidly away to be eventually followed by the other planes.

They had survived the first attack and perhaps they were not going to sink, yet they knew the Japs would be back and that was only a matter of time.

The Japanese returned later that day after refuelling and bombing up and homed in on the long plume of smoke drifting across a placid sea. Pressing home their attack with four consecutive flights of aircraft over a four-hour period, Capon coolly manoeuvred the *Empire Star* so effectively that only one bomb found its mark.

Plunging through the deck it exploded in a cabin next to the engine room causing little serious damage.

Against all odds they had won through and as the enemy aircraft left the ship's crew and passengers broke out in a series of cheers as they hugged and laughed to celebrate their escape from an unthinkable death in the waters of the Strait.

Captain Capon was informed of the two Australian Army Nursing Service Sisters who had attended the wounded during the action and late that afternoon, as the ship made good headway towards Batavia, he asked the passengers to assemble. He commended the actions of Anderson and Torney, saying they had done a very brave thing, especially the shielding of the wounded with their own bodies when they came under direct attack from Japanese aircraft. There was no doubt in his mind that their ministrations had saved the lives of many.

In closing he spoke of his participation in the evacuation of French and British forces from the beaches at Dunkirk, saying he had never experienced anything at the time that would match what they had all been through that day.

He urged them all to remember and to be thankful for their deliverance.

" Given the normal outcome of these attacks, you should all be swimming out there right now."

He waved his arm in a sweeping gesture toward the never-ending sea about them.

"So, remember this day and remember it with reverence. Thank you all and …. well done."

Some one from the crowd yelled. "And thank you Captain." and they all broke out in applause as Capon smiled and nodded before striding away in the direction of the bridge.

It was February 14, 1942 when the *Empire Star* sailed into Batavia Harbour, on the island of Java.

Capon immediately went ashore to arrange for temporary repairs to his ship before attempting the voyage to Fremantle.

Anticipating repairs would take some time and not wishing to compromise the safety of the Australian Sisters and their patients, he ordered them to disembark and join a small Dutch freighter that was due to sail that day.

The Dutch authorities however, informed the Captain his ship would be ready the next day and so Capon rescinded his order and bringing the nurses back on aboard the *Empire Star* sailed the following day in company with another ship.

The Empire Star arrived in Fremantle on the 23rd of February

There its people learnt of the evacuation from Singapore, by sea, of the 2/13th, 2/10th and 2/4th C.C.S. on the night of the twelfth.

Thrilled to hear of their companions' escape they began to look forward to celebrating their arrival, assuming their ship was only a few days behind the *Empire Star.*

Unknown to them fate had already intervened dealing their friends a brutal blow, how brutal they were not to learn for three and a half years.

ESCAPE FROM SINGAPORE

Thursday 12th February was no different from any other at St. Patrick's Boys' School, apart from the shortage of staff, which made it increasingly difficult to cope with the flow of wounded. With all of the wards filled to capacity, stretcher cases were placed in rows on the lawns surrounding the building as the Japanese kept up a constant bombardment of the area with both mortars and artillery.

The medical staff, in a superhuman effort to contain the situation, worked round the clock. The theatres operated 24 hours a day.

Vivian, exhausted from lack of sleep, was walking mechanically down the corridor unaware that she had passed Major Hunt until a hand gripped her firmly by the arm.

Startled, she let out a sharp cry of alarm and turning looked into the face of Bruce Hunt.

He appeared agitated and was speaking to her very quickly, his words flowing together, almost meaninglessly.

Shaking off her weariness, Vivian forced herself to concentrate on what he was saying. " Did you hear me Sister? I said, get your things together, you're being evacuated to Ceylon."

Still clutching her arm in his excitement, Hunt went on to explain that the remaining Sisters were going out on the last ship and there was only time to pack one small bag and get herself downstairs.

Aware of the urgency in his voice, Vivian snapped a "Thank you, Sir." before taking off down the corridor at the run hearing his "Good luck" as she headed for the Chapel ward.

Jenny Ashton was attending to a young soldier when Vivian found her and she whispered the news of their evacuation, not wanting to alarm the patients around them.

Unperturbed, the stalwart Sister continued her work while suggesting Vivian should go pack and that she would join her shortly.

As Vivian started back towards the door she felt a sudden rush of guilt sweep over her. She was running away. They were leaving these boys to the Japanese; turning their backs on them at a time when they were needed most. Orders or not, it was wrong and as she looked across the rows of beds, with their occupants smiling at her as she passed, Vivian, for the first time in her life, felt ashamed and was on the verge of tears.

An hour later, a dejected band of Australian Army Nurses, some sobbing uncontrollably, climbed into waiting ambulances and with cries of "Good luck!" and "Godspeed!" from the doctors and orderlies, slipped out of the hospital's grounds and into the shell-swept streets of Katong.

Winding its way through the rubble, the convoy finally came to a halt at St. Andrew's Cathedral. It brought back memories to Vivian of that wonderful night at Raffles, just down the road. No sooner had they left the vehicles than air raid sirens began to moan and from somewhere within the cathedral's grounds an anti-aircraft gun barked as bombs exploded several blocks away.

Treading carefully through the hundreds of wounded lying on the lawns around the church, the Australian nurses made for the comparative safety of the building in search of the 2/10th and 2/4th girls.

The planes went off in search of fatter targets amongst the godowns and docks and this allowed the contingent of Sisters, now numbering 65, to mount the vehicles and set out for the docks.

As they left St. Andrew's, Betty Jeffrey from the 2/10th summed up their feelings,

"We had to walk out on those super fellows and not one of them complained, as a matter of fact, they told us it was a relief for them to know that we would be safe. It's the most rotten thing I have ever done in my whole life and I hate it."

Nearing the docks it became impossible for the vehicles to negotiate the rubble.

The women picked their way on foot through the burning debris, suitcases held up to their faces to protect them from the intense heat of the fires that surrounded them.

Clouds of dense black smoke, fuelled by burning rubber stocks, billowed upward from shattered godowns and glowing sparks fell like golden rain onto the tightly packed throng of people flowing towards the harbour and the last evacuation ships.

Marching in the midst of this fear-ridden crowd were the Australians, disciplined, heads held high.

Approaching the main gates to the dock, the military police recognised their uniform and waved the Sisters through before continuing their check of the sea of documents frantically being waved in their faces by the pressing horde of civilians.

Once inside the gates Vivian and the others passed an incredibly long line of European women, many with children, who were patiently waiting for their papers to be checked by a group of naval and police officers seated at a table.

'Why', she asked herself, 'did these people leave it to the last minute to evacuate?'

It was obvious to her, that given the few ships in the harbour and the number of people waiting, plus those who continued to arrive each minute, for the majority there would be no escape from Singapore.

A hoarse shout of alarm, immediately followed by the screams of women and children, brought a halt to the frenzied activity.

A group of men plunged headlong through the crowd, oblivious of those they knocked to the ground. With eyes wide with fear, they were bearing down on the ferry that was carrying approved passengers out to the last ships and it was obvious they intended seizing it to effect their own escape.

Military police drew revolvers and took aim at the onrushing men. A command to halt was ignored and shots rang out sending men, women and children, sprawling onto the wharf.

Overriding the sounds of revolver fire were the screams of mortally-wounded men; then silence.

A small number of survivors from those who had charged the ferry, stood frozen amid the bodies of their fellow-conspirators, their mouths slack from shock, arms dangling loosely at their sides in abject capitulation.

Facing them with arms outstretched and holding their revolvers steady, ready to resume firing on the command, were the military police.

People began to get to their feet and reform queues. The bodies of the would-be hijackers, sprawled on the wharf, appeared not to worry them.

Perhaps they had seen death in abundance over the past weeks, or were their minds set on the ships in the harbour, the last hope of escape from a rampaging victorious army that would be free to rape and butcher at will?

The survivors of the would-be hijack party, defeated, made their way dejectedly back toward the main gate and the burning city as the air raid sirens warned the mass of people on the wharf of the approach of enemy aircraft.

Pandemonium broke out and, panic-stricken, the crowd scattered in a desperate search for cover. It was into this mass of humanity that the first stick of bombs fell.

Exploding with a deafening roar, the shattered bomb-casings instantly converted to deadly razor-sharp shards of steel, which scythed their way through vulnerable flesh and bone, killing and mutilating all in their path.

Large sections of wharf disappeared in a flash and chunks of wood, concrete and body parts rained down on the people nearby.

As the All Clear sounded the Australian Sisters stared in disbelief at the scene around them.

The wounded, shrieking, lay among the dead and dying as frantic mothers, clutching at the stumps of their children's severed limbs, watched their lifeblood drain away. Shocked and dazed survivors wandered aimlessly through the carnage calling to loved ones as the fires along the wrecked wharf raged anew.

Without a command, the Australian nurses moved quickly among the injured, stopping to tie off severed limbs and bandage gaping wounds. For dressings they tore up garments salvaged from the shattered suitcases which littered the wharf. As they worked the nurses murmured words of encouragement to each wretched person knowing that many if not all who were seriously injured would die. Hospitals not already in the hands of the Japanese were overflowing, with civilian and service wounded overwhelming facilities and medical staff.

Vivian, attending to a young woman at the time saw a well-dressed young man, ten paces from her, sitting beside the bloodied body of a young woman. Slowly, and with great tenderness, he rolled her over and leaning forward, gently picked up a baby from where it lay shielded by its mother's body. Vivian watched him gather the small one in his arms and, with tears streaming down his cheeks and without a backward glance at the dead woman, walk slowly along the devastated wharf to join a long line of people reforming for evacuation. Vivian prayed this man would be given passage and reach the safety of Australia where the little one could start a new life which had been bought at the cost of its mother's.

ORDERED OUT

Colonel Derham, Assistant Director Medical Services, Australian 8th Division, his Deputy, Lieutenant Colonel Glyn-White and the Transport Officer, Captain Abramovich, arrived at the evacuation point following a hazardous car ride from headquarters. The chaotic scene that greeted them was typical of what was happening all over Singapore.

Anxious to locate the Australian Sisters before they embarked, the three officers pushed their way through long lines of frantic people.

They found Matron Olive Paschke of the 2/10th Australian General Hospital and Glyn-White confirmed that her nurses, together with those of the 2/13th and 2/4th, were to be evacuated to Ceylon.

He added. "You should not be leaving...it is far too late; the Japanese have complete control of both the air and the seas."

Matron respectfully reminded him they had been ordered to leave. "And this runs against the wishes of myself and my nurses," she said, indicating the reason why they had left the men of the Australian 8th Division.

Glyn-White could only agree and informed her they were concerned for their safety and both he and Colonel Derham were on their way to see the General Officer Commanding the AIF Malaya.

He assured Matron they would make their best representations in their endeavour to persuade Bennett to rescind the order and allow them to stay with the Division.

An hour or so later the three officers returned to the wharf and a downcast Glyn-White confirmed to Matron the GOC's order stood; they were to be evacuated by sea immediately.

A disciplined woman, Paschke gave them a respectful look of disapproval, simply by raising her eyebrows, before stating she would assemble her nurses for boarding the ferry. Bidding the officers a cheery goodbye she stepped smartly over to where Matron Drummond waited with the remaining element of the 2/13th.

Falling in, the grey-uniformed Australians stood out as they marched down the dock towards their ferry each clutching one small suitcase representing their entire possessions.

As the crowd parted to let them through they heard the loud remarks passed by expatriate women waiting in the seemingly endless line. "There go the nurses....follow them and we'll get through." shouted one, "How dare they go before us?" commented another.

Ignoring the many insults and hostile looks directed at them, the Australians marched with heads held high, secure in the knowledge they had carried out their duties in the highest traditions. With jeers from some sections of the crowd they filed aboard a waiting tugboat which promptly cast off and headed out into the harbour.

Looking back, Vivian watched thick, black plumes of smoke billow from the massive conflagration consuming the godowns and oil storage tanks ashore fed by constant bombing, shelling and mortar fire. In the smoke-distorted half-light she listened to the sounds of battle waging in the streets of Geylang and Katong as the British and Commonwealth forces made their final stand against the Imperial Guards. She thought of St. Patrick's and the wounded crammed into its wards and corridors, and lying on the lawns around the make shift hospital.

Turning away she looked into the tear-streaked faces of her fellow Sisters and knew they too were thinking of the young boys of the 8th Australian Division who never complained of their wounds and always waited patiently for their turn to be attended to - now, who would care for them?

The tug nosed its way through waters littered with the burning hulks of stricken ships until it found one unharmed and riding at anchor.

Changing course the little craft headed for it.

Through the heavy haze Vivian saw the familiar shape of their evacuation ship appear ahead and she called to Nancy Harris, "It's the *Vyner Brooke!*"

Nancy, who remembered the delightful candle-lit dinner shared with the ship's officers, called back "It's just like old home week."

Jimmy Miller greeted them warmly before showing the two below.

"This cabin," said Miller, "is yours while I am on duty," adding they were to help themselves to his cigarette and booze stocks as well.

Brushing aside their protestations he led them topside reuniting them with the others who had chosen a living space forward of the upper deck.

The ship which normally catered for 12 passengers, now carried over 300 men, women and children.

Life-preservers were handed out with the instruction to put them on and keep them on.

Struggling into hers, Vivian said to Nancy. "I hope this thing works because I can't swim."

Nancy gave her a strange look,. "Don't worry about it Bully....I'll look after you."

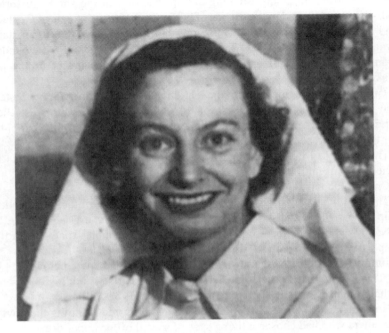

Sister Vivian Bullwinkel at Saint Patrick's
Boys' School Hospital, Singapore, 1941.
(V. Bullwinkel collection)

(Photo on opposite page)
The 2/4ᵗʰ Casualty Clearing Station Malaya, 1941.
Left, Back Row: Sisters Hilda Dorsch, drowned, Bessie Willmott, shot, Wilhelmina
Raymont, died as POW, Elaine Balfour-Ogilvie, shot, Peggy Farmaner,shot.
Front Row: Sister Dorothy Gardam, died as POW, Matron Irene Drummond, shot,
Sister Mavis Hannah, the only surviving member.
(Australian War Memorial photo by Sergeant Major J.D.Emmett.)

58

Enjoying a cup of tea on the verandah of ward C1, Australian General Hospital, Tampoi, Malaya, 1941.
Left to Right: Sister Vivian Bullwinkel, Matron Irene Drummond, Sisters Margaret Anderson and Margaret Selwood.
(Australian War Memorial Negative Number P 1344/12/08)

Sisters and Staff Nurses of the 2/13ᵗʰ Australian General Hospital on the lawns of Saint Patrick's Boys' School, Katong, Singapore, 1941.
Left to Right Back Row: Sisters Gladys Hughes, Annie Trennerry, Lorna Fairweather, Jean Ashton, Bess Muldoon, Vivian Bullwinkel, Matron Irene
Drummond, Sisters Maude Spehr, Bessie Taylor, Unknown, Marie Hurley, Mary McGlade, Florence Casson, Veronica Clancy, Harley Brewer:
Front Row: Sisters May Rayner, Ada Bridge, Minnie Hodgson, Nellie Bentley, Betty Garood, Loris Seebohm, Janet Kerr, Ewin Wittwer
(Australian War Memorial Negative Number P1344/12/01)

Saint. Patrick's Boys' School, Katong, 1941.
(By courtesy of the National Archives, Singapore.)

Saint Patrick's School 1994.
(Author)

Civilians being evacuated, by ship, from Singapore, 1942.
(By courtesy of the National Archives, Singapore.)

European women and children boarding an evacuation ship
watched by husbands and service personnel. Singapore, 1942.
(By courtesy of the National Archives, Singapore.)

Japanese troops cross the Batu Pahat River on the West Coast of
Malaya in their drive south to Singapore Island. January, 1942.
(By courtesy of the National Archives, Singapore.)

Japanese assault troops enter Kuala Lumpur
along Taman Pasir Road. January, 1942.
(By courtesy of the National Archives, Singapore.)

RUNNING FOR SUMATRA

Captain Richard Borton, Master of the *Vyner Brooke,* planned the escape-route carefully, taking in the likelihood of both Japanese Naval and Air Force units ranging south of Singapore.

Hugging the island chain southwards, steaming only at night without lights and sheltering during daylight, Borton intended to reach Sumatra to take on provisions before sailing to Java and eventually to Fremantle.

If Sumatra had fallen to the enemy he intended to press on to Java via Bangka Strait.

Concluding his briefing, Borton gave the order to slip anchor and, on the night of February 12, 1942, in company with three other ships, the darkened *Vyner Brooke* picked its way through the British minefield and to the open sea.

****

Vivian woke at dawn. She felt revitalised after her sleep despite the hard deck beneath her.

For some time she stood watching the new day, absorbed in the beauty of a tropic dawn at sea. There was a calmness within her, a lightness, a touch of joy; emotions she had not experienced in months, and the war began to recede from her thoughts, becoming more a half-forgotten nightmare than reality.

Clouds streaked the sky highlighted by the rays of a rising sun which appeared as a ball of angry fire low down on the horizon. When the breeze died, it would be like sitting in a furnace for the three hundred souls crushed together in the confined space of the *Vyner Brooke*

For Captain Borton, daylight was fraught with danger and he anxiously scanned the sea ahead for a place to hide

An hour later he took his ship alongside a small jungle encrusted islet and dropped anchor.

With the ship secured, both passengers and crew settled down for the long, sweltering wait until nightfall. The majority stayed below while those on deck searched for, or improvised, any kind of cover to protect them from the searing heat of the sun.

For the Australian Sisters there was no rest as the two Matrons had organised them into district nursing teams responsible for defined areas of the ship. Each Sister was to ensure proper discipline and good morale was maintained within her area of responsibility.

Should they come under attack they were to attend to the wounded and if the ship was sinking their instructions were to evacuate the wounded and all passengers.

Matron Paschke made it quite clear to them that in the event of the ship being abandoned they were to be the last to leave.

"Check the ship thoroughly for anyone who could be left behind," she said to the assembled Sisters, "and when all is clear wait for the order to leave, which will come from either Matron Drummond or myself." Matron went on to advise them that the ship's lifeboats would not cater for the number on board, they would have to sustain themselves in the water with their life-jackets, adding that the crew would throw life-rafts over the side.

"Remember," concluded Paschke, "remove your shoes, hold your life-jackets down firmly and jump into the water feet-first. If you don't hold your jacket down it can come up and hit you under the chin with the possibility of breaking your neck."

Later in the morning, following an inspection by the two Matrons, they were again assembled and told there was a problem with rationing the passengers. The ship's stores could not cater for everyone and most of the passengers had not thought to bring food with them. In the circumstances both Matrons had decided the Sisters would pool their issue of rations and distribute them to all on board.

The women spent the remainder of the day pinning syringes of morphia inside the pocket of their uniform, preparing field dressings and attending boat and evacuation drills, supervised by their Matrons, until the light began to fade.

****

It was late in the afternoon and the decks of the *Vyner Brooke* were littered with the bodies of dozing people who had come on deck to escape the heat and humidity below.

A distant droning on the darkening horizon caught the attention of the few who were not asleep.

One man pointed to a small black spot low on the horizon.

It was a lone aircraft and Vivian knew only the Japanese had planes.

The single engine fighter dropped down to almost sea level and headed straight for the *Vyner Brooke*.

No one moved, transfixed at the sight of the onrushing aircraft, until the command, from the bridge, "Take cover!" galvanised them into action. Scattering, they sought the protection of other side of the bridge.

From her position of comparative safety Vivian saw the Jap fighter loom large and fireflies were dancing along the leading edges of its wings, creating parallel lines of small water spouts in the sea. These ran quickly across the surface towards the ship impacting in a storm of steel upon the hull, then the upper structure, sending ricochets screaming off the iron plating to smash into the soft wood of the lifeboats.

With a thunderous roar the Jap plane screeched over their heads barely clearing the ship's mast and climbing away, lazily circled to gain altitude before heading back in the direction from which it came.

Miraculously, there were no serious casualties among the passengers and crew, wounds being restricted to superficial cuts caused by flying woodsplinters.

Several of the ship's lifeboats, however, had been severely holed. Should they be sunk, the majority of people on board would have to abandon ship with only their life-jackets and a few rafts in waters known to be shark-infested.

It was obvious the Japanese would be back in force.

Borton gave the order to get underway.

Weighing anchor in the gathering dark and running without lights, the freighter slipped away from the islet on a course set for Bangka Strait.

They had been steaming for some time through waters dotted with small islands when a brilliant shaft of white light pierced the inky blackness surrounding them. Other beams now joined the first and together they began to sweep the surface of the sea.

Captain Borton ordered complete silence on board and shut down the ship's engines.

They began to drift as the searchlights, which they assumed came from either one or several warships, continued to grope for them.

Considering his options, knowing that eventually they must be discovered and sunk, the Captain decided to make a run for it, positioning an island, which the map indicated was ahead and slightly to starboard, between them and the lights.

As the *Vyner Brooke's* engines came to life and the vessel began moving, the fingers of light dashed to and fro in a bid to pick them up.

A darker than the night shape loomed up ahead and Borton brought his command back on course for Sumatra, placing the island between him and the prowling Japanese warships.

ATTACKED FROM THE AIR

It was Saturday February 14, and Second Officer Miller stood by the railing with Vivian, pointing to a long, low strip of coastline barely distinguishable in the early morning haze.

"That's Sumatra." he said as Vivian, following his outstretched arm, squinted in an effort to bring the blur into focus.

"Is that where we are going?" she asked

"Well, no, not quite, we enter Bangka Strait first, some time today. Then, we'll slip down the coast, cross to the mouth of the Musi then up river to Palembang."

"As simple as that," she said, adding, "and as long as the Japs let us."

Miller told her of the Captain's decision to take a risk and press on during the day in the hope of reaching Sumatra earlier than planned.

Vivian went off to find Nancy and when they had completed their rounds the two joined the other Sisters and passengers in the main saloon

There was a shout from the bridge warning of approaching aircraft.

The deck above her head clanged with the sound of running feet as the crew ran to man their action stations and the small-calibre anti-aircraft gun. The engines begin to pound as they worked their way up to full speed and the deck canted to port as the Captain began to manoeuvre the *Vyner Brooke* to escape the bombs.

The first bomb exploded, in the water, alongside the *Vyner Brooke*. The shock wave pounded against the hull, the noise so horrendous that Vivian was momentarily deafened and unable to hear what Lorna Fairweather, sitting beside her, was trying to say.

This near miss was rapidly followed by a series of explosions, which battered the ship, shaking it violently, as women and children screamed out in terror. Adding to their fear was the banshee shrieking of aircraft engines as they passed low overhead, the constant barking of the anti-aircraft gun and the violent tilting of the deck that tossed them into jumbled heaps as the Captain pitted his seamanship against the falling bombs.

Vivian was astounded to see Sister Jessie Simons propped against the wall, serenely reading a book with the cover title *Cactus*.

Jessie appeared to be completely absorbed in what she was reading and apparently oblivious to the mayhem going on around her. 'How can she do that?' Vivian asked herself, turning to attract Nancy's attention to their fellow Sister's indifference. In that instant the cacophony of sound stopped and the ship came back onto an even keel. The planes had gone and people were starting to sit up, some smiled; others laughed as they showed their relief in the fact that the ship had survived the attack without being hit. Yet as the civilians congratulated one another the Sisters exchanged sombre looks for they knew the Japs would not give up.

At 2.00 p.m. the same day a flight of Japanese bombers returned to strike again at the fleeing *Vyner Brooke*. As people on the upper deck sought cover the first stick of bombs left the bellies of the leading aircraft and plunged toward the little ship.

This time, luck deserted them.

A large bomb plunged down the funnel and exploded in the engine room.

In the saloon Sister Wilma Oram, lying prone on the floor alongside Vivian, was lifted bodily into the air by the force of the explosion. Slammed back onto the deck she saw a large section of bulkhead abruptly disappear to leave a gaping hole through which she could see the ocean.

Mortally hit, the *Vyner Brooke* shuddered and began to loose headway, her engines dead.

The second bomb slammed into the aft section where it exploded between decks.

Many passengers were killed instantaneously. Panic, broke out and hysterical survivors, ignoring the bleeding wounded, stampeded for the stairs in one wild fighting, shoving mass to escape the in-rushing sea.

The Australian Sisters, immediately following the first explosion, proceeded to their designated areas of responsibility and calmly went about the task of attending to the wounded and assisting in their evacuation to the main deck.

Sylvia Muir, a 2/13th Sister from Queensland, bent over an elderly gentleman who had received a stomach wound. One glance at the depth of his wound told her there was nothing she could do for him. As she patted his hand his steady grey eyes looked into hers and he began to sing in a weak voice, *Rule Britannia*. Sylvia stood up and hurried away, looking for others she could assist.

Below decks, Vivian moved from one prone figure to another searching for any vital signs when, above the fearful racket of exploding bombs she heard one of the girls cry out, "Over here, Wight and Halligan have been wounded."

Pushing her way through the half-crazed passengers who were trying to get topside, Vivian arrived at the spot where several nurses had gathered to tend the needs of the two wounded Sisters.

Both were trying to get up from where they lay on the floor, blood pouring from shrapnel wounds to their buttocks. "We can manage," said Rosetta Wight. "Yes, really we can," added Clarice Halligan.

The others would not hear of it and after dressing their wounds helped them to gain the upper deck.

The stricken ship was settling in the water, her list becoming more pronounced, as Jessie Simons headed for her post. Dashing out of the crowd, a wide-eyed woman gripped her by the arm with such desperation as to make the Sister wince with pain.

"You'll take care of me, won't you Sister?" pleaded the fear-crazed woman.

69

Disengaging herself from the steely grip she looked calmly into the woman's eyes. "Now, you are going to be perfectly all right." she said reassuringly before dashing off.

Looking down at her arm she wondered why she had not noticed the shrapnel wound until the woman had grabbed it.

Another stick of bombs straddled the sinking ship, one penetrating the deck and exploding, as the Australian nurses went methodically about searching the ship for people who might have been left behind.

Vivian, with Iole Harper, Louvinia Bates and Jessie Simons, fought her way along a sloping companionway in semi-darkness, where deck and deckhead were slowly changing position. Forcing open cabin doors she called out, stopping to listen for a reply, yet hearing only the sound of water rushing below her feet. The *Vyner Brooke* did not have long to live.

With difficulty they made their way to the deck which was now almost at right angles to the surface of the sea.

They slid more than walked to the ship's railing where the crew were lowering a lifeboat, crowded with women and children.

There was a sharp crack and a seaman shouted a warning as the loaded boat lurched and, dropping at one end, spilled its screaming passengers into the sea.

For a moment the boat hung precariously by its remaining line, but the excessive weight was too much and it parted with a sharp report and it plunged down upon the heads of the unfortunate people below.

Vivian watched for survivors and saw several rise to the surface and cough up water. A number of others, who reappeared, drifted away, heads lolling from side to side in their life jackets.

The crew by this time had readied and loaded a second boat which they began lowering.

All was going well and it was about to touch the surface of the water when suddenly, it came to an abrupt halt. Despite frantic efforts by the crew the obstruction could not be cleared and the packed boat remained suspended, some twenty feet above the water, held tightly to the ship's hull by a mass of twisted rope.

The Australian Sisters now lined the railing, their faces turned towards the two Matrons, waiting for the order that would send them over the side and into the sea.

Olive Paschke looked, with pride, at her nurses.

"It's time to go, girls."

The order given, some Sisters climbed the railing and leapt into space while others sat down on the sloping deck and methodically removed their shoes before jumping. One Sister was heard to complain it was all a waste of time removing one's shoes because she was going to drown anyway being a non-swimmer.

Betty Jeffrey, who never did like heights, decided the most dignified way of leaving the ship was by way of one of the many ropes dangling over the side.

Kicking off her shoes she grabbed the nearest line and, from where she stood on the rail, swung herself outward before slowly relaxing her grip. The thick manila rope whipped through her hands burning deep furrows in the palms and ripping the flesh unmercifully. The excruciating pain forced Betty to let go altogether and she plunged the last few feet into the sea, crying out in agony as her torn and burnt hands came in contact with the salt water.

Wilma Oram went over the side with her friend Mona Wilton who was a non-swimmer. Hitting the water, Wilma was propelled under for several feet before the buoyancy of her life jacket popped her back to the surface. Momentarily disorientated, it took a little time for her to identify where she was and to begin swimming around looking for Mona.

She heard a shout from above and looking up, saw a life raft hurtling down upon her.

Too late to avoid it, the heavy object struck her a glancing blow forcing her under the water. Surfacing dazed and bleeding from a deep scalp wound, she had barely time in which to take a gulp of air before being hit for a second time by a falling raft.

With lungs bursting and her head throbbing from the wounds inflicted by the two rafts, Wilma broke the surface alongside the ship and seeing the raft that hit her floating nearby, swam over to it.

Hauling herself up she crouched down and began paddling with her hands to get clear of the sinking ship and search for Mona

"May I join you?" asked a voice and looking down Wilma saw a woman clutching at the side of her raft. "I don't care what you do." she replied rather bluntly. With that the woman climbed aboard the raft and sat silently while she caught her breath.

'I'm Mrs. Gibson." she volunteered eventually.

Ignoring her, Wilma resumed paddling for she had no intention of being sucked down by a whirlpool created by the sinking *Vyner Brooke* as she scanned the survivors in the water hoping to see Mona Wilton.

As Vivian removed her shoes she thought about not being able to swim and the faith she would have to put in the life-jacket around her neck.

Stories had been circulating about their dubious qualities, someone even claiming that, following a period of immersion, the cork within the jacket became water-logged turning it into a dead weight much to the detriment of the wearer.

'Well,' she told herself, 'I don't really have a choice.' She climbed onto the railing and remembering to hold the jacket firmly down, jumped.

The coolness of the water came as a shock as the momentum of her fall carried her down into the depths.

Deeper and deeper she plunged as, for the first time in her life, Vivian experienced the absolute silence and loneliness of being under water.

The vastness of the ghostly green void of half-light frightened her and she wondered if destiny, by some quirk of fate, had marked these unfathomed depths as the place of her death, knowing her fear of dying alone.

71

Her chest hurt as she strained to hold the air within her lungs. 'Perhaps,' she thought, 'it was time to let it out and have it over and done with?'

"No, hang on." said something in her head and her body became lighter, rising toward the diffused light above. Breaking the surface, she took in a deep and grateful gulp of fresh air then turned to see where she was.

The *Vyner Brooke's* hull was so close she could have reached out and touched it. Craning her head backwards, as far as the preserver would allow, Vivian looked up at the awesome shape of the ship looming above her.

Someone was calling to her to get away from the ship's side before it rolled.

Stirring herself she began to dog-paddle, as best she could, away from the settling hulk.

Matron Paschke, seeing the last of her girls leave the ship, removed her shoes and climbing onto the railing paused to look down at the bobbing heads of her nurses.

"Here I come girls," she shouted, "look out for me, remember I can't swim." With these words Matron launched herself into space holding the collar of her life jacket down as she had instructed her girls to do.

When she surfaced a number of willing hands seized her and towing her over to a life raft they pushed and hauled Matron up onto the floating platform.

Matron Drummond, assisted by several Sisters, loaded a quantity of medical supplies into one of the remaining shrapnel holed lifeboats and launching it, rowed away from the ship, its crew furiously bailing with whatever came to hand in a frantic effort to keep the craft afloat. The *Vyner Brooke*, listing badly, was still afloat. The thick fuel oil from her ruptured bunkers began to spread wider on the surface of the calm sea, coating the living and the wallowing dead with its viscid blackness.

High above the tragic scene wheeled the formation of Japanese planes responsible for delivering the ship's death-blow. As the survivors watched several broke away from the formation and, dropping down to sea level, sped toward them.

When the aircraft were within machine-gun range the pilots opened fire. The bullets lashed the sea around the rafts and people in the water tried frantically to push themselves under the surface to escape death or injury. This was to no avail for the buoyancy of their life jackets kept forcing them to the surface where they were at the mercy of the guns. For those sitting on or clinging to life-rafts there was no escape.

They watched as thousands of miniature waterspouts ran across the top of the water to finally engulf them, smashing men women and children violently into a reddening sea.

The strafing aircraft held their course letting their lines of fire run through the survivors and on to the stricken ship where they impacted on the bridge and open deck killing the few still on board.

Lifting at the last possible moment they roared over the *Vyner Brooke,* climbed away and on rejoining the others flew off in the direction they had come from.

Vivian, escaping from being hit by the maelstrom of fire, concentrated on reaching an overturned lifeboat which was surrounded by oil-blackened heads. Kicking vigorously she was eventually able to grab a hold on the rope running around the gunwale and resting, caught her breath.

Clinging to the upturned boat were several sisters from the 2/10th, who Vivian recognised, but could not put a name to. Then there was Wight and Halligan who had been wounded during the air attack on the ship; an elderly couple who clung desperately to one another, and an oil- streaked face that was very familiar.

"Jimmy,?" she croaked, "Jimmy Miller?" His haggard face with its sad eyes, relaxed in a smile as he recognised her. "Viv, thank God you're safe."

At that point someone said "There she goes" and everyone looked to the *Vyner Brooke*.

Slowly at first, then with gathering speed the ship rolled over, crushing the lifeboat packed with women and children held fast to its side. The stern rose high out of the water, revealing its propeller, then quickly it slid from sight.

Several large air bubbles broke the surface bringing with them packing cases, luggage, sections of railing, doors and the dead.

The bodies of little children and babes-in-arms, too small for life jackets, floated briefly amongst the debris before disappearing back into the depths, while life-preservers, supporting the bodies of adults, drifted away.

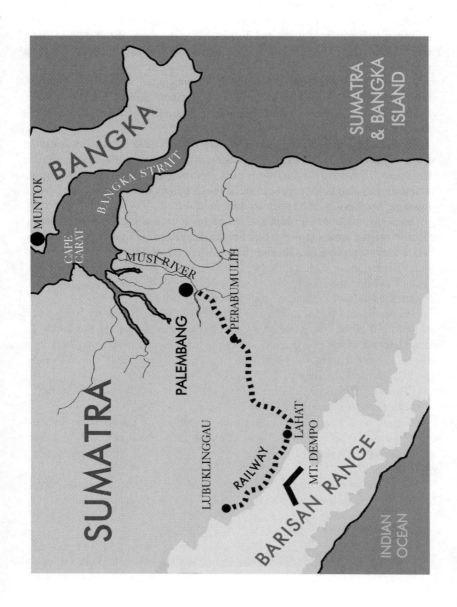

SUMATRA & BANGKA ISLAND

BANGKA

MUNTOK

BANGKA STRAIT

CAPE CARYT

MUSI RIVER

PERABUMULH

PALEMBANG

SUMATRA

LUBUKLINGGAU

RAILWAY

LAHAT

MT. DEMPO

BARISAN RANGE

INDIAN OCEAN

LEFT TO THE SHARKS

The sun was beginning to set and Vivian became aware of the pain in her hands, which were cold and puffy from immersion, and her legs ached from the constant kicking. Yet, like the others, there was no slacking, for to stop was to give themselves over to the strong currents.

Earlier, one of the nurses had voiced her fears about sharks being attracted by the thrashing of their legs and this caused the others to look constantly about them.

Jimmy Miller pointed out it was unlikely there would be a shark within twenty miles of the place, given the number of bombs dropped in the sea.

Reassured by his words they went back to concentrating on their paddling and the jungle-clad coast crept closer as the last light vanished.

Looking up, Vivian could only wonder at how vast an enigma the universe was, with its unfathomable depth of nothingness extending forever and how pitifully insignificant she was by comparison. "There's a light," said Miller.

Vivian saw the glow of a bonfire which, she believed, could have been lit by the first to land as a guide for them. With spirits high and sharing a feeling of renewed hope the small band of survivors aimed the waterlogged boat in the general direction of the fire and continued paddling.

It was almost ten o'clock. They had been in the water for seven hours and had lost sight of the beacon on shore. Resting momentarily from her kicking Vivian became aware of a tingling feeling in her toes followed by a dragging sensation. Immediately she knew what it was and standing up called to the others, "I can feel the bottom."

At the urging of Jimmy Miller they let go of the boat and stumbled toward the strip of beach now visible in the soft light.

Weakened legs gave way, sending some sprawling in the shallows as the rest reeled out of the water to collapse upon the sand. Halligan and Wight, the two wounded Sisters, were assisted ashore by the other nurses and made comfortable.

It was some time before they could speak. Miller suggested a small party should try to locate the beacon so they could link up with the other survivors.

This was agreed and Vivian, together with two other Sisters who had also volunteered, and led by Miller set out along the beach.

It was not a long journey and the four soon came upon the fire to be greeted by Matron Drummond and a number of nurses. With them was the First Officer, Bill Sedgeman, a few of the crew from the *Vyner Brooke*, about 40 British servicemen and some civilian men, women and children.

Vivian told Matron of their escape from the ship, of the exhausting hours in the water before coming ashore and the wounds sustained by Halligan and Wight.

Anxious for the two wounded Sisters, Drummond, taking Vivian with her, sought out a Chinese doctor she knew to be among the civilians. Locating the medico she asked if he would accompany them to the other camp to treat the two nurses.

To their dismay he refused on the grounds the main body needed him and if the women required treatment they must be brought to him.

Matron, who was visibly controlling her temper, pointed out it would be inhuman to expect them to attempt the journey without first receiving medical treatment. With an edge to her voice she added that both these nurses, once attended to, would be invaluable in the care of the sick and wounded in the main group.

Again the doctor declined to accompany them.

Without even bidding him goodnight Matron turned and strode off down the beach forcing Vivian, who had been caught by surprise at her sudden departure, to scurry after her.

Drawing abreast of the furious woman she heard her say, "Calls himself a doctor? indeed!"

The last word literally exploded from her.

In Matron's absence, Sedgeman and Miller decided to bring as many survivors as possible, into one big group. They could then send a party out to look for a native village and food and make contact with the local authorities.

This was agreed and Miller set off, returning some time later with his small group, including the two wounded nurses, the latter having suffered great pain and discomfort during the journey.

The main group, settling down for what remained of the night, was disturbed by a series of large flashes out to sea, which lit the horizon with the intensity of an electrical storm. This was accompanied by the sound of gunfire and explosions and the sailors amongst them thought they were witnessing a naval battle.

Several hours later a ship's lifeboat came out of the darkness to ground itself on the beach. Aboard the little craft were men, women and children and a number of servicemen, some of them wounded. After making them as comfortable as possible in the circumstances the group tried to get some sleep with what remained of the night.

At first light Sedgeman called a meeting of survivors and suggested he lead a party in search of food. With all in agreement he then asked for volunteers, choosing five British seamen off the ill-fated battleship *Prince of Wales,* who had also survived the sinking of their evacuation ship, plus five women, including Vivian. The latter, he thought, would gain a measure of sympathy from the locals.

Taking a narrow trail they discovered near the landing point, the foraging party started out briskly. This soon waned as the roughness of the track bruised bare feet and the heavy humidity made walking an extreme effort.

The track wound through thick jungle and ultimately led them to a native kampong, or village, set in a small clearing. The scene appeared peaceful enough.

Smoke curled lazily into the still air from several cooking fires which, the party saw, were attended by village women. Children ran happily about the collection of huts idly watched by three elderly men who sat in the shade provided by a simple attap-covered structure.

Sedgeman decided to approach the three men alone. This he did, greeting them as he drew near.

Using arm and hand gestures, he explained they were part of a large party who had been shipwrecked, that many others were on the beach and in need of food, which they were willing to pay for by way of a promissory note against His Majesty's British Government.

Vivian watched the parley from where she and the others stood beneath the leafy canopy of a large tree. She saw one of the old men momentarily wave his arm toward the far end of the village, where a track disappeared into the jungle, following which Sedgeman bowed and headed back to the party.

It transpired the old boy had refused them food, suggesting they take the track to Muntok where the Japanese would feed them.

"So," said Sedgeman, "it's obvious the Japs are already here on Bangka."

After discussing what they should do next, a decision was made to return to the main party to reach a collective agreement as to their next move.

On their arrival back at the main camp Sedgeman called everyone together, choosing the spot where the wounded lay, beneath the palm trees, so they would be a part of the decision making process. The alternatives, as Sedgeman saw them and which he put to them were:

Take to the sea again hoping the tides would carry them to an island unoccupied by the Japanese. Move deeper into the jungle and endeavour to survive with the help of local natives or; Surrender to the Japanese.

The first two options were immediately eliminated on the grounds they would have to leave the wounded and, additionally, the elderly among them would not have the physical stamina to face either the sea or the jungle.

Although it was a well-known fact amongst the service personnel present that the Japanese did not take prisoners, the majority reasoned, that with a large number of women and children in the group, the Japs would have no alternative but to take them prisoner.

"Besides," they added, "the wounded need hospital treatment."

It was unanimous; they would surrender.

A party consisting of two survivors from HMS *Prince of Wales*, led by Sedgeman, would start at once and make contact with the nearest Japanese troops, bringing them back to the beach so the surrender could be effected.

Vivian's innermost thoughts became depressive and, unwilling to share her fears with the other Sisters, she decided to busy herself by tending to the needs of the wounded.

As Vivian went about her task of fetching water, from a nearby jungle stream, a large section of the civilians had met and agreed on a further course of action.

It was proposed the women and children, accompanied by some of the men, would immediately follow on behind Sedgeman's party

Their rationale was, it would save the Japanese time in transporting them to a prison camp thus freeing the trucks earlier to rescue the wounded and take them to the nearest hospital.

Matron Drummond, on hearing of the women's intention to leave, called the Sisters together and told them of their decision. "Their duty," she said, "was to remain with the sick and the wounded."

Others who also elected to remain behind included: Jimmy Miller, some 50 to 60 British servicemen and an elderly Englishwoman who insisted on staying with her injured husband.

The large party of men women and children left immediately in an endeavour to catch up with the first group while those who were left settled down to wait.

MASSACRE ON THE BEACH

Around mid-morning of that day Sedgeman emerged from the jungle with a contingent of Japanese soldiers.

In strict patrol order, with their officer leading, they crunched across the yellow sand coming to a halt at the place where the wounded lay and the other survivors were now assembling.

"These are the people I told you about," Vivian heard Sedgman say to the officer. "they want to become your prisoners of war."

The officer's face, she noticed, was devoid of any emotion, except for a slight narrowing of the eyes as he took in the scene around him.

Turning stiffly to a soldier at his side he spat out an order in rapid Japanese.

There was a loud metalic clicking as each soldier loaded a round into the breech of his weapon and brought it to the ready. Vivian felt a sickness well within her and bile flooded into her mouth as the ugly snouts of sub-machine guns and rifles, fitted with bayonets, were levelled at them.

Automatically the survivors moved toward each other for mutual protection as Sedgman began to protest. Moving forward menacingly, the Japanese soldiers used the tips of their bayonets to separate the men from the women, herding the men into a group before marching them up the beach towards a promontory at the far end. They went silently, sullen, with heads bowed.

Frantically Vivian searched the ranks of men for Jimmy Miller finally identifying him when he turned to face her. His eyes searched for hers and finding them, a brief boyish smile flashed across his sad face as he acknowledged having seen her, then he was gone, blending with the other naval, military and airforce uniforms as they tramped down the beach to vanish behind the small headland.

Watching them go, his legs spread arrogantly apart, with both thumbs imperially hooked into his sword belt, the Japanese officer's gaze was fixed on the backs of the men as they were marched away. As they waited silently for whatever was to happen Vivian looked the Jap over. By the cut of his uniform, his badges and insignia, he was obviously an officer, possibly a Lieutenant. Of medium build, his young, expressionless face gave her the impression he was detached from the proceedings and possibly bored if not impatient to get all this over and done with so he could be on his way.

Several muffled shots echoed throughout the bay, startling the women, then silence.

Some five minutes passed before the soldiers reappeared from behind the headland, bunched up, and obviously talking amongst themselves, they strolled back along the beach.

As they chatted each cleaned his bayonet with a small rag and occasionally a laugh reached the Sisters. Not one of the British servicemen followed.

"Bully," Vivian heard the voice of Jenny Kerr, who was standing beside her, "they've murdered them all!"

Vivian found herself unable to answer Jenny for along with all of those fine young men had gone two friends, Jimmy Miller and Bill Sedgeman and she felt devastated.

Nancy Harris spoke to no one in particular "It's true then, they aren't taking prisoners."

The soldiers put themselves into some kind of order as they approached their officer and when they came to a halt in front of him he snapped an order which caused them to quickly form a semi-circle around the nurses.

Vivian looked at the sun glinting off the steel of their bayonets and wondered if they were to be the instrument of their deaths. Instead, the soldiers used them to turn the women around so they faced the bay in a line. Then, prodding them with the sharp tips of their bayonets, they forced the women to walk into the water including the elderly British lady who had elected to stay with them. The two wounded Sisters, Wight and Halligan, helped to their feet by friends, were half-walked, half-carried down to the beach to join the extended line at the water's edge.

As she felt the sea wash over her feet Vivian kept asking herself, 'Why? Why did they have to die? And what God given right did the Japanese have to take their young lives?'

"Bully?"

The sound of her nickname broke through Vivian's mental accusations and she became aware that Alma Beard was walking beside her.

"Bully" she heard her say again, "there are two things I have always hated in life, the Japanese and the sea, and today, I've got them both."

The sun was climbing toward its zenith and a light breeze played across the surface of the bay's tranquil waters, reaching out to stir the tall, green palms lining the golden shore.

On the beach, watching impassively as the single grey line of women waded into the sea, were seven heavily-armed men.

There were no pleas for mercy from the Australian women, no sounds of sobbing or, a cry of anguish, only the sharp slapping sound of water striking their bodies as it reached to their thighs.

Thrusting herself forward against the resisting pressure of the sea, Vivian concentrated on the picture postcard perfection of the bay and she sighed dejectedly, as the words came into her mind, 'How could anything as obscene as this happen in such a beautiful place?'

It was at that moment, as she searched for an explanation or, even a reason, that her mother's face came to her.

'Oh! Mother,' she cried out in her mind, 'I am so sorry you will never know what happened to me.' She saw a smile spread over the familiar face and a deep look of tenderness flood into those beautiful blue eyes and suddenly, she felt relieved of her anguish.

'Anyway, it will be great to see Dad again Mum.'

The presence of her mother and the thought of meeting her father, brought an inner calm to Vivian and composed, she turned to share her peace with the other girls.

To her surprise she saw they had already found the truth. Each one returned her smile in a strange and beautiful way, radiating the strength of their togetherness, for as one, on this day, they would share the final experience in life and discover the secret of whatever lay beyond.

"Chin up girls, I'm proud of you and I love you all." It was Irene Drummond's voice, the words spoken so softly they came as a whisper and, hearing them, Vivian's love went out to her Matron

The roar of weapons' fire shattered the stillness, startling Vivian and sending flocks of jungle birds screeching into the air. The water around the line of women was lashed into white foam as the furious storm of high velocity bullets churned it over. Many of the Australian women were immediately flung forward as they were hit in the back while others folded over, like limp rag dolls and slid beneath the surface.

Vivian stood perfectly still in waist deep water, petrified by the harsh barking of rifles and sub-machine guns crashing and echoing throughout the bay as the Japanese soldiers 'walked' their fire up and down the row of women. She waited for death, watching as the crystal clear waters about her turned crimson and the metallic hammering of breech blocks continued, unabated, as the rounds groped for those still alive amongst the floating inert bodies.

Then it happened as she knew it must.

A huge fist smashed into her lower back, crushing the breath from her lungs, slamming her forward. Instinctively, she flung her arms out to stop from going under, but the blow was so severe it carried her below the surface into a world of silence away from the guns.

'So this is what it is like to get shot and die.' she thought.

The acceptance of death both calmed and relaxed her and her body rose to the surface of the bay to float face down and she gratefully accepted the blackness that enveloped her.

Vivian wanted to vomit and turning her head to one side she did, then automatically sucked sweet air into her lungs.

'I'm not dead,' she told herself before throwing up again.

The realisation of where she was and what had happened overrode any elation she may have felt in discovering she was alive and, clearing her mind, she began thinking about her situation.

She was floating on her stomach, head to one side, which allowed her to breathe. The wound in her back was burning with the intensity of a white-hot poker and without being able to look at it, she had no idea how serious it was or how much blood she had lost.

As for the Japanese, she couldn't hear any sounds coming from the shore that might suggest they were still there and watching. Then again, she dare not risk raising her head to have a look in case movement brought more shots.

It was also obvious to her the nausea she felt was a result of having ingested a large amount of seawater and her vomiting fits would continue.

Giving some thought to this, she decided to continue floating, her head to one side for breathing and voiding purposes, and to control excessive movement in her shoulders when forced to throw up. This way she would continue to appear dead.

Resigned to this course of action and exerting a great deal of self-control, she allowed the current to carry her where it may.

Time was meaningless as Vivian drifted in and out of semi-consciousness and a gentle swell carried her in a rhythmic rise and falling motion in and out of the shallows until eventually, it slid her up on to the beach.

Wide-awake, she lay perfectly still, the waves lapping around and over her. She heard the sea, the crying of the birds and the wind rustling the palm trees, but nothing else; it was time to act. Gripping the sand with both hands she summoned her last reserve of strength and, pushing herself up into a sitting position, faced the shore.

The beach was deserted. Quickly she turned to scan the waters of the bay, steeling herself against what she would see.

Nothing!

Stunned, Vivian again searched the sea and its shoreline only to confirm that the bodies of her friends were not there. It was as if the whole terrible thing had not happened, but the pain in her side told her differently.

There were several possibilities she told herself, one being the removal of the bodies by the Japanese. This she immediately discounted because, if that had been the case, why didn't they attempt to take hers? The more reliable answer, when she came to think about it, was the bodies had been caught in a rip and taken out to sea.

Accepting this her thoughts turned to her current predicament.

She assumed the Japs would be back to check the area and so her first priority was to get off the beach and into the jungle where she could hide.

But would her wound allow her to walk?

Gingerly, she slipped her hand around to her back and found where the bullet had entered, high on the left hip. Turning now to her stomach she saw where it had exited on the left side.

As there was no profuse bleeding, coupled with the fact she felt well in herself, Vivian concluded the bullet had gone cleanly through her body without damaging any vital organs.

Heartened by this she rose painfully to her feet and stood swaying on weakened legs before attempting a step. With one hand clamped to her wounded side, Vivian started toward the distant jungle

Several times she was forced to stop and rest before reaching the first group of palms, and urging herself on, she limped and stumbled over the remaining stretch of sand to the jungle, where, blundering her way through the dank undergrowth, she found a large fern tree.

Burrowing deep within the sanctuary of its wide lush fronds, she collapsed on the dank undergrowth and curled up into a tight ball. Physically exhausted and drained emotionally, Vivian embraced the blackness that swept over her and she slept, deeply, safe in the jungle and the gathering dark from the accursed men of Japan.

A MAN CALLED KINSLEY

Opening her eyes, Vivian was at first confused by her surroundings. The wound in her side was throbbing and her mouth was parched.

Adding to her craving for water was the heavy humidity around her.

Cautiously she pushed aside the drooping fronds that secured her refuge, and peered out. Not far away was the track they had used to find the village and it was off this track that the fresh water stream was located. "Thank goodness." she thought and tensed her leg muscles before attempting to get to her feet.

A metallic click sent her cowering deep within the shadowy fronds of her fern tree for as the sound caught her attention so did the flash of light off a bare bayonet.

It was then she heard their voices, chattering in Japanese, so loud that they obviously considered the area safe and under their control.

She held her breath as the Japanese patrol came down the track and filed past her hiding place beneath the fern. With her heart pounding so loudly she was convinced one of them would hear it, Vivian stared into the face of each soldier as he ambled by, willing him not to look in her direction.

Recognising them as being the same soldiers who had murdered the men and her fellow Sisters caused Vivian to shake uncontrollably for to be discovered by these men meant instant death

Her luck held and the last soldier went by without spotting her, the patrol disappearing down the track and on to the beach where they headed for the promontory.

Petrified at the thought of them returning and catching her in the open, Vivian fought her thirst and remained under cover for some hours before she was forced to seek out the stream.

Locating it she knelt beside the crystal clear waters and cupped her hands and lent forward.

"Where have you been nurse?"

Startled by the male voice, Vivian spun around to see a young man, propped up on one elbow, legs splayed, wearing a British Army issue khaki shirt and shorts staring intently at her.

"Who are you?" she asked sharply, not having appreciated the way in which he had revealed himself to her.

"Private Kinsley," he answered in a weak voice, "I was one of the stretcher cases brought ashore. I saw what they did to you girls; then they came back to put the bayonet into us wounded."

"I'm Sister Bullwinkel," she said formally.

He told her that the Japs had moved away after bayoneting the wounded in their stretchers and despite having being run through twice, he was able to crawl to a small derelict fisherman's hut. Here he spent the night, leaving at first light to drag himself to the stream for water. When he heard the patrol returning he crawled into the jungle and hid.

"No," he said when Vivian asked the question, "I don't know what happened to their bodies."

While she listened to his narrative, Vivian drank her fill from the stream before sitting back to study the man. She noted the blood-soaked shirt and a field dressing on his upper arm that was both bloodied and bedraggled.

"You're wounded, aren't you nurse?" he asked.

"Yes," she said, brushing the question aside, "but let's have a look at you."

Kneeling beside the British soldier she unbuttoned his shirt and gently removed it.

The fleshy under part of the left upper arm had been sliced off, exposing the bone, which he said, in answer to her question, had been caused by a bomb fragment. The holes in his upper and lower midriff were obviously bayonet wounds. There were early signs of infection in all of his wounds.

In her opinion, based on the war wounds she had treated, this soldier required immediate surgery and intensive care if he were to live. In their current situation this was impossible and so all she could do was to make him as comfortable as possible and stay with him until he died.

Her first task was to clean and redress the wounds and optimistically she asked if he had any unopened field dressings, which he did not. This decided her to go back to the beach and search around to see what could be used. When she told him of her intention a look of alarm appeared on his face and he warned her to be careful for the Japs could come back this way and put an end to them both.

Reassuring him, Vivian set off, stumbling along the track in bare feet, the rough path with its spiny tufts and sharp twigs making her journey both painful and exhausting.

On the edge of the jungle she paused to carefully scan the beach before moving down to the water's edge where she hoped to find medical supplies either washed up or, dropped by survivors coming ashore.

A dark object in the shallows further down the beach caught her eye and she moved toward it. As she got closer she realised it was a body and her first thought was it could be one of her fellow Sisters.

The long black hair of the young Asian girl, strung out, floated like seaweed in the gently lapping water, her once beautiful face bloated by days of immersion in the sea.

There was no doubt in Vivian's mind that this girl, caught up in the frantic evacuation from Singapore, drowned trying to reach the island after her ship had been sunk.

Vivian moved back along the beach, going higher, more to the edge of the jungle.

She found an army water bottle half-buried in the sand and two life-jackets.

Retrieving the jackets she pulled the bottle from the sand by its strap and headed for the stream, pausing to pick up a quantity of coconut fibre from beneath the palm trees along the jungle's fringe.

Kinsley looked relieved when Vivian returned to throw the jackets on the ground with the explanation they would make very good pillows. Easing herself down she began to tease the coconut fibre in to long strips and when he asked what she was doing she told him it was for dressing his wounds

Completing the task, she gently washed and cleaned his injuries before strips of fibre were applied and bound in place with thin vines from the undergrowth.

Turning to her own wounds she padded and secured them before lying down to rest from her exertions; Kinsley having already drifted off in to semi-consciousness.

****

Following their rest, Vivian raised the question of where they were going to hide.

She was in favour of moving deeper into the jungle while Kinsley wanted to return to the fisherman's hut, which would provide them with a shelter from the tropical rains.

Vivian objected on the grounds that the hut was too obvious and the first place a patrol would look; also they needed to be near the stream.

The discussion became heated until brought to a head by Vivian's ultimatum that she was going to live in the jungle where she felt more secure and he could live in the hut.

Kinsley replied as forcibly as his weakened condition would allow that they should stay together for mutual protection and company.

Ignoring his directive Vivian struggled to her feet, picked up a life jacket and prepared to leave.

At this point Kinsley capitulated.

His willingness to go along with her wishes lifted a load from her mind for the last thing she wanted to do was leave him at a time when he needed her. Besides, she dreaded the thought of being alone in the jungle.

"Thank you Kinsley," she said with genuine appreciation, "we had better get moving then, before it gets dark."

Leaning heavily upon one another the two made their way slowly down the track, then branched off into the jungle where they found a suitable site in a section of very dense rain forest.

Here Vivian set down the soldier and placing a life-jacket under his head told him to get some rest. Picking out a spot for herself, Vivian slumped to the ground and looking around at the gathering gloom, felt more at ease.

Awake as the first patches of light appeared amongst the breaks in the jungle canopy Vivian was thinking that it was only a matter of time before Kinsley succumbed to his wounds; in the interim it would be up to her to find a way of feeding them both.

The only edible thing she had seen so far were the coconuts high up in the palms which she couldn't possibly reach, and those that fell on the ground she had nothing to open them with.

She had no skills in trapping birds and small animals, or in detecting which jungle berries could be safely eaten. Her last meal had been bully beef and biscuits aboard the *Vyner Brooke* and no doubt Kinsley's situation would have been similar. They would have to eat today.

The more she turned these facts over in her mind the more she was convinced there was but one way to feed the two of them; she would have to walk to the native village and plead for food.

Further more, she told herself, she would have to do it today, before her strength gave out.

"Kinsley," she called, "are you awake?"

Propped up by her life jacket she looked over to where he lay and saw his eyes open.

"I'm awake."

"I have decided to follow the path back to the village and ask the head man to give us food."

"What if he turns you in to the Japs?"

"That's a risk I'll have to take."

He seemed to digest this and when he did speak it was not with any conviction in his voice.

"We could give ourselves up."

To Vivian this was not an option and she said so.

"You know as well as I do…the Japs don't take prisoners."

They both fell silent for a while and then Kinsley told her she was right and the only person who could save them from starvation was the village chief.

With both in agreement Vivian decided she would set out as soon as the light was stronger, meanwhile, to take his mind away from the pain of his wounds she questioned him about his background.

Was he married? Yes, he was, to a woman he called Elsie and they lived in East Yorkshire.

The conversation evidently had sparked him up for it was his turn to ask Vivian the questions and she found herself telling him about Kapunda in South Australia, where she was born and where her Grandfather Shegog served as a senior police constable.

She reminisced about the time she went to live with her grandparents, when she was six, and how her grandmother, a very adventurous lady for her day, took her to see Australia play a test series against England.

On another occasion it was to see Pavlova dance, prompting her desire to be a World-famous ballet dancer like her idol.

She found herself telling him that her name, Bullwinkel was indeed German, her great-grandfather, having been born in Hanover, eventually settling in London where he was naturalised in 1849 and became the publican of the *King's Arms* in Whitechapel.

They even discussed her brother John, Kinsley commenting on the irony of him engaging in a war in the Far East while her brother flew Spitfires in England.

The sun was, by this time, climbing inexorably towards its zenith and it was time for Vivian to leave.

****

Eva Bullwinkel sat alone at the dining room table in her small, neat house in a suburb of Adelaide, South Australia.

Beside her, on the table, lay an airmail card dated Singapore, 5th February, 1942 and a cable bearing the next day's date; both were from Vivian reassuring her everything was alright.

What disturbed her was the sudden gap in Viv's correspondence, which was the reason why she was writing again so soon after the last letter she sent.

My Dear Vivian,

I was so glad to receive your cable Saturday morning I have been, and still are, terribly glad to know you are still safe and well. I notice your cable was handed in at six o'clock on the 6th inst. and I received it at 9.30 the next morning so that was very quick.

The last airletter I received from you, you wrote on the 5th of February and has only just arrived, so I hope I will get another from you very soon.

I listen to the wireless for every bit of news about Singapore. In this morning's paper it says the Japs have secured a foothold on Singapore. I am worried however when I receive your letters things always seem a little brighter, when your letters do not come my hopes go down to zero again.

Adelaide is all blacked out at night now so I do not go out after dark.

I received a cable from John a few days ago with birthday greetings and saying he is well. He sent the cable from some place called Woking.

Thanks awfully darlingist for your kind wishes for my birthday, fancy you thinking of it when you must be frightfully busy and so much for you to think about.

How is your pal Jim Austin, I do hope he is well and quite himself again.

I am looking forward to your letters if you have time to write letters, there should be quite a lot to write about.

Well darling I must stop now. Sincerely hoping that Singapore will be able to hold out until reinforcements arrive, which I hope will be very soon.

Hoping and praying you will come through safely.
With fondest love to your dear self from.
Mum.

Slowly Eva folded the pages and placed them in a sky blue envelope, sealing
it, before dipping the nib of her pen in a bottle of ink and addressing it to:

VX S/N Bullwinkel. V.
13th AGH
AIF SINGAPORE

Taking a nine-penny stamp she attached it to the airmail letter before walking
down the hallway and out the front door on her way to the post office.

****

Vivian's heart was pounding as she followed the winding jungle track.
Shoeless, without stockings, wearing only a grey cotton uniform stained with
bunker oil, mud and her own blood, she forced herself forward, every step a
smarting, stinging torture to her bare feet, every step tearing at her wounded
side.

Mile after mile she fought the desire to stop and lie down, goading herself
on with a fierce determination to reach the village.

Arriving at the kampong, which she remembered from her previous visit
with the Sedgeman party, both parched and considerably weakened from her
long walk she paused to take in the scene before moving over to where the
women were.

They were tending their cooking fires and they eyed her impassively as she
approached and asked to speak with the headman. Dispatching a young girl
to fetch him they stared at the white woman swaying before them until an
elderly man walked over and bluntly asked what she wanted.

Through dry and cracked lips, her voice thick and husky, she spoke of her
injured companion and their desperate need of food and asking if the village
could spare a small amount for them each day.

The old man shook his head, saying he could not help and it would be better
for them to give themselves up to the Japanese.

Vivian pleaded with him but he ignored her and turning away he walked off
flinging his final words over his shoulder. "You give up to Japan man get
food."

Panic hit her and she spun around to face the women. "Please." she said
extending her arms, "please, just a little food."

She saw their eyes shift from her to their cooking pots and at that moment
knew she had lost.

The enormity of their refusal and its consequences struck her and she faced
reality, death by starvation, and there was nothing she could do. Resigned,

89

she turned in the direction of the path and holding her side, walked with deliberate dignity from the kampong

Vivian's spirit was at its lowest. Her bitter failure, coupled with her waning strength under a harsh tropical sun, was sapping her will to go on.

Rounding a bend in the track she shuffled to a halt having seen a movement in the jungle.

'Was it a Jap patrol?', she asked herself and stood stock still, transfixed with fear, staring at the wall of green as several large fronds moved, then parted.

Stepping out into the open were two smiling native women. Quickly they bent down, placing two packages on the ground before melting back into the shadows. In an instant they disappeared as if they had never existed for not a word did they speak.

Vivian staggered over to the parcels and picking one up opened the banana leaves to discover a large portion of cooked fish, accompanied by several handfuls of boiled rice, with big chunks of pineapple.

Retrieving the other parcel she turned once more toward the hide and Kinsley, her heart lighter, her steps firmer.....for she had not failed after all.

****

Carefully Vivian divided the food into a number of portions, one to be consumed immediately, with the others for future meals.

She calculated they had enough for four days and before they ran out she would make another trip to the village in the hope the women would again provide for them.

Both she and Kinsley were in high spirits following her return with the food parcels and the consumption of their first meal in days, yet despite the relief of knowing they could sustain themselves for at least four days, Vivian despaired for their future

'How long could they rely upon the native women to provide for them? What would happen to her once Kinsley died? How many years would she be forced to live in the jungle alone until the war was over?' These were the questions she asked herself knowing all along that they lead to only one sensible answer.

"Kinsley," she said aloud, "I think we should give ourselves up to the Japanese."

There! she had come out with it.

Surprisingly enough he didn't reject her idea outright but gave her an alternative.

"We are alive for a reason", he said in a soft, halting tone, "so why not take it a day at a time, Nurse?"

For some reason she could not understand, Vivian exploded. " Do not, I say again, do not, call me nurse, I am a Sister in the Australian Army Nursing Service and as such you should address me as Sister."

The shock of her rebuke had its effect upon Kinsley who was obviously at a loss to understand the reason for this outburst, for all he could do was make a stumbling apology and say how much he appreciated all she had done for him.

"I'm sorry too Kinsley, it was silly of me."

She knew now what it was that had upset her. It was an inability to come to terms with the sudden and savage deaths of Matron, her friends and a desperate inner struggle to suppress the memory of it. Then, there was the guilt. Together they had walked out to sea knowing they were going to die, yet they were unafraid, for they were sharing a common fate. Then she was spared, she was alive. 'Why wasn't she with the others? Why wasn't she dead?'

Vivian looked at her soldier companion her eyes pleading for an answer to the question that burned to the very depths of her soul.

"Kinsley, why was I spared? Why me?"

"I don't know Sister," he said softly almost apologetically, " I don't know."

Several days later, in a tropical downpour, Vivian set out once more for the native kampong where again the old headman denied her food. Uncertain but hopeful, she walked slowly back along the track until reaching the approximate spot where the native women had previously emerged from the jungle. A few minutes passed as she stood waiting expectantly, the thought crossing her mind that perhaps they were not coming this time. A stirring of the foliage announced their presence and the two women stepped out on to the path handing her two large, leaf wrapped, parcels.

Exchanging smiles with her they quickly turned and vanished within the green forest, leaving Vivian to continue her journey, relieved and eager to get back to Kinsley to share the precious gifts.

The days that slowly passed were repetitive and wearing for Vivian as she carried out the daily tasks under extremely primitive conditions.

Since her near discovery, following the massacre, they had not sighted a Japanese patrol and this encouraged her to venture more often down to the beach where she spent a great deal of time walking the shore in search of anything that may have been washed up.

It was on one of her late afternoon trips, with Kinsley sleeping fitfully in their hide, that Vivian lay down in the cool, tranquil shallows of the bay, and unbuttoning the front of her uniform, checked her wound.

Gently she explored the perimeter of the purplish hole noting there was no evidence of gangrene, in all it was coming along nicely and even the pain had begun to recede.

Looking at the exit wound she wondered at her miraculous escape from death.

She had continued to think about this a lot and had come to the conclusion she had been saved by her height.

The Japanese, she reasoned, would have aimed for their backs, being the tallest of all the girls, the bullet meant for her entered lower down the back, more to the hip and away from the vital organs such as the liver, intestines, stomach and lungs. The quick healing of the wound, without infection, she put down to the hours spent in salt water.

Even given this practical solution as to how she survived, Vivian could not understand why only one bullet had struck her? Why the Japs hadn't seen her vomiting in the water? Why she was not swept out to sea with the other bodies? and why hadn't at least one Jap, in the patrol that passed her hiding place, discovered her?

It was then that she became aware of a need to talk with God.

Vivian was not overly religious, attending church on an irregular basis.

Yes, she had thought about praying, but dismissed it on the grounds that the world was at war and hundreds of thousands of people were dying or suffering the most hideous experiences, each and every day. The Lord, she assumed, would have been flat-out listening to their pleas for deliverance and her cry for help would have been but one more tiny voice amongst the multitudes.

Now, at a time when every last vestige of hope had been drained from her body and her spirit spent, she had a deep yearning to pray.

Kneeling, she lifted her head to the heavens.

"Lord, I haven't really prayed to you before, but you know I believe in you. I don't understand why you spared me when all of the other girls used to go to church regularly, you must have your reasons. I am sorry to worry you, because there must be a lot of others asking for your help right now. I don't want a miracle, all I want is your guidance, I want you to help me know what to do. You see, there's Kinsley, I think he is going to die. When that happens, I will be on my own and Lord, you know how much I fear being alone, I couldn't bear that, I can't be on my own. Tell me what I should do, please show me the way."

Vivian remained kneeling, willing herself to hear a voice, desperate to receive a sign, but she heard only the sound of a restless sea and the cry of a seabird.

Getting to her feet she took one last look at the beautiful bay before trudging through the sand, making her way toward the palms with thoughts of what she had asked still milling around in her mind.

She had asked for guidance, a way in which to see there was some hope of their survival.

An old familiar saying flashed into her head. "God helps those who help themselves."

The thought persisted. "Of course," she heard herself saying aloud, "that's it." And she quickened her pace, anxious to share her thoughts with Kinsley, as an inextricable and unexpected lightness came over her, for now she knew what had to be done.

****

Arriving back at their hide Vivian woke Kinsley from his restless sleep. "Kinsley," she said, gently shaking him, "we must talk about our future." When assured he was listening she went on.

92

"We have been here eleven days and eventually we are both going to die here. I know we made a pact not to surrender, that it was better to die free, but it's taking too long and if you go first....I'll be alone and I don't want to die on my own, I want to be with my own people.

Kinsley, I want to surrender to the Japs now, I want to take the chance and find out if they will take us as prisoners or kill us.... either way it will be a relief."

He had obviously been listening carefully to what she said for without hesitation, he agreed, adding that, "if it comes to the worst I hope the Japs do a better job of it this time."

Relieved that he was in agreement, Vivian suggested an early morning start taking the track to the kampong and linking up with another, which should lead them to a Jap post.

It was then that Kinsley asked if they could defer their departure until the following day. When asked why by Vivian, he explained that tomorrow was his birthday and he would like to celebrate it in freedom.

"Well of course we will stay," she said and getting up carried a food portion to him. "now I want you to eat this and get some sleep, it's going to be a big day tomorrow for the birthday boy."

Vivian rolled on to her good side and using her arm for support, heaved herself to a sitting position before getting to her feet.

It was daylight and a light mist hung heavily in the forest. She made her way to where the food was kept and rummaging around found what she was looking for.

Holding the small, leaf wrapped object in her hand she walked over to where Kinsley lay and knelt beside him. "Kinsley wake up."

At the sound of her voice his eyes opened and focused on her face.

"Good morning and a happy birthday Kinsley."

She held out the parcel to him which he unwrapped, revealing a small amount of rice which had been moulded to the shape of a cake with a single twig embedded in the top representing a candle.

His eyes brimmed as he looked at her, "Thank you, Sister." he said simply, but with emotion.

Vivian made a remark about not eating it all at once then went on to explain how they were going to fill in the day by preparing for tomorrow's journey. Having divulged her plan to him she set about achieving it.

Starting with the redressing of his wounds, using fresh coconut fibre, Vivian went on to scrub his shirt with a combination of sand and fresh water to ensure the bayonet holes in it were not so obvious and finally she gave her uniform a good wash.

At the completion of her chores Vivian turned and looked at Kinsley with critical eyes.

****

93

The cables and letters from Vivian had ceased altogether and Eva Bullwinkel had no idea what had happened to Vivian following the news reaching Australia of the fall of Fortress Singapore.

Conscious of the fact that it may never be delivered, Eva, nevertheless, sat down and wrote to her daughter convinced the very act of doing so would keep her alive where ever she may be.

My Darling Girl,

The suspense of the last couple of weeks has been dreadful not knowing how you are – where you are and what has been happening to you.

I have rung Mrs. Drummond several times but they have not received any word from Matron Drummond at all. Mrs. Drummond seems to think some of the nurses are still on Singapore Island. There is only one comfort the Japanese have, from all accounts, respected the Red Cross in Malaya and my only hope is that the nurses will be well treated. Even if you have left Singapore the dangers are so great that one feels in constant fear of what may happen.

Oh Viv dear, if only you were back in Australia. Every day I have been hoping for a cable from you. Betty Garrood, Nell Bently and two other girls have sent cables to their mothers. Those girls are in Java. I am going to the Red Cross to see if they can find out where you are.

I have not heard from John for some time so cannot give you any news of him.

Darling I cannot write more in this letter. If you ever receive it you will understand.

I wonder if you received my cable which I sent to Singapore. It was dispatched on the 10th February. I do hope and pray I will receive some news of you very soon – good news.

With fondest love to your dear self and may God guard and protect you, is my constant prayer.

Your loving mother.

****

"Do I pass inspection Sister?" asked Kinsley conscious of her critical examination of him as he stood before her.

Vivian's heart was full of compassion for this British soldier. He leant on a stout stick salvaged from the forest, his long, matted hair and unkempt beard failing to hide the hollow cheeks and haggard face beneath. His shirt, now laundered, was carefully tucked into Bombay Bloomer shorts, which revealed wasted legs disappearing into a pair of large army issue boots.

How he kept standing, with terrible wounds, let alone attempt an arduous journey of unknown distance amazed her. Here, she thought, was a man of great fortitude.

"Do I pass Sister?" he repeated hopefully.

"Kinsley, you look great, now what about me?"

The tall, blue-eyed, attractive young woman stood upright, shoulders back, her face devoid of make up, her light brown hair a thick, tangled mess. The plain grey uniform, despite having been washed, still bore the stains of oil and blood while her legs were covered in cuts and scratches. Having discarded her shoes and stockings before abandoning the ship her feet were both cut and mudstained.

"What are you going to do about that." he asked pointing to the neat round hole in her uniform with its tell-tale bloodstain.

Triumphantly she bent down and, picking up the army water bottle, swung the strap over her shoulder positioning the bottle over the tell tale hole. "There! how's that?" she asked.

He nodded his approval, "Very good Sister, very good."

"Then we leave tomorrow morning; Let's get some rest."

Vivian gazed around their sanctuary with a feeling of fond familiarity and thankfulness for having hidden them for so long, however it was time to leave for the grey light of dawn was filtering through the thick jungle canopy above them.

She moved over to where Kinsley stood and placed an arm around the small of his back at the same time she felt his encircling arm and his weight as it pressed down on her left hand side.

Prodding the ground in front with his stick, Kinsley attempted a step, then another and at a slow, halting pace they started forward and on reaching the track he stopped to rest.

Worried by his physical weakness, Vivian was concerned that he did not have the ability to attempt such a strenuous journey and she contemplated leaving him in the hide while she went ahead to contact the Japanese. She conveyed these thoughts to him, drawing a response, which confirmed his determination to undertake the march. So they set out, arms entwined, Kinsley leaning heavily upon Vivian and his staff, their gait ungainly, but with hope in their hearts.

The blazing sun beat relentlessly upon them as the two staggered along the rough, stone-strewn surface of the road to Muntok.

Having stopped earlier at the kampong, where the old headman was very helpful once told they wanted to surrender to the Japanese, they were given food and shown the road they must take to reach Muntok, the main seaport on Bangka Island.

They had been walking for several hours and the soles of Vivian's feet were broken and bleeding and Kinsley's weight was beginning to drain her, when she heard the sound of footsteps. "There's some one walking behind us." she whispered and they slowly turned round to confront the person following them.

He was a small man in his thirties, his style of dress suggesting he was Indonesian.

As they looked he raised his arm and waved it in a greeting.

"Hello." he called out in perfect English, "good morning to you."

Reaching them, the diminutive chap asked, very politely, where they were bound and Vivian replied they were going to Muntok to surrender.

Nodding his head and smiling he agreed this was indeed the best thing they could do because the Japanese had internment camps there with lots of women who wore Red Cross armbands and grey uniforms just like her.

Vivian was overwhelmed with a feeling of euphoria at his description of the women for, unquestionably, he must be referring to Australian Army Nursing Sisters and it also confirmed the Japanese were taking prisoners.

Thanking the stranger for this information they said their good-byes and the little man strode off to dwindle into the distance ahead.

****

It was well past noon when a whining sound behind them grew louder and they identified it as an approaching motor vehicle.

Instinctively they moved to the side of the road to allow it to pass. Butterflies fluttered in the pit of Vivian's stomach, for she knew the only people who could possibly be driving a vehicle on this island would have to be Japanese.

As the fear built within her, for an instant, she wanted to run and hide in the jungle. A voice in her mind warned her not to, so she stood her ground, supporting Kinsley, waiting for her second meeting with the men of Japan, her would-be murderers.

Suddenly, remembering her wound, she reached down and grabbing the water bottle held it tightly to her side as, with a grinding of gears, the old open tourer came to a halt beside them.

Sitting stiffly to attention behind the wheel was a Japanese soldier, beside him, in a more relaxed attitude, was a naval officer.

Eyeing the two dishevelled westerners with some suspicion the officer spoke rapidly to the driver in Japanese who promptly slid out from behind the wheel and opening his door ran around the car to where Vivian and Kinsley stood.

Carefully he searched them for weapons and finding none, apparently reported this to the officer, for the latter rattled off a string of Japanese prompting the soldier to scramble back behind the wheel before turning to them.

"Get in."

His hesitant, barely understandable English took them by surprise and they were slow to react.

"Quick." he commanded and with some effort she got Kinsley into the back seat before climbing in herself. No sooner were they settled than the driver found first gear with a grinding 'thunk' and the tourer lurched off down the road.

96

Enjoying the luxury of travelling in an open car with a cooling breeze blowing in her face, Vivian stretched her long legs out to ease their aching muscles and her bare feet came in contact with something under the front seat.

Looking down she saw it was a large bunch of ripe bananas.

Leaning forward she addressed the driver.

"Excuse me, would you ask your officer if he would permit me to have one of his bananas."

She waited expectantly while the driver briefly translated this to his officer who grunted a reply.

"Yes." said the driver, without turning his head and Vivian swooped down to rip one from the bunch. Peeling it and breaking it in half she give one section to Kinsley before sitting back to enjoy hers as the veteran tourer bumped its way along the pothole littered road to Muntok.

****

Muntok was located on the north western coast of Bangka Island, its substantial buildings dominated by a towering white cement lighthouse and a long iron roofed customs shed which stood at the beginning of one of the longest jetties in the Far East.

Negotiating the narrow streets of the main residential area, the tourer came to a halt outside an impressively large bungalow.

Looking up at the wide verandah, that ran the entire length of the building, Vivian caught her breath for standing on it, near where they had stopped, were a number of Japanese men clad only in G-strings.

Their driver jumped out and ran around to the passenger door and opened it for his officer who dismounted and entered the building before turning to where they sat.

"Out." he snapped and with a superhuman effort Kinsley, with some assistance from Vivian, lurched from the vehicle to stand swaying in front of the bungalow, the sweat rolling in rivulets down his gaunt face.

Motioning them to follow, the soldier led them up the wooden steps to the opposite end of the verandah to where the Japanese men were. Here he indicated they were to be seated at a cane table.

Time dragged in the heavy humidity of the afternoon as they listened to the desultory conversation of the men at the end of the verandah who occasionally shot glances at the two captives. This left no allusions for Vivian as to who they were talking about.

Their conversation ceased abruptly when six Japanese men, beautifully attired in tailored kimonos, strode on to the verandah from within and headed purposefully for Vivian and Kinsley.

They stopped in front of the pair and the elder in the group signalled to the soldier, who had remained nearby, to come to him.

Marching over he bowed and the older man barked an order at him whereby he turned and facing the prisoners said in atrocious English, "The Colonel wishes to know how many British soldiers in Singapore?"

This stunned Vivian for she reasoned Singapore must have fallen soon after their departure and therefore they should know the answer to that question.

"I don't know, I am a nursing Sister and know nothing of military matters." she replied.

This was swiftly translated to the Colonel who cut the soldier short with a few sharp words leading Vivian to suspect the old boy understood English..

Then it was Kinsley's turn to answer and he carefully explained he had arrived on the last troop convoy into Singapore and had been in the fighting for only a few days before being evacuated.

When this was reported to the Colonel he grunted several words, prompting the interpreter to ask Kinsley if he would work, to which he said he would.

He then turned to Vivian and repeated the question and she said, "Yes, providing I can work in a hospital."

At this stage the group retired inside the bungalow, having evidently concluded their interrogation of the two prisoners, shortly after which a soldier appeared with a tray of biscuits and hot tea and set it down in front of a surprised Vivian.

Famished, the two quickly consumed the biscuits followed by the tea.

No sooner had they finished when they were approached by one of the kimono clad men who handed Vivian a rolled up bandage and sitting beside her flung his leg up and on to the table.

She understood immediately that this was a test and so began to bind his ankle aware of his eyes watching every movement as he assessed the dressing.

When she had finished he took his leg down and withdrew inside.

One of the men, standing at the other end of the verandah, detached himself from his comrades and came over to their table. Leaning across it he addressed Vivian in Japanese at the same time pointing to her neck.

His tone was aggressive and he obviously wanted something as he kept pointing at her. Reaching up she groped around her collar and felt the familiar shape of her Australian rising sun badge.

'So this is what he wants.' she thought, then looking him firmly in the eyes she said aloud. "No."

His voice became icy, demanding, as he placed his hands on his hips signalling his rising belligerence.

"Give it to him Sister, he means business."

Kinsley's whispered words cut through the tense atmosphere and seeing their wisdom, she unpinned her badge and handed it to the Jap with a look of disdain on her face.

He inspected it carefully, turning it over with his fingers, even holding it up for the others to see, then with a swift motion he closed his fist on it and turned to leave.

Vivian's reaction was like that of a striking snake. Leaping to her feet she threw herself in front of the startled Jap.

"That," she spat at him. "is mine and I want it back."

The silence that was to follow was both deep and deadly until a voice of command cut through it.

From the corner of her eye Vivian could make out the figure of the Colonel standing in the doorway.

He snapped a string of Japanese at her detractor, who sullenly opened his hand and held it out to Vivian, his steely black eyes glinting with frustration.

"Thank you." she said coolly, retrieving the coveted badge, immediately pinning it back on her collar with hands that trembled slightly.

As she took her place at the table Kinsley whispered to her. " I don't think you've made a mate there."

****

Later in the day their tourer driver reappeared and told Kinsley to follow him. Moving to the foot of the stairs with Kinsley following as best he could the Jap halted and looked expectantly down the road.

Exhausted by the short walk and the descent of the stairs, Kinsley flopped on to the bottom step. Seeing he was distressed, Vivian rose from the table and holding the water bottle strategically at her side, negotiated the stairs to sit beside him, her back to the railing to hide the hole in her uniform.

Her arm encircled his hunched over shoulders and slowly, he raised his head to look at her.

She saw the deep lines of exhaustion etched in a ravaged face with eyes clouded by constant pain. He had achieved so much in an incredible fight to stay alive but Vivian knew his battle was nearly over. What was more he knew it was over, for it showed in his face...he was ready for peace.

"Kinsley," she whispered, " I want you to know that I admire you very much and I feel a great pride in having had you as a companion."

He looked into her clear blue eyes, which had, during their time together either cajoled, goaded, scolded, placated or reassured him.

"I would never have made it this far if it hadn't been for you, Sister." he said slowly.

In the distance they heard the familiar rattle of the old tourer as it rounded the corner at the far end of the road.

" I used to look at you," he went on, " and wonder, what with everything that happened to you, where you got your strength from to go on. You set the example Sister, you made me determined to be like you."

The car came to a halt opposite the two and the interpreter beckoned to Kinsley to get in the back.

The two rose and clasped hands.

"Goodbye Sister and may God always bless you."

"Goodbye Kinsley, I hope we meet again."

They looked deeply into one another's eyes, with mutual respect and affection, before he turned to shuffle over to the car. Controlling his pain as much as possible, he climbed in and flopped against the back of the seat.

Vivian closed the door as the interpreter jumped into the front seat beside the driver and with a jerk, the old tourer chugged off down the dirt road.

She watched the back of his head, as it rolled from side to side with the motion of the car, until it grew very small to finally disappear around the corner.

With a thumping heart she sat down at the foot of the steps as a feeling of utter loneliness enveloped her, for now she was alone, alone with the people who had tried hard to kill her.

'What was it Alma Beard had said on that day? Bully, there are two things I have always hated in my life....the Japanese and the sea and today I've got both of them.'

Again she heard the gunfire explode in her head.

"Don't be afraid Sister, the Japanese are really very kind people."

Startled by the near perfect English of the female voice she turned and looked up at the verandah.

Standing there was a woman in her early fifties. Of medium height, she was imposing rather than attractive with short dark hair and a slight figure that was dressed in the European fashion of the day.

"You are European?" asked Vivian unable to identify the slight accent.

"Yes my dear," came the reply. " to be more precise, Vichy French."

Vivian knew Vichy France had sided with the Germans, which made them an ally of the Japanese, which explained why this woman looked well treated and at ease.

"Ah," said the woman, clapping her hands "here comes your present."

A guard had walked on to the verandah holding a small, brown monkey, which he placed on the back of a chair at the table.

"Are you not coming up to make his acquaintance?" cooed the woman.

Vivian stirred herself and dragging her travel weary legs up the steps, went over to where the monkey sat.

"He is for your amusement my dear," said the woman, "so you can see how thoughtful the Japanese can be."

Her condescending attitude was beginning to annoy Vivian and it was fortuitous that, at that moment, she heard the clatter of the car returning, at the same time a guard ran out of the bungalow and indicated she should follow him.

With her water-bottle still in place she retreated backwards down the steps, bowing to the near naked men still congregated at the end of the verandah.

She hated herself for bowing to them but it was necessary if she were to hide the hole in the back of her uniform where the bullet had entered.

Climbing in to the idling car Vivian lent lightly against the seat rest and wondered where she was being taken.

With the usual revving of the motor and crashing of gears the car took off and they headed in the same direction Kinsley had taken only a short time before.

The substantial buildings and makeshift shanties of Muntok blurred as they sped through its streets with the driver leaning on the horn to warn the droves of pedestrians that he had the right of way.

Vivian was tired, so very tired, and the afternoon sun, still with a bite to it, added to this lethargy. Content to relax and watch the passing scene, accepting what fate had decreed for her, she began to nod off when the tourer bounced around a corner and almost collided with a column of marching men.

Taking evasive action the driver swung the vehicle to the opposite side of the road and continued on past a long line of allied servicemen accompanied by Japanese guards.

In ranks of three abreast the men moved like automatons, their faces stubbled and gaunt, wearing uniforms representing several countries and varying services, shredded and filthy.

To Vivian, now fully awake, it was a heartbreaking sight. All these fine young men, the pride of their countries, overwhelmed and defeated in such a short space in time, being marched off to a prison camp.

Dust billowed from the back of the tourer sending choking clouds of grit rolling over the marching men who, ignoring it, tramped on.

The rhythmic swaying of the little car, combined with the heat from the sun, soon saw Vivian's eyes close and she dozed.

She was abruptly awakened by the squealing of the car's brakes and a jerking stop. Snapping her eyes open the first thing she found herself staring at was a woman filling a bowl with water from a tap; she was European and wore a Red Cross armband.

Looking about her Vivian could see they had stopped at a wall in which was an arched doorway.

It was toward this that the driver now herded her. Emerging on the other side she found herself in a large open area ringed with huts, in various stages of disrepair, surrounded by the high stone wall.

A very long hut, with a rusting iron roof, stood at the far end of the compound and it was from this direction that a tall young man wearing the remnants of a British army uniform, was hurrying to meet her.

Striding up to where she stood he held out his hand to her.

"Welcome to the Coolie Lines, Sister, and it is indeed a pleasure to see you."

His voice was cultured English upper class and the badges of rank on his uniform told her he was a Captain.

"Me too," she answered as she took his hand in hers.

He pulled a field notebook from a pocket then a pencil stub, at the same time asking if she would be good enough to supply him with some information.

Agreeing, he suggested they head for the large shed and while they were walking he asked for her army number, AGH and the ship she had been on.

She answered his questions at the same time looking about her. There was a set of large gates to one side from behind which a blur of faces were ogling her. Too indistinct to identify whom they belonged to she put it down to inquisitive natives.

The Captain had just asked her where she came ashore and in company with whom, when a woman's voice cried out. "It's Bully!"

At the sound of her nickname Vivian stopped in her tracks and a hot flush rushed through her body.

"Some one over there knows me." she heard herself cry out as she looked wildly about her.

"Hey, Bully, over here!" the voice yelled.

With her mind in a frantic turmoil, Vivian began to stumble toward the gate where she had seen the faces and the Captain called for her to wait until he had finished interviewing her.

"Not now," she flung over her shoulder, "somebody over here knows me."

Inhibited by her wound and torn bloodied feet, she lurched toward the sound of the voice.

The gate began to move, as if under pressure from the other side, then it was flung open and revealed Australian Army Nursing Sisters running to meet her.

"You're alive!" she shouted at them, "you're alive!"

They collided in mid-compound, a hugging, kissing ecstatic mass of women, their spontaneous affection drowning out for Vivian all of the loneliness and horror of the weeks gone by.

She was back amongst her own and it was a wonderful, joyous, feeling.

Initially she did not recognise individuals for no-one was wearing uniform but were dressed like natives in sarongs and small halter neck tops. Carefully searching their faces she realised they were all from the 2/10th.

"Come on Bully, the rest of the girls are over at the Coolie Lines," said a familiar voice.

Instantly Vivian recognised it as belonging to Betty Jeffrey, who had been good to her during her attachment to the 2/10th in Malacca. Flinging their arms around one another and with the others bunched around the two, the smiling, laughing group moved toward the large iron shed.

Sister Jenny Ashton, the Senior Sister, had assumed the role of Acting Sister in Charge of the surviving members of the 2/13th in the absence of the Sister in Charge, Florence Casson.

A tall, imposing woman, she was gentle by nature yet firm when it came to nursing discipline and was held in high esteem by her fellow Sisters.

In company with Sister Veronica Clancy they watched the bunch of high-spirited women approach and soon they were able to identify the tall figure of Vivian Bullwinkel in their midst. Calling the other 2/13th girls together they went out to meet her.

The excited women showered Vivian with questions, eager to hear news of friends. Where had she been for all these weeks? Had she seen the others? Where was Matron Drummond, Jenny Kerr, Mary McGlade, Kathleen Neuss, what happened to Matron Paschke? The names went on as Vivian's smile faded and she stood silently staring back at them.

The voices faltered and the questions stopped as an ominous hush settled over the crowd of nurses as they waited for Vivian's answer.

Vivian couldn't bring herself to tell them what had happened on the beach, the words would not come out, all she could do was look at the faces before her and see the anticipation in their eyes, they wanted her to speak and she couldn't.

The silence was painful for all of them.

"Bully, where are the others?"

It was the gentle, encouraging voice of Sister Ashton that reached her.

Vivian looked at Jenny and heard herself speaking to her in a hollow voice. "They're all dead."

"How could they all be dead?" asked an incredulous voice from amongst the shocked nurses.

Vivian wanted to run, to get away from the questions and the pain they brought her. To some extent she had buried the horrific tragedy deep within her and now that wound was being re-opened, she was being forced to remember it. She knew her fellow Sisters had a right to know for they were all family but how was she going to tell them?

"We surrendered to the Japanese after coming ashore," her voice was low and steady as she began to relate, to her hushed audience, the events as they had happened.

"They took the men away and bayoneted them all and as they walked back the Japs were wiping the blood off their bayonets with bits of cloth."

Several women audibly caught their breath while the others looked numbly at her as if not believing what they were hearing.

"Then, they told us to line up, the whole twenty-two of us, even Halligan and Wight who were wounded, and we were forced into the sea......then.... they shot us."

A loud gasp went up from the horrified nurses and several called out, "No!"

"They were all killed, I was hit, but not seriously," she moved the water bottle aside so they could see the bullet holes and the blood stain on her uniform, "I played dead in the water."

Quietly she went on to tell the shocked nurses of her survival, the meeting up with a wounded British soldier, of her fight for food and the days in the jungle before the final decision to surrender.

As she told her harrowing story many of the girls broke down and wept openly while others, stunned by at what she had said, stared, wide eyed at her unable to either cry or talk.

When she had finished Vivian, surprisingly, felt calm and composed as she listened to the stifled sobbing around her as Sister Ashton moved to her side and placed an arm around her shoulders.

"Come on Bully, I'll show you where you can sleep."

Surrounded by the sorrowful women, Jenny and Vivian walked slowly toward the big shed, the silence, testimony to the grief they shared at the loss of 21 Sisters.

****

The shed was one big open space with a concrete floor that sloped from the edge to the centre, where a sewer drain ran the entire length of the building.

A cement sleeping-platform jutted out from the inside wall, approximately two feet off the floor, and ran down either side. Above this it was open to the elements and overhead, an old sheet iron roof ensured the place would be like an oven during the day.

A repulsive stench, from the central drain, pervaded the place at all times.

As the group of nurses neared the shed they were approached by two Australian Officers who, asking for Vivian, introduced themselves as Wooten and Quinn from Army Intelligence.

Word had already reached them of the massacre they said, via the camp's bush telegraph, or word of mouth. They asked Vivian to confirm that it had happened and that she was the only survivor.

She gave them a brief account of the fate of the men and the shooting of the nurses, at the conclusion of which one of the officers cautioned her and the others. "Talking about it," he said, "could lead to Vivian's death, if not all of you, because the Japanese would not want witnesses." He went on to say the Japs had committed a major war crime and when the war was over they would prosecute the guilty and to do that, they needed witnesses so they were to treat this episode as top secret and to discuss it with no one.

Turning to Vivian he held out his hand. "Sister you make me feel very proud to be an Australian....good luck."

With that the two officers departed, letting the group continue on to the shed where Wilma Oram found a vacant sleeping shelf for Vivian. Promising to see what she could do about getting her some 'civvy' clothes, Wilma told her to get some rest while she was away. Wearily Vivian climbed up and stretched out on the bare concrete surface and soon fell asleep.

The lighthouse at Muntòk, Bangka Island, where many survivors of sunken ships came ashore.
(Author)

Muntok Beach and Bangka Strait. The Vyner Brooke *was attacked and sank some 16 kilometres out from this point.*
(Author)

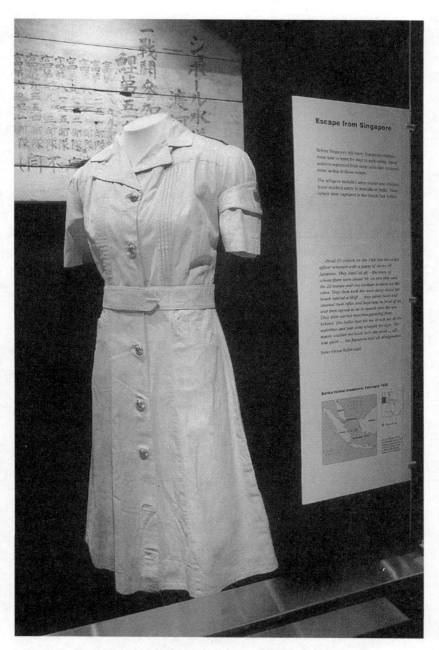

The Australian Army Nursing Service uniform, with its Red Cross armband, worn by Sister Vivian Bullwinkel sole survivor of the massacre of 21 fellow Sisters by the Japanese on Bangka Island in February 1942. The uniform is displayed in the Australian War Memorial Canberra. (By courtesy of the Australian War Memorial)

THE COOLIE LINES

The Coolie Lines had been constructed long before the war to house the Chinese coolies who worked the ships in Muntok.

When the Japanese occupied the town they turned it into a make shift prison for civilian prisoners . The conditions were deplorable. A single stagnant well was the only water source and an open drain, located behind the big shed, served as a communal latrine, the contents of which flowed sluggishly through the camp giving off an offensive odour.

There were neither baths or showers and one shack, set aside as a hospital, boasted several doctors but no medical supplies or equipment to treat the sick and injured.

Many arrived at the camp, having survived the sinking of their ships, with only what they wore. These people were forced to sell watches and jewellery to those who had time to prepare for their internment, having worked on plantations or held a civilian or government position.

Thirty surviving Sisters of the 2/10th, 2/13th and three from the 2/4th Casualty Clearing Station were imprisoned with the civilians in the Coolie Lines, all of them still suffering the effects of the sinking of the *Vyner Brooke*.

Some had sustained raw necks from chafing life jackets, others deep burns to their hands from using ropes, and there were multiple lacerations and light shrapnel wounds inflicted by the bombing. All had lost their luggage and shoes.

Bereft of soap, tooth-brushes, combs, make-up, mirrors, bedding and the other niceties of life they scrounged or rummaged the camp, for any bits and pieces they could make use of.

Someone found an old toothbrush in a drain and after cleaning it, shared the mangy brush with five other Sisters. An old milk tin served as a food plate and a rusted shoehorn a spoon.

As to the assorted clothes they were wearing, Wilma explained to Vivian that these were made from remnants left behind in the old Muntok cinema by allied servicemen and discovered when they were incarcerated there after coming ashore near the lighthouse.

Those amongst them who could sew converted the slacks, shirts and greatcoats into shorts and tops, their uniforms folded and carefully put aside for special occasions.

Food, in the form of boiled rice, which was frequently burnt, was issued once a day at ten o'clock in the morning and the Sisters partook of this away from the rest of the camp. This was not born out of aloofness, or a feeling of superiority, but an automatic routine. They had been accustomed to sharing each other's company which they had been doing since joining the army and they could see no reason for discontinuing the enjoyable custom simply because they were in a prison camp.

For her first few rice rations Vivian, having arrived with nothing, shared Wilma's utensils until she was able to scrounge her own.

The next day was spent bringing Vivian up to date with what had happened following the sinking of the ship.

Jessie Simons, with both hands heavily bandaged to protect her rope burnt palms told her story.

Sliding down a rope and into the water Jessie struck out for a life raft and reaching it hauled herself aboard joining two British sailors and the radio operator from the *Vyner Brooke*. One of the sailors had been badly burnt. Later she was joined by Patti Gunther and Winnie Davis and toward dusk three women swam over to the raft, one soon after drifting away unconscious, while the remaining two, who turned out to be mother and daughter, held on grimly.

That night the burnt sailor slipped off the raft. Powerless to stop him because of their weakened state, they watched him float away.

Drifting with the current, they hit an anchored merchant ship loading Japanese troops into landing barges. Their raft scraped along the ship's side, yet no one on board appeared to have any interest in them and the tide swept them on past the ship and down the coast. Later they saw a fire on shore and made a final effort to swim the raft toward the light but again the current beat them and they drifted until dawn to find they were in the middle of yet another Japanese invasion fleet.

A landing craft, with two Japanese sailors, was returning from the beach empty and in response to their waving, it altered course, came along side and took them on board.

Coming ashore near an ammunition unloading party, comprising of a number of G-string wearing men, one corpulent fellow broke away from the others and waded over, offering his extended hand to Jessie. Still weak from her exertions and not having regained her land legs as yet, Jessie toppled into the Jap's arms when she tried to stand.

"So", she told the others, "I maintain I didn't fall into the hands of the Japs....I fell into their arms."

They spent that night in a deserted pig-sty, roughly twelve feet square, with Patti going to sleep gripping an iron bar for she reasoned anything could happen in a place such as that.

The next day they were marched through the jungle to be locked up in the Muntok cinema before their ultimate removal to the Coolie Lines.

"Bully, Bully wake up."

Vivian fought her tiredness as she came out of a sound sleep at the sound of some one calling her name. Fuzzy-headed and unsure of her surroundings, the putrid smell that assailed her nose told her she was in the shed within the Coolie Lines.

"What is it?" she asked, recognising Wilma.

"There's a Chinese chap here, says you're wanted over at the hospital."

Wide-awake by now, Vivian went outside to where a young Chinese man waited and she followed him over to the shack that served as a hospital, there to be met by a British nurse.

"Over here Sister." she said leading her down a central aisle, in the darkened hut, to either side of which were raised platforms supporting the sick and wounded. Stopping halfway down she indicated an inert shape, "He is sinking fast, and has been asking for you."

Vivian sat on the edge of the wooden platform and lowered her face to his as the British nurse walked away.

"Kinsley," she whispered, "I'm here."

Stirring, his eyes fluttered open in a bearded face saturated by perspiration and he turned his head toward her, his dry, cracked lips parting. "Sister?" he breathed more than spoke the word.

She took his hand in hers and squeezed it.

"Yes, Kinsley, it's me."

A wave of sadness engulfed her as she looked at this intrepid man who had endured so much for it all to end like this, in a dark, squalid hut thousands of miles from his loved ones in England. He drew a hacking breath and as he fought to speak she recognised the familiar rasping, liquid sound, of pleuropneumonia.

"Thank you…. for everything Sister."

She felt a light pressure on her hand as he tried to squeeze it.

Vivian smiled at the dying soldier and said softly, "Thank **you** Kinsley."

"You…. had better…. go now." he said in a barely audible voice and weakening visibly he closed his eyes.

It was tragic and heartbreaking for her. She had seen so many young men die these past few months; some slipped quietly away as if welcoming the coming peace while others, for some unknown reason, fought death to the very end. In war soldiers die and nurses, such as herself, had to accept that, as she must now accept Kinsley's death.

Yet this man was different, for they had found each other at a time when they believed they would die alone in a hostile world. Together they had shared the horror, the hunger, the pain and the despair of their adversity and had fought, as two human beings, to retain the dignity of their race. They had survived through the solace of their comradeship; now the physical presence of that fraternity was passing, the memories to linger in time, never to be forgotten.

Sitting in the dimness of the native hut, in the primitive Coolie Lines, in a small, remote town, Vivian found herself searching for the words of Florence Nightingale. 'What was it that great woman had said, in that hospital full of dying men on the Crimean Peninsula, so long ago?'

She groped for the elusive words learnt as an exuberant young nursing student and, finding them, nodded to herself as they echoed clearly in her mind. *'No soldier should die alone upon a foreign soil.'*

She bent down to where he lay, her firm hand holding his, and whispered.

" I'll stay with you for a little while longer Kinsley."

Twenty minutes later the British soldier, Kinsley, died.

****

Around three o'clock that morning, Japanese guards woke the camp with flashing torches and with fixed bayonets they prodded the inmates out of the huts and into the compound.

Snatching up their meagre possessions, consisting mainly of a uniform and eating utensils, the nursing Sisters assembled outside in the blackness, asking all about them if any one knew what it was all about.

The rumour was they were shifting camp and were headed for Palembang on the island of Sumatra. This movement was later confirmed when they were issued with a portion of rice for breakfast and another paltry amount, wrapped in a banana leaf, and herded aboard a fleet of open-backed trucks fitted with wooden cattle rails.

Loaded to capacity, with standing room only, the convoy lurched out of the camp and into the streets of Muntok, the passengers swaying from side to side with the motion of the trucks as a pale streak of peach-coloured cloud heralded the coming of another hot day.

Arriving at Muntok wharf the prisoners were quickly off-loaded and told to go to the end of the jetty and wait.

It was a sad parade of people who made the journey along the two to three mile length of the jetty. Many carried loaded suitcases and dragged tired young children by the hand, while women on their own were left to struggle, as best they could, with both and for some there was the added responsibility of a babe in arms.

The Australian group, reaching the end of the jetty settled down, some to sleep, others to pass the time in light conversation or simply stare out to sea absorbed in private reflections.

Vivian had noticed the bandages on Betty Jeffrey's and Iole Harper's hands and thought now was as good a time as any to find out what had happened.

They told an amazing story of endurance. It started when they left the sinking *Vyner Brooke* by way of a rope, which caused the deep burns to their hands. In the water they went looking for Matron Paschke, who could not swim, and although they met up with a lot of the girls there was no sign of Matron.

After spending some time hanging on to a stretcher, which they shared with

110

Patti Gunther and Win Davis, the two struck out through the thick oily sea for a raft.

To their joy and amazement they found it was supporting not only Matron Paschke but Sisters Caroline Ennis, Annie Trennery, Gladys McDonald, Hilda Dorsch and Mary Clarke. Caroline was holding two little ones, a Chinese boy of around four and an English girl of three. With the Australians were two Malay sailors and five civilian women.

"Matron was as pleased as punch she had made it that far," said Iole briefly interrupting before Betty continued with her narrative.

They were well organised in shifts which allowed the sick and injured to remain on the raft while the others took turns hanging on in the water and resting on top. Iole frequently swam around the raft counting heads and encouraging people to kick a little harder and get further away from the sinking ship. At one stage, after the ship had gone and it was getting dark they saw a fire on shore and put in an extra effort to reach it but the current caught them and they were swept back out to sea.

Later that night they picked up the flashing beam of a lighthouse and steered their craft toward it.

The current however was too strong and it carried their raft through the dark shapes of a Japanese invasion fleet where they cannoned off the hulls of several troop ships before floating free and being again carried back out to sea.

Daylight revealed them to be well out from the coast and miles further down. From their raft they could just make out the shore and the shapes of trees and following a discussion amongst Matron and the Sisters it was decided Betty and Iole, two of the strongest swimmers amongst the survivors, together with the two Malay sailors, would attempt the swim to shore.

As soon as they landed they would seek assistance to mount a rescue for the others.

They were no sooner in the water and swimming when a current hit the raft, spinning it around, taking it swiftly away and over the horizon with its human cargo shouting at them.

Betty and Iole, staying within a relatively close distance to one another, struck out for the distant shore in company with the two Malay sailors who, several hours later they found they had lost contact with. As the two young women swam on they called out to one another to ensure they kept together.

Iole was in a different current to that of Betty and was the first to reach shallow water where she waited for her companion. They finally linked up several hours later and finding a small strip of land crawled ashore. The trees grew right down into the water and were so thick that they were impenetrable. The girls rested by hanging off the boughs before continuing their search for a landing place. Kicking off again the two swimmers found the mouth of a river, which they spent the rest of the day investigating together the many tributaries that came down to meet it. There were no beaches to be found, only mangroves with razor-sharp tree spikes sticking out of the black water.

111

It was beginning to get dark and the tide was going out exposing the river bottom covered in mangrove roots. They must find a place in which to spend the night. Splashing around in what water was left Betty and Iole felt the tree spikes lacerating their legs, arms and stomachs while their deeply burned hands throbbed with intense pain. Both were physically exhausted.

Betty called out to Iole, who was some 15 yards ahead, and asked what her name was. Iole, a Western Australian, was with the 2/13th and the two had never met. Betty recounted to Vivian how she and Iole stood in the mangrove, up to their thighs in black water, swapping names and addresses and looking one another over.

The exchange calmed them and looking around they chose a suitable swamp tree and spent the night sitting in a fork swatting at hordes of mosquitos and trying to keep from falling into the water.

Both women hallucinated during the long night.

Betty saw Sister Win Davis give an orderly a glass of water and direct him to where she sat precariously in the tree; as she reached out both the glass and Win dissolved into blackness

Iole looked down on a perfectly comfortable bed that had been correctly made up with pure white sheets and a fluffy pillow. It was just below Betty and Iole began urging her to get in it and go to sleep. When Betty, who could see nothing below her except swamp water, refused her companion got 'really scotty' and refused to talk to her for the rest of the night.

Next morning, with the tide in, the two women painfully lowered themselves back into the water and swam up river for several hours during which time they spotted several crocodiles lazing on the bank. Although disturbed at this sight it did not deter them from going on, there was no alternative until they found solid ground.

Later in the day they saw a patch of green shoreline, about thirty feet wide, which looked most inviting, so swimming over to it they climbed up for a rest.

The green bank turned out to be a floating island made up entirely of vegetation, into which they sank several feet.

Gathering up several armloads of palm fronds from nearby, which they had to break off with their elbows because of the injuries to their hands, they placed them on the floating vegetation to form a mattress and promptly lay down and fell asleep.

Mosquitos, sand flies and the nearby coughing of a wild jungle animal ensured they did not enjoy a full night's sleep and at first light they wearily flopped back into the water and headed up river from whence they had heard a dog bark during the night.

They had been swimming for some time when a boat full of natives rounded a bend in the river. Spotting the women in the water they hauled them aboard and took them back upstream to their village.

As the boat pulled alongside a primitive makeshift jetty, Iole nudged Betty and pointed to the sandy beach on which lay the bodies of some thirteen sharks. It was a sobering thought to think they had been sharing the same river for the last two days with these killers.

The people of the village could not do enough for the two Australian women and they were fed as well as having their many injuries treated. It was then, while resting, that they met a Chinese gentleman, whom they nicknamed Charlie Chan after the famous Hollywood movie detective. Dressed in an impeccable white suit and speaking perfect English he looked the part.

Apparently, so the local villagers told them, he escaped from Singapore only to be arrested on Bangka by the occupying Japanese while attempting an escape to Java. They had not imprisoned him which implied they tolerated him for some particular reason.

Charlie Chan informed them there were a number of white prisoners in Muntok and urged their surrender for, "to remain in the village," he said, "is to endanger the lives of those who have sheltered you." As neither woman wanted this they agreed to surrender and Charlie went off to fetch the Japanese, returning within the hour with a truckload of soldiers.

Betty told Vivian they got along fine with each other. The soldiers spoke fluent Japanese, they spoke fluent English and the conversation concluded when the Japs stuck the tips of their bayonets against their stomachs and indicated they should get in the truck.

Arriving at the Coolie Lines Betty said they were confused when they saw what they believed to be a number of Malay women walking around and not an Australian nurse in sight. As they passed two sarong clad women, one addressed her, "A bit haughty today aren't we, old thing."

The broad Australian accent made them look closely at the two 'natives' and they saw it was Jennie Greer and Beryl Woodbridge. At last they were back amongst Australians and the occasion felt like a good old-fashioned homecoming.

CAMP ONE....BUKIT BESAR

The ships to transport them to Sumatra did not arrive until the next morning, forcing the large group of captives to spend an uncomfortable night attempting to sleep on the timber decking of the Muntok jetty.

Both twin-deck river craft, the boats had seen many years of work in the tropics, if the depth and extent of their rust was any indication. Several launches began ferrying the waiting people out to where they rode at anchor, the men to one, the women and children to the other.

With the loading completed the ships headed out in company and into the Straits, their decks packed with hot, flustered and perspiring passengers as an angry sun climbed halfway toward its noonday zenith.

Vivian, perched on top of a large pile of wood destined for Japanese cooking fires, was enjoying the fresh sea air. Leaning back she watched the rolling swell sweep by and her thoughts turned suddenly to her mother. The heart-rending bitterness she felt was because she knew where she was but her mother didn't. Dispirited and frustrated Vivian could only stare at the sea and live the last few weeks again

The two old vessels found the mouth of the Musi River and proceeded upstream, keeping to the middle of the channel, the decaying mangroves giving way to grassy fields, native huts and finally isolated villages.

The further they journeyed up river the more water traffic they encountered and Vivian watched the procession of small boats, propelled by paddle wielding natives slip by.

They docked at the ferry Station in Palembang around five o'clock that afternoon and were held on board while a handful of Japanese, stripped to the waist, supervised the unloading of both ships by a team of natives.

Except for the activity on the wharf there was little else to see apart from several dilapidated godowns and two corrugated iron sheds at the far end.

With the unloading of the cargo completed, a squad of Japanese soldiers rushed on to both vessels and began moving the captives down the gangways to the wharf where they were ordered to line up.

Here they remained for two hours, under a still blazing hot sun.

Ultimately the sound of truck engines announced the arrival of transportation and quickly the guards unhinged the rear cattle gates and indicated that the prisoners were to climb aboard. The loading was quickly executed and the convoy moved off and wound its way through the streets of Palembang.

At one point a number of Japanese soldiers were in the process of assembling a crowd of local people, evidently to show off their prisoners and humiliate the great white race.

As Vivian's truck drew abreast of the gathering crowd the Japanese began urging those by the roadside to jeer at the prisoners and several, as if afraid not to, reluctantly broke into some low-key heckling.

This infuriated the Australian Sisters who, spontaneously, responded with booing and catcalls. The reaction they got from the crowd was more than they had hoped for. The locals stopped jeering and stood stunned, mouths agape, as the white women hurled abuse at them and even stuck their tongues out in a most unrefined and crude manner. The Japanese renewed their efforts in an endeavour to get the crowds to demonstrate but with little result for the people had become sullen and silent, still shocked by the white women's outburst.

As the convoy picked up speed after leaving the scene of the demonstration the Sisters, their spirits restored, burst into laughter at the memory of the shocked look on the faces of the people and the incensed guards, who began shouting and hitting out at the totally bewildered natives.

The line of vehicles came to a halt in front of a Chinese school where a group of British and Dutch officers waited. A British officer, introduced himself, adding there was a big pot of stew waiting for them.

There was no need to repeat the offer for the back of the truck quickly emptied as the Sisters scrambled down and led the push into the school building.

After they had eaten, the officer who had met them split the new arrivals into groups of 40 allocating each a classroom where they were to sleep the night on bare boards with Japanese guards patrolling constantly.

The next morning saw them all with puffy, almost unrecognisable faces, the result of mosquito bites. Following the issuing of a small ration of rice, the nurses were visited by the Senior British Officer, Air Commodore Modin.

He stood at ease just inside the doorway to their room surveying them casually. A man in his forties and of medium height, he was a career airman who suddenly found himself in command of a mixed bag of civilian nationals, including a bunch of Australian Army Nursing Sisters who looked more like the local natives than nurses. He had just finished protracted negotiations with his Japanese counterpart concerning the future of the Australian nurses and he was there to inform them of the outcome of that meeting.

It had been his intention, he told them, to have the Japanese agree to their military status. This meant the nurses would be accorded the privileges of their rank, be entitled to accompany the service personnel when they left and be paid as serving officers during their detention.

Unfortunately he said, the Japanese refused to acknowledge that they were members of the military and insisted they were to remain with the civilian prisoners, which, they informed him, were to be moved that day.

"I am sorry I was unable to persuade them to let you go with us," said

Modin, "but I can assure you it wasn't from a lack of trying." Wishing them good luck he left the room.

Sister Mavis Hannah, from the 2/4th CCS, wanted to know, "If we aren't Army Nursing Sisters, what the hell are we?"

A spirited discussion on this topic followed until the Senior Sister, 2/10th, Nesta James, suggested their time would be better spent preparing for the move that day.

It was early afternoon before the guards ordered every one out of the school and onto the road where they were lined up in ranks of three and marched off. This time there would be no motor transport.

The Australians stayed together as a group on the rough road and Vivian, in an effort to relieve the pain in her bare feet and side, concentrated on the happy memories of Sunday picnics in Broken Hill under the gum trees and beside the river.

The sky was beginning to darken as they reached the camp which appeared from out of the thick vegetation as a row of houses. The guards split the Australians up, allocating 15 to number 26 and 17 to number 24.

The houses were large, in a good state of repair and had electricity connected.

The investigating nurses assumed Dutch people had lived in the houses and had been forced to leave in a hurry for there was European food on the kitchen table as well as in the kitchen cupboards.

The bedroom wardrobes were full of adult and children's clothing, giving credence to the quick flight theory and much to the satisfaction of the occupying women. There were even squeals of delight when the bathroom yielded up a cake of precious soap. Yet the most exciting find of all was made by the girls in house 24.

It stood in the kitchen, the door open wide for the admiring circle of women to glimpse its cavernous interior, while the handsome top gleamed from constant and dedicated cleaning. It was the grandest electric stove they had seen in a long time.

Vivian, in 26, chose a sleeping spot before joining the others in the main room for a conference called by Jenny Ashton.

After setting the house rules the Acting Sister in Charge allocated tasks, one of which was to build a fireplace and oven in front of the house for cooking. Another was to investigate a small store up the road to see if they could buy food there, especially eggs.

Mavis Hannah announced she had ten dollars, Singapore money and volunteered to go.

At this point their meeting was interrupted by a knock on the doorframe and several women trooped in, each laden with loaves of bread and bunches of bananas which they set down on the table. In a thick Dutch accent one of the women welcomed them to Bukit Besar and went on to say they could get more supplies from a Mrs. Blake in house number 7.

Following a flood of words of appreciation from the Sisters the Dutch women departed, bidding them to enjoy what they had left.

Before they could resume their meeting a diminutive native woman walked in, her white teeth flashing a smile as she announced. " Me Seetee."

They watched wide-eyed as the woman went to the table and placed a large bowl and a kettle beside the food already there saying she had brought them rice and beans and hot tea.

Again a chorus of "thank you" rang out from the appreciative Sisters and with a delicate bow the gift-bearer left as silently as she had entered.

Intoxicated by the sight of so much food, and with spirits soaring, they rushed to conclude the meeting and their allocated chores in anticipation of the feast to come, their first substantial meal since leaving Singapore.

Daily life in the camp at Bukit Besar began to take on a new meaning for the Australian nurses because they were able to augment their daily ration of rice with other food from the camp store.

In addition, through diligent bartering, they obtained other essentials such as toothbrushes, clothing, cushions, furniture, playing cards and even a chess set.

They formed District Nursing Teams with sections rostered on a daily basis. These teams, each of two Sisters, visited all within the camp bringing a measure of comfort to the sick despite the scarcity of even the most rudimentary medicines. Vivian and Wilma Oram operated as one of the teams. When not on duty the women busied themselves by cleaning house, searching for firewood, fetching rations, preparing meals and repairing clothing.

Because they kept busy the Japanese guards did not overly interfere in their routine although one incident gave the Australians cause for concern.

It occurred when a Sister was bathing in the bathroom and happened to look up to see a guard watching her. She froze with fear as he minutely inspected her nakedness, then unexpectedly he laughed and walked out of the house.

Discussing the encounter that night the women thought it significant enough to be raised with the others for it posed the question of possible mandatory relations being forced on them by the guards. It was agreed the situation should be closely monitored in future.

How quickly this situation was to develop and from an unexpected quarter was not realised at the time.

A Japanese non-commissioned officer, in company with a European woman interpreter, visited the nurses several days later and proceeded to tell them, through the interpreter, that they were to vacate both houses immediately as the Camp Commander wished to convert them into an Officers' Club. The nurses, he said, would be accommodated further up the road. Meanwhile, they were to clean the houses thoroughly and await instructions as to what entertainment they were to provide.

At a later conference of all the Australian nurses they discussed the implications of this order and agreed it plainly inferred they were to become comfort girls for the officers. The meeting also confirmed that a plan should be prepared, one that would prevent them from being forced into prostitution, at the same time avoiding reprisals by the Japanese against them, or the civilians in camp. Meanwhile as there was no sense in upsetting their captors prematurely they set about stripping and cleaning the houses.

Working in the humidity of a threatening downpour and with sweat glistening on arms and faces, they methodically removed the furniture, flywire, light cords, curtains, floor coverings and the electric stove. Then standing out in a thundering rainstorm they jested amongst themselves as they passed each item along the human chain they had formed which extended from their old accommodation to the new. Iole Harper suggested they should rename the place Lavender Street. When asked why, she explained that, "seeing the Japs are going to open an officers' brothel here it should be named after the well known red light district in Singapore." The suggestion was greeted with roars of laughter from the line of rain-soaked women.

"Oh, and by the way," yelled Iole over the rolling thunder, "it's my birthday today."

The laughter turned to cries of "happy birthday" and their boisterous voices could be heard above the noise of the storm by the civilians, huddled in their houses, who shook their heads and questioned the sanity of the crazy Australians.

Several weeks passed before news was sent, via the woman interpreter, that the opening of the Officers' Club was mooted for that week and the Australian Sisters were to attend. Failure to comply with this order would see all food rations to the camp stopped.

Sister James, highly indignant at the order, told the woman interpreter to inform the Camp Commander that the Australian Sisters would not be attending their Officers' Club.

When she repeated this to a meeting of the women later that day a cheer went up and they agreed unanimously to face the developing situation together and damn the consequences.

For the next four days the Japanese withheld all rations from the prisoners in Bukit Besar putting a heavy demand on individual food reserves. Despite this and the pleas from all sections of the camp to give in to the Japanese, the Sisters resolve did not weaken and they continued to defy their captors.

It was all brought to a head the following day when the Japanese Commander sent the interpreter to deliver an ultimatum to the Australians.

An inquiry, announced the interpreter, was to be held in the Officers' Club the next day and the Australian nurses were to attend, individually, the first being Sister Winnie Davis.

The Sisters decided to go along with the interviews and after attending the first one Win Davis recounted what had happened to a hushed audience of her colleagues.

On entering the room Win saw there were four Japanese Officers seated behind a table, the one in the centre she recognised as the senior officer in camp, the others she did not know.

Following an exchange of bows the youngest of the three passed her a sheet of paper and indicated she should read it.

Poorly typed, apparently on a typewriter with an ancient ribbon, it was very difficult to read and the ungrammatical English further exacerbated this.

Having got the gist of the document and with her self control beginning to slip away, Win slammed the paper down and with all the contempt and vehemence at her command she flung one word at her captors.

"No.!"

The senior man took up a pencil from the table and offered it to her saying in halting English that she was not thinking correctly and she should sign.

"Can't you understand?" said Win, " n – o spells no!"

This time one of the others leaned forward and fixing her with his dark viperish eyes hissed.

"No sign…you die."

Win, now composed, reminded them that they were Australian Army Nursing Sisters with the rank of Lieutenant and not prostitutes. Further more they would not give of their bodies in return for food privileges no matter what the consequences.

With a low hissing of breath, as he sucked air through clenched teeth, the senior officer dismissed her.

Jessie Blanche was then called only to reiterate what Win had told them, others followed and all repeated the same word, "No."

Finally, realising that the Australian women were not going to sign the document agreeing to be comfort women, the Japanese stopped the interviews.

On the morning of the announced opening of the Officers' Club the Australians were visited by two Englishmen, a Mr. Tunn and a Mr. Stevenson, accompanied by the lady interpreter.

Tunn said the Japanese were demanding that six women from their ranks were to attend the Club that night. If they did not there would be dire circumstances for all. He went on to say that both he and Mr. Stevenson were told they were to run the bar in both houses, therefore they could keep an eye on things and ensure they were not left alone with the Japs. In conclusion, he implored the Australian women to reconsider their stand for the Japanese had made it quite clear to him that, if they did not agree to attend they would start executing prisoners from within the camp.

From what he had said the Sisters knew he had both their interest, and that of their fellow prisoners at heart and that the Japanese had placed him in an unenviable position.

Without hesitation, they agreed to send Sisters to the Club that night.

It was time to implement their plan.

As their strength lay in numbers all the Sisters would go except for the very attractive ones, such as Pat Gunther, the rest were to make themselves as unattractive as possible.

Greeted by squeals of delight they set about their collective preparations with enthusiasm.

Both Vivian and Wilma decided to wear their uniform, for the loosely hanging, one piece garment hid the curves of the body. The finishing touches included twigs in their hair, dirt rubbed on face and arms, with Vivian going barefoot and Wilma slipping into a borrowed pair of men's boots.

When they were ready the women inspected each other and so successful were their attempts at creating ugliness that they fell about in fits of laughter declaring they were more than ready to vamp the honourable oriental gentlemen of the Officers' Club.

At precisely eight o'clock 22 women assembled outside one of their former houses and marched in to confront six very surprised Japanese Officers.

The two groups stood facing one another, the men eyeing with disbelief, the dishevelled and unbecoming appearance of the women gawking at them with imbecilic expressions on their dirty faces.

The silence was overpowering until an officer stepped forward and in halting English, offered them a drink to which they replied, " we would like some milk."

The Jap said there was no milk, only spirits, to which Blanche Hempstead, who hailed from Queensland and could drink and swear with the best of the cattle drovers, replied in a sweetly innocent voice that, "Australian girls were nice girls and did not drink alcohol."

If Vivian had not immediately controlled herself she would have burst out laughing at this ridiculous statement of Blanche's.

The awkward silence that followed was thankfully broken by a tinkling of glasses and the appearance of Mr. Stevenson bearing a tray full of soft drinks, which he distributed to the ladies.

Vivian soon woke to the fact that only one Jap had a slight grasp of English, for, following another period of silence, he asked why they did not wear lipstick and powder and, if they wanted to, they could go to Palembang and buy some.

In answer to this the perplexed officer was told Australian women did not wear face make up.

Another long silence until Mr. Stevenson returned with biscuits and peanuts, which the women pounced on and started consuming while the Jap officers sipped their drinks and openly ogled them.

Without warning and catching the girls by surprise the six officers rose to their feet and the English speaking one demanded that 6 of the women go to the house next door. A dangerous situation was now beginning to develop.

Remembering their preset plan, which called for them not to be split into small groups, half the Sisters stood up and immediately left the room for next door. This prompted the bewildered officers to break into rapid Japanese while Vivian and the others centred their attention on the peanuts. At the end of their exchange of words the English speaking officer abruptly told them to go.

The amazed but relieved women jumped to their feet, bowed and fled into the darkened street outside.

In the house next door a similar scene was being played out except the Japanese officers dismissed the women and demanded four remain.

Mavis Hannah, from South Australia and the forceful one of the 2/4th CCS, volunteered to stay and she was immediately joined by Sisters Eileen Short, Val Smith and Blanche Hempstead all Queenslanders from the 2/13th.

Reassured by Mavis that they would be alright the other Sisters reluctantly left the house and adjourned to the opposite side of the street to take up a watching position from behind some shrubbery.

It was here that Vivian and her group joined them and together they stared silently at the house tense and apprehensive for it needed only one scream for the lot of them to have gone charging in.

As soon as the door had closed behind the departing Sisters, the four inebriated young officers lurched over to where the girls sat and, hauling them to their feet, led them through the doorway out into the street.

Mavis was first to grasp what they had in mind and voiced this to her companions.

"The creeps are taking us back to their quarters." she whispered.

It was then, in desperation, they hatched a plan designed to cool the Jap's ardour.

Blanche hit on the idea of pretending to have tuberculosis, a disease highly feared by the Japanese, and Val Smith, a heavy smoker, broke in to a hacking cough which would have convinced any doctor that she was in an advanced stage of TB.

Immediately Blanche, following Val's example, threw herself at the Jap holding her and went into a violent coughing spasm.

Horrified, their captors pushed the two aside and whipping out handkerchiefs clamped them firmly over their mouths before staggering off down the road.

This was the cue for Blanche and Val to depart in the opposite direction which left Mavis and 'Shorty' Short contending with their would be paramours.

Shorty had formulated her own plan. Seizing her very tipsy, overweight Jap, she told him they were going for a brisk walk to sober him up and proceeded to drag him up the road at a brisk pace, ignoring his protests.

Reaching the top of the hill she whirled the puffing officer around and marched him back down the street shouting orders at the top of her voice. The physical effort was all too much for the corpulent Jap who, disengaging himself from 'Shorty's' grip, headed off into the night leaving her to escape.

Meanwhile, as Mavis watched 'Shorty' drag her Jap up the hill, an encircling arm warned her there was mischief afoot. Instinctively she turned and shoved the drunken officer in the chest with both hands.

Propelled backward by the unexpected force of her rejection, the Jap struggled to maintain his balance until the long Samurai sword at his side thrust itself between his legs sending him crashing to the roadway. Here he lay, limbs flailing in the air, as Mavis, seizing the opportunity, took off.

All this had been viewed by their compatriots hidden behind the hedge, who, despite the seriousness of the events, could not suppress their laughter at the antics of 'Shorty' Short and the other girls.

They talked late into the night about what had happened and the possible reprisals to be expected next morning.

Finally, they agreed to take their story to Air Commodore Modin so he could intervene, on their behalf, at the highest level.

A delegation, to include Nesta James, Jenny Ashton, Wilma Oram and Vivian, was elected to contact the camp doctor, who also visited the servicemen's camp and ask if he would carry a message to Modin.

The doctor, once informed of the attempt by the Japanese to coerce the Australian women into prostitution, said he would pass this on to Air Commodore Modin during his next visit, which, in due course, he did.

Although frustrated at the stance taken by the nurses the Japanese did not carry out serious reprisals which could have been through embarrassment, instead they chose to cut off their rations, including purchases from the shop and gifts of food from other inmates.

By the second day they were out of food and the decision was made by the nurses to divide the group into pairs, each to scour the camp for anything edible, but to avoid asking for or, receiving food from fellow captives.

The hunt met with a measure of success, Jessie Simons and Mavis Hannah coming up with the best result.

Not only did they dig up a large tapioca root, they were also given ten Guilders by a friendly native and news from Australia.

Evidently, they told their attentive audience later that day, the native had not only been watching them scratch around with a sharpened stick but knew the Japanese had cut off their food supply.

Calling them over to the barbed wire fence he spoke in very good English, saying he knew of their plight and would lend them ten Guilders to buy food, through the wire, from the local people. He went on to say he had a secret radio and listened to the news broadcasts and a few days ago there had been mention of Australian Army Nurses arriving back in Australia on the ship *Empire Star.* This was greeted with cheers from the Sisters who spontaneously decided to celebrate their colleagues' escape with whatever there was to eat.

Browsing through a backdated copy of the *Australian Womens' Weekly*, which one of the girls had discovered in a cupboard, Vivian came across a picture of herself with Sisters Gunther, Rayner, Glover, Bridge and Tait, relaxing while off duty at the hospital in Malacca.

The smiling young women, dressed in starched uniforms and large white veils, seemed to belong to another time for so much had changed since the photo was taken. Some had returned safely to Australia, others were dead and a few were prisoners of the Japanese. For Vivian they were memories too bitter to revisit.

It was Jenny Ashton who brought her the good news.

Walking into the house, Jenny looked at Vivian and the other girls and with a hint of triumph in her voice told them there had been a visit by a Japanese General. Following an inspection of the camp he ordered the Officers' Club closed and then informed the camp officers they were all to be transferred immediately.

This much she had learnt from the camp doctor who had accompanied the General.

Evidently, so the doctor reported, the Air Commodore had been furious when he had told him of the Japanese efforts to obtain the Australians as comfort women. Storming off to see the General he remonstrated with him as to the integrity of his officers trying to force Australian Army Nursing Sisters into prostitution and concluded by saying "It's not cricket Sir! and furthermore, it's not on."

What's more, the Jap General agreed.

The news broke the tension of the last few days as they realised everything would revert to comparative normality and their rations would be reinstated.

CAMP TWO....IRENELAAN

Vivian woke to the sound of running feet and shouted commands. It was still dark and she heard the others stir when a Jap guard entered the house and screamed something at them in Japanese before departing. Then the questions started.

"What's going on?"

"What's all the noise about?"

The answer came from a Dutch woman who told them they were on the move again and warned that the Japs were confiscating knives and scissors.

Those who possessed such valuable instruments hid them as best they could among their miserably small collection of clothes and utensils. Vivian, who possessed neither scissors or a knife, snatched up her small bundle, slipped on a pair of clogs she had been given and shuffled outside.

Quickly assembled into two ranks by the guards they were marched away wondering where they were going and how long it would take for dawn to break, and food was still two hours away.

The march, much to their surprise, was over in a matter of minutes for they were halted at the top of the hill on the *Padang* or, open ground. Here they could faintly make out the shapes of men women and children standing in ranks, with luggage at their sides so it was plain to all that the whole camp was on the move.

Standing in line with the other girls, Vivian watched the night sky turn to a delicate pink before dissolving into a bright red which in turn was absorbed by a fiery orb that climbed aggressively higher, radiating the heat of a thousand furnaces. 'It was,' she decided, 'going to be one of those heavy days.'

The children were the first to feel the heat and many began to whimper or cry, while conversations among the adults dwindled and stopped. Those without head protection suffered intense headaches and the Australians remembered stories they had heard of brains boiling under similar conditions. Vivian asked herself 'Why were the Japs keeping them out in the sun?'

It was to be eight hours before her question was answered and it came in the form of their guards who, during the long wait, had been seated under the shade of the surrounding trees. Now they came forward and pushing their way through the rows of heat exhausted people began shoving the men to one side creating two groups.

At first people were slow to see a reason for the culling of the men, the heat of the day having dulled their senses, then the truth struck home and the separated women began to wail, their cries of anguish mounting as others realising what was happening joined in.

Leaving no time for farewells, the Japanese guards quickly marched the men away, the shock of the sudden and unexpected separation showing in their faces as the cries of their distraught wives and children followed them until they were out of sight.

Vivian and the group of Sisters watched the heartbreaking scene unfold, unable to comprehend why the Japanese would do such a thing. It was outrageous enough that they imprisoned innocent civilians let alone separated them, keeping husbands, wives and children ignorant of each other's fate. To Vivian it was not only diabolical, it was calculated torture and an act she would mentally record adding to the list of crimes committed by a callous enemy.

A further half-hour under a torturous sun passed before the women and children were formed up in two ranks and marched off in the direction of Palembang. The Sisters, in a group, fell in behind. It was the first of April 1942.

It was late afternoon before the footsore and weary women and children reached a group of houses, which appeared to have been constructed within the last twelve months.

Halting the column, the Japanese N.C.O. summoned the woman interpreter who translated for him saying they were to be accommodated, for one night, in the houses in front of them.

The street sign identified the place as Irenelaan and the houses, built for the Dutch, would have comfortably suited three people. Each had two bedrooms, a lounge-dining area, a bathroom and a small kitchen to the rear. There was no furniture, electric light or cooking facilities and the guards packed 23 people or more into each house.

The Australians quickly sorted themselves out the 2/10th moving into one house and the 2/13th and 2/4th girls taking the one next door

Before they had a chance to settle in the guards allocated a further five women and three children, with luggage, to the house occupied by the 2/13th and 2/4th

Too tired and hungry to argue, the worn-out Sisters picked their individual positions on the bare floor and fell asleep, oblivious to the swarms of mosquitoes that attacked their bare flesh and the flashing torches of the watchful guards.

The statement by their captors that their stay at Irenelaan would be overnight, was proven to be false when early the next day a convoy of trucks arrived and soldiers began unloading a large number of wooden poles and a quantity of barbed wire.

Before nightfall a security fence surrounded the settlement clearly indicating to the inmates that they were there to stay.

Several days later a large party of women and children arrived from Muntok. Wasted by severe dysentery, they told of the primitive conditions and food shortages they were forced to contend with during their imprisonment at the gaol and of the long, debilitating march to Irenelaan.

The 18 houses and one garage made up the camp's accommodation. There were, 300 English, Dutch and Asian prisoners crammed in the tiny compound.

This had a serious impact on the septic system which had been built for 50 people. It overflowed sending raw sewage down the two storm-water drains on either side of the main street. The drains overflowed, threatening an epidemic.

The Australians met to discuss the problem. Their first move was to elect Nesta James as Spokeswoman, Pearl Mitz Mittelheuser, House Captain, 2/10th and Jenny Ashton, House Captain, 2/13th & 2/4th CCS.

A list of duties was compiled, together with a daily work roster, and the women were allocated to teams. Each team was responsible for a specific task, such as emptying the septic tank and clearing blocked drains, housekeeping, rationing, gathering supplementary food, cooking, light entertainment, district nursing and the manning of the dressing station, the latter being located in a garage and run by Doctor Jean McDowell.

The most important task was to clean up the effluent.

With this under control the camp settled into a routine, the children went to school, the Sisters carried out their daily duties according to the team roster and on Sunday everyone attended the church service conducted by the women missionaries.

****

Vivian and Wilma, rostered for district nursing duty, came out of a house they had been visiting and Viv was all smiles at what one of the Asian women had said to her. It stuck in her mind, "We know you, we like you and we trust you." the woman had said. It was her way of saying thank you.

They were walking toward the next house when Vivian's attention was attracted by the cries of a young girl seated beside a fire. Standing over her, kettle in hand, was an elderly woman who was pouring boiling water on the screaming girl's head.

"She'll scald that little girl's head," said Vivian as she strode over to remonstrate with the woman.

The elderly lady identified herself as the child's grandmother and told Vivian to mind her own business for she was treating the sores on the child's head as the result of sandfly bites when they came ashore at Jelabo after their ship had been sunk.

Vivian tried to convince her that this was not the way to treat head sores but the old woman would not listen, adding that she would decide what was best for the girl.

"Not on this occasion." said Vivian, her determination clearly expressed by the set line of her mouth and her piercing blue eyes. Grabbing the girl by the arm Vivian led her away.

"What's your name?" she asked when they were out of earshot of the grandmother, "Betty Kenneison," came the reply.

"I'm Vivian Bullwinkel but, you can call me Viv."

126

As the girl looked up at the tall woman walking beside her a sly grin began to form around her mouth and she confessed she had seen Viv. before.

Intrigued, Vivian asked where she had seen her and the little girl admitted it was the day she came to the Coolie Lines and the other nurses made such a fuss over her. Vivian laughed and said she was going to fuss over her this time and would treat the head sores each day until they cleared up. "The treatment young lady will begin tomorrow."

Happy with this offer Betty said goodbye and skipped back to her Grandmother and Vivian and Wilma continued with their house visits.

*****

Edith Kenneison was born at Batu Caves, outside Kuala Lumpur, on the 26 November, 1927. The family always used the pet name of Betty. She lived with her parents until she was five at which time she was sent to a convent school as a full time boarder.

Six years later her parents divorced and Betty, together with her two brothers and a sister entered a convent on Penang Island where they stayed until the outbreak of war.

When the Japanese juggernaut rolled down the Malay peninsula and threatened Penang Betty was evacuated to her grandparent's home in Kuala Lumpur where she was told her father had joined the Royal Air Force as a pilot and her eldest brother was with the British Army.

As the situation deteriorated her Grandfather and Step-Grandmother decided it was time to take Betty with them to Singapore and then on to Australia.

Managing to obtain passage on the Chinese coastal steamer *Giang Be* they slipped out of Singapore on the 12th of February in company with the *Mata Hari*, *Kwung Wo* and *Vyner Brooke*.

Their ship lost contact with the *Vyner Brooke* during that night and on the following evening was discovered by Japanese warships, attacked, and quickly sunk. Some 200 souls went down with the *Giang Be*, including her beloved Grandfather.

Fifty-six survivors, including Betty and her step-Grandmother, crammed into a lifeboat and beat off the clutching hands of drowning people who threatened to capsize them in their frenzy to be saved. Betty was forced to listen to their cries as the current swept them away into the darkness.

A Japanese cruiser, its engines throbbing, loomed out of the night and swept the scene with a searchlight. As the grey monster drew closer to the lifeboat Betty heard a familiar sound coming from the warship. At first she was unsure, then looking at the Japanese sailors crowding its deck she realised to her astonishment, that she was right....they were laughing....laughing at their deaths.

The obsceneness of it all sent her cowering to the bottom of the lifeboat, shivering and vomiting, as she tried to understand what was happening to her.

When the sun rose it revealed an oily sea and a lone lifeboat surrounded by flotsam from a sunken ship. In the light of day the survivors saw land low down on the horizon and several picked up the oars and began rowing towards its promised shelter and safety.

After three torturous days the boat was beached at Djaboe, a small bay on the northwest coast of Bangka Island where they camped for three days until found by friendly Malays. Taken to a Chinese village they were sheltered for five days until found by the Japanese. Roughly manhandled the stunned and weary survivors were placed in cattle trucks and driven to the Coolie Lines of Muntok and abandoned.

It was during this trip that Betty discovered a terrible truth; her Step-Grandmother blamed her for the death of her beloved Grandfather.

Hurt and bewildered by the accusation Betty searched her memory for the events that led to the sinking of their ship in the hope she could convince her Step-Grandmother she was not responsible for his death.

Betty remembered fighting her way on deck with her grandparents and her Step-Grandmother yelling for her to "take Grandfather's hand and don't let go under any circumstances, look after him."

People were pushing, shoving and even fighting for a place in the few lifeboats that were left and Betty held his hand ever so tight as he guided them through the desperate pack of humanity.

It was then that another shell struck the ship, blowing off a section of the bridge, sending lethal shards of steel and wood cutting through the air, killing or wounding all in their path.

Those who escaped injury became hysterical, and wide-eyed they stampeded for the ship's railing carrying all before them. Betty, propelled forward by the weight of an avalanche of bodies, felt her hand slip from that of her Grandfather's and she fought desperately against the pressure of the crowd to again link her hand with his. The slightness of her young body and a slippery deck prevented her and she lost sight of the man she idolised. Battling to stay on her feet, fearful of going down to be trampled on, Betty was swept forward together with her Grandmother. Engulfed by people, she became aware of a big man suddenly looming up in front of her. Reaching down he caught her up in his strong arms and bulldozing his way through the hysterical mass lifted her over the ship's railing and dropped her into the sea before doing the same to her Grandmother. They did not remain in the water for long as a passing lifeboat stopped to haul them both aboard.

Ignoring the weeks that had passed since the sinking of their ship, Betty was convinced that one day her Grandfather would stride through the gate of the Coolie Lines, therefore she must be there to greet him.

Taking up her usual spot near the gate and in the shade of a large tree, Betty watched unconcernedly the comings and goings of the camp guards until the unfamiliar figure of a young woman appeared. She watched as the stranger stopped, just inside the gate, and looked about her as if uncertain as to what she should do next.

Tall and very thin, with hair cropped short and matted with jungle growth, her sad face did not hide its gentleness expressed by a generous mouth and soft blue eyes. Betty's gaze dropped to the woman's bare and bloodied feet and deeply scratched legs and knew immediately she had suffered. Her dress, badly stained, was barely identifiable as a uniform but it was similar to that worn by the other Australian Army Nurses in camp.

When the tall woman whom Betty now believed to be an Australian moved, she favoured her right side, indicating some sort of injury, and was evidently heading off to meet the English officer coming for her.

There was something about this person that made Betty tingle all over and, as young as she was, she knew instantly there was empathy between them regardless of the fact they had never met.

Like herself, this woman had suffered a great loss and Betty was determined to meet her and become friends.

****

The Australians went to a lot of effort to prepare rice meals that had some variety and broke away from the endless boiled rice. One additive was a weed called Gula Java, which grew around the Irenelaan compound, to this they added coconut milk before mixing with the rice.

Infrequently the Japanese would slaughter a pig and dump it on the ground outside their huts, dissecting it with a sword. The various rationing committees collected the hunks of meat, hauling them off to be cooked up that night.

Another variant was eggs, which occasionally could be purchased from the locals, but only at the risk of all their lives for the Japanese strictly forbade dealing in food.

The guilders needed to make these purchases were earned by making grass hats and bags or crushing soya beans to which was added vanilla essence, to produce a very credible soya milk drink which was sold to the camp's inmates.

It was an egg, however, that brought tragedy to their door.

The guards dragged the frail old local man to the centre of the compound and tied him to a post with barbed wire. Before leaving they warned the women against giving the old man water or food, as he was under punishment for dealing in food, and any one caught doing so would share his fate. As the soldiers marched away the women looked at the half-conscious man hanging by his wire bonds, head lolling to one side, mouth swollen and bruised, a large cut to his head, all indications of a brutal beating handed out by the Japanese. His crime had been an attempt to sell several duck eggs to the undernourished and semi-starved women prisoners.

As the merciless sun beat down on the elderly man, caking the blood that seeped from his many wounds and dehydrating his body, he lapsed into semi-consciousness and began hallucinating.

The Sisters were forced to listen to his verbal ramblings and cries of anguish hour upon hour knowing they dared not help him.

His pleading for water continued well into the night and was heard throughout the camp, until finally he fell silent, having fallen into unconsciousness.

Around noon of the second day a woman's scream brought the Sisters from their house to see what was happening. A middle-aged woman, whom they recognised as being from the British group, was lying spread-eagled on the ground and standing astride her was a Japanese soldier wielding a sheathed Samurai sword. The woman let out a long drawn-out howl as a blow glanced off the side of her head opening up the flesh and causing blood to flow.

As he raised his sword to deliver another blow, Jenny Ashton, in a loud and authoritative voice, commanded he cease at once, and strode toward him followed closely by the other Sisters.

Pausing, with his arms raised to strike again, the soldier looked at the advancing women and sneering at them, landed one more blow to the woman's head before stalking off.

Gently they lifted the bleeding woman from the roadway and bore her to the shade of the verandah where they tended her wounds. When this had been done and the distressed woman given a cup of precious tea she was asked, "what had sent the Jap off his face?"

It appeared she heard the old man's pleas for water and could no longer stand listening to his suffering and so she had brought him water only to be discovered by a guard.

"If that Jap had stopped to take the sheath off his sword you would be dead," said Jenny, "and whatever you do it will not save the old man because they are determined to make an example of him."

Tenko, or the daily count of prisoners, was called at the usual time next morning and the camp assembled on the *padang* in front of the post which held the old man. Slumped over and held from falling to the ground by his barbed wire bonds, it was clear to them all that he was dead.

The prisoners stood mutely looking at the frail little body before them, as a small party of Japanese approached from down the road.

Halting in front of the assembled three hundred, a short, dapper officer, with a western style haircut and neatly barbered black moustache, stepped forward.

"Good–morning," he said in passable English, "I am your Camp Commandant, Captain Miachi. Doctor McDowell has been appointed your civilian commandant. You want something, you go to her and she will come to me. That is all."

He paused to eye the women, then with a quick movement he turned and walked away from the parade, continuing on up the hill.

As soon as his officer had left the senior Japanese non-commissioned officer marched forward, halted and screamed, "Tenko!" which was the cue for the

House Captains to leave the ranks, count their house members and report to him.

Jenny Ashton and 'Mitz' Mittelheuser carried out this duty and bowing to the Jap, gave him the count of 23 and 24 respectively before rejoining the others. After receiving the counts from the other House Captains and satisfied with the overall figure, he dismissed the parade.

Both Wilma and Vivian were hobbling back to the hut when Jenny joined them and queried the state of their feet.

Inside, she insisted on examining them and confirmed what they already knew, they had tinea, a crippling fungal skin disease probably contracted during their earlier Coolie Lines days and while working in sewage with badly cut bare feet.

The Acting Sister in Charge insisted they see Doctor McDowell that day, whom she said, would most likely admit them to the hospital in Palembang for treatment.

They were about to leave when one of the civilian women living in the same house as the Australians, barged into the room and confronted the three Sisters.

Placing her hands on her hips in an aggressive manner she demanded a room for herself and the others, saying, "it was no use them putting on any fancy airs and graces because it wouldn't wash with her and they were determined to take over the large bedroom for their exclusive use."

Jenny, in a calm and conciliatory tone, tried to reason with the large woman, the wife of a British serviceman, stating that they should sit down and discuss the matter rationally.

"Rationally", the word exploded from the woman, "why you stuck -up bitch, you always take the best for yourselves and cheat us on rations. So high and mighty, why you're only playthings for the officers!"

"That of course," said Jenny imperiously, "is pure nonsense."

"Nonsense is it? I'll show you nonsense!" screamed the furious woman, launching herself at Jenny. Knocking the surprised Sister aside, she rushed into the bedroom and began pitching the possessions of those who lived there out on to the floor of the main room, while screaming obscenities at the startled Sisters who had gathered to see what the noise was all about.

Wilma was the first to react and with her temper rising she hobbled over to the bedroom and told the woman to "cut it out."

When this had no effect Pauline Hempstead strode over to the door and in the strong language of outback Queensland told her to "belt up or there would be a bloody big blue."

This had an immediate effect upon the rampaging woman who, letting out a piercing shriek, flew at Wilma with extended hands, raking both cheeks with her fingernails.

As Blanche advanced, her face set for a fight, two more civilian women burst in, one grabbing Blanche's hair and giving it a violent tug.

131

Seeing this Wilhelmina Raymont headed for the fracas saying the odds needed evening and was promptly greeted with a blow to the head by one of the women. 'Ray' responded by flinging her arms around her attacker, locking her in a tight bear hug and pinioning her arms to her sides.

As the antagonists struggled with one another a young woman thrust her way through the watching Sisters to stand in the middle of the ring. In her hand was a large knife.

Shouting an expletive she announced her intention of sticking the Australians with the blade.

At the sight of a knife being wielded by the daughter of one of the assailants, the fighting stopped and the room became hushed as everyone waited expectantly for the next move.

It came from a least expected quarter.

"That will be enough."

The crisp command cut through the tense atmosphere and all eyes turned to see Doctor McDowell standing in the doorway, her handsome features contorted with a mixture of annoyance and frustration.

Demanding an explanation she listened to both sides before resolving the dispute by allocating the smaller bedroom to the civilian women over the protests of the Australians closing with, "I don't want any more trouble from this house, is that understood?"

Before leaving, the doctor examined Vivian and Wilma's feet and confirming the tinea, told them to be ready for transfer to Palembang and the hospital the next morning.

The doctor was as good as her word for Captain Miachi granted permission for Oram and Bullwinkel to be taken to hospital and they were dispatched the next day in a very old and dilapidated ambulance.

It was a hot and uncomfortable trip over primitive roads before reaching a small building in Palembang where they were met by a Dutch nun who, with a handful of Dutch doctors and Sisters, ran Charitas Hospital.

It was to this hospital that the seriously ill from the surrounding districts and prison camps were sent for treatment. Initially the staff was able to effectively treat cases with a supply of drugs hidden prior to the Japanese occupation. These stocks had quickly been consumed forcing them to become dependant on the capriciousness of their captors who released small quantities to the hospital on an irregular basis.

Escorted to their room they discovered a small area crammed with eighteen beds, none of which were occupied at the time. It was the beds however that attracted their attention. Although the base was a simple wooden bench, a thin mattress and pillow sat on top of it and to Vivian and Wilma, who had not slept in a bed with a pillow since the *Vyner Brooke,* this was as good as a suite at Raffles Hotel.

The nun introduced herself as Sister Renelda of the Order of St. Francis Xavier and while the two changed into the white gowns that were lying at the foot of their beds, she told them, in a thick Dutch accent, of some Australian Diggers down the hall.

"Ah, they are so naughty," she said clucking her tongue.

"Naughty?" exclaimed Wilma.

"Ja, naughty," she scolded.

"No, you must be mistaken, Sister," said Vivian lightly seeing the humour in it all, "they're a little playful, but not naughty."

"Ja, naughty," persisted the little nun, "they got me in big troubles."

"What trouble?" asked Wilma as both she and Vivian fought to control the laughter within them from bursting forth.

"Vell," said the nun forcefully, "yesterday I search for insects under the beds of the Australian soldiers, like I do in other wards because there are many here. They ask me what I am looking for and I tell them, I am looking for bugs, and they laugh and tell me I not say it correctly that in proper English it is buggers and that I should say I am looking for buggers. So I finish in the wards and I go to the Priest's room and say Father I have come looking for buggers. He became very angry with me and when I told him what the Australians had said he explained what are buggers and said I should not listen to them again. Australian soldiers are very naughty boys I think."

No longer able to contain themselves Vivian and Wilma burst in to howls of laughter, momentarily bewildering the little nun. When she realised it was her story they were laughing at she turned, and in a fit of pique left the room, flinging one word over her shoulder as she went. "Australians!" This appeared to explain everything.

Vivian's departure for the hospital in Palembang was the day Betty Kenneison considered to be the day she lost her best friend.

The tall young nurse was the object of her complete devotion, not because she cured the sores on her head with tender attention, but for being the source of constant wonderment.

Each day Betty would follow her as she walked the camp on grossly infected feet, giving freely of herself, radiating calm with her broad smile and infectious laugh, giving hope to the ill and dispirited, bringing a little sunshine into an otherwise dark and miserable life.

To Betty, Vivian was a fairy Godmother whose aura of light could turn the bitterness of a worthless strand of glass beads into a priceless string of pearls, such was the power of her magic. Where there had been the frustration of captivity and a deep sadness at the loss of her Grandfather, now there was the game, a game even the Japanese could not stop her from playing and it had been Vivian who had taught her the secret.

They had been walking together around the perimeter of the camp on a very clear night and for some reason that Betty didn't understand, she was feeling miserable. Vivian appeared to have sensed this unhappiness for she rested a hand lightly on her shoulders and said, "Don't walk looking down at the ground Bet, look up to the stars, imagine you are there, imagine you are free."

She did look up and her eyes swept the heavens taking in the myriad of light that winked at her out of a black vastness and suddenly she knew not everything in this world was a prisoner of the Japanese. Lots of things were free, she told herself, and if she were to concentrate a little bit harder she would see them all around her; in the beautiful blooms of the flowers that grew in the compound; in the cry of a wild bird as it darted from tree to tree high above the encircling barbed wire; it could be seen in the glow of the fireflies and in the orderly line of little insects scurrying under the wire.

Freedom was everywhere if you knew where to look for it and Betty now understood that the key to it lay in her mind, to be called on at any time, to escape to for as long as she wished.

Since learning the secret Betty would run quickly to the wire if she felt depressed and walking close to it, stretch out her arm allowing her hand to pass between the barbed strands, holding it there, she would say to herself, "My hand is free and one day all of me will be free."

****

The children of the camp, along with the adults, were expected to work and their daily duties included the collection and disposal of rubbish, cutting kindling wood for the cooking fires and picking up the rice ration which they hauled up the hill to the kitchens.

A task the children hated was working in the vegetable gardens, for the total crop went to the Japanese and if any of the plants died they were severely beaten. Either way there was nothing to gain for them or their mothers.

Between duties they attended the house of a missionary lady, a Miss Prouse, who by chance had discovered on her arrival at Irenelaan a volume of the complete works of William Shakespeare. Each day she would read an excerpt from the Bard's works to the children as they sat on the ground outside her house.

Most of her audience found the words of Shakespeare confusing and boring and were relieved when Miss Prouse took them for spelling and writing lessons.

Using sticks that had been sharpened and burnt to charcoal in a fire, the children wrote on pages torn from a Dutch telephone directory. They scratched their words in the clean margin around the edge of the pages and this amused Betty when she thought that the Malays wrote from right to left, the Chinese from bottom to top while she wrote in circles.

When lessons became too boring Betty would play her mind game for a while before resorting to the fashioning of small mud balls for the boys to use in their slingshots.

This was very serious work for in the war games they played it was the side who had the most mud balls who won. Just like the real war, Betty reasoned, when the Japanese must have had more mud balls than the British because they won and now she was in prison with not enough to eat.

The images of food controlled Betty's thoughts constantly for she went to bed at night and woke up in the morning with a gnawing hunger in the pit of her stomach which stayed with her for the rest of the day.

In the little time she had left between rummaging for extra food, her school and camp duties, Betty would take up her position at the main gate to Irenelaan. It was not her Grandfather she waited for this time but the tall Australian Army Nurse, Vivian Bullwinkel, her friend.

Time moved slowly for Betty and it was three weeks before Vivian returned to the camp, which to her seemed more like three months. She saw her coming through the gate and ran to her side. They walked together chatting avidly until reaching the nurse's house where she was welcomed back by the other girls.

Wilma, had not been cured of tinea and the pain in her feet and legs had persisted, requiring her to remain in the hospital for ongoing treatment.

Vivian saw there was an addition to the furniture, a veteran piano. It had been given to the Australians by a Dutch House Captain who said no one played the instrument and besides, they would welcome the additional sleeping space once it was gone.

Also during her absence, a paper called *The Camp Chronicle* had been produced, in both Dutch and English, on an old typewriter scrounged from somewhere in the camp. The first edition, under a masthead featuring a barbed wire background, was eighteen pages and covered community announcements, games, gossip, fictional and humorous stories as well as a cooking page. This proved to be one of the most popular features amongst readers, containing dozens of recipes submitted by fellow prisoners. These described mouth-watering dishes with several ingenious ways to present rice, which made it more appealing and palatable.

The latter was well received for they were approaching their first Christmas in captivity and there was a need for something different in which to celebrate the festive season.

That week the Japanese marched in a large number of Dutch children accompanied by their teacher, a nun, who ran the local school. With a population of four hundred and thirty-five people in accommodation designed for seventy-two, it would be difficult finding room for the children, and yet this was achieved within hours of their arrival.

Some relief from the overcrowding was forthcoming when the Japanese released several neutrals and a number of Asians. This started a number of rumours concerning the release of prisoners of war. One, claiming a Japanese officer as its source, confirmed talks were underway with the Americans and that there would be a large exchange of P.O.W's, the details of which would be released within two to three weeks.

Amidst the speculation and hopes of their fellow captives, the Australians remained sceptical, ignoring the rumours linked to their imminent release because they had heard them before, and given the track record of the Japanese they knew they would never be released.

The proximity of so many people in a restricted space did have repercussions throughout the camp and the Australian Sisters were not immune to its effect. Although perfectly content with each other's company, because of the years spent in training, working and living together in hospitals and later barracks, the Sisters were intolerant of undisciplined outsiders.

This had been the cause of their previous confrontation with the civilian women sharing their accommodation and it was only by avoiding any social contact that a precarious and uneasy peace had since existed between the two groups.

Inevitably old resentments and current frustrations would combine to create a volatile situation, as the Sisters were about to experience.

****

Sister Ashton thought it would be a treat for the girls if she made a pot of jam from the fruit and sugar she had purchased through the wire that morning.

Gathering up a battered saucepan and the ingredients, she went outside and set about building a fire. With the pot carefully balanced over the flames she stirred its contents with a piece of wood which had been roughly shaped in the form of a spoon. It was approaching the hottest part of the day and squatting beside the fire, native style, she was thankful for her two piece sun frock and bra, made from curtain material, and the broad-brimmed grass hat on her head.

Vivian at the time had just completed her ablutions following an early morning start on the task of cleaning out the sewage pit and drains. Slipping into a pair of wooden clogs, which little Bet had insisted she needed a beginner's permit to learn to steer, she made her way with some difficulty across the living room becoming more aware of the sound of raised voices.

Joining with the other inquisitive Sisters in the house she went out onto the verandah from where she was able to see Jenny Ashton crouched by the fire with two of the women involved in their previous altercation. They stood in front of the kneeling Sister their hands placed aggressively on their hips with facial expressions clearly communicating their anger.

One of the British women thrust her head forward and screamed like a banshee at their colleague, telling her to put the fire out. Continuing to stir the contents of the pot Jenny requested the woman to control herself, explaining that she was simply making some jam. It was the other woman's companion who replied accusing the Acting Sister in Charge of lighting a fire that sent smoke billowing into their bedroom almost suffocating them.

Fixing the two with a patronising look Jenny suggested they may have been exaggerating the situation. "Exaggerating?" the word exploded from the mouth of the larger woman, who at the same time launched her ample frame at the fire aiming a savage kick at the pot which sent it flying, to land some feet away and on its side, spilling the contents on the ground.

Angered by the thoughtless waste of food Jenny sprang to her feet and took a step toward the gloating women.

"You wretched woman," she said with force, "get away from here."

"We don't take orders from officers' whores," was the reply.

With a determined look on her face Jenny advanced with the clear intention of settling the matter. However, the smaller of the two women, who had been standing to one side while the verbal exchange was going on, took that moment in which to charge the Australian nurse. Moving quickly she surprised Jenny with a body blow to the side which sent her sprawling in to the patch of jam soaked earth and almost to the feet of her other antagonist.

With a crude cackle the big woman leaned down and grasping the Sister's bra top, ripped it from her body, holding it aloft as a symbol of their victory, a triumphant grin spreading across her face.

The colour in Jenny's face deepened either through embarrassment or fury, or perhaps a combination of both. Springing to her feet the now angry Australian flung her arms around the startled Brit and gripping her in a tight bear hug spun the woman around on the spot several times before letting her go. Desperately the weighty woman tried to regain her equilibrium as she pirouetted twice out of control before finally crashing to the ground where she lay winded.

A cheer went up from the Australian Sisters on the verandah as Jenny recovered her top and was about to put it on when her colleagues shouted a warning. As she turned Jenny received a blow to the head from a lump of wood wielded by the smaller of the women and she went down on to her knees, blood flowing from a wound above the left eye.

Shocked by the cowardly attack, the watching Sisters advanced in a body as Blanche Hempstead voiced an opinion they all shared.

"You two tarts need to be taught a bloody lesson, one you won't forget."

Fear sprang into their eyes as they saw the solid line of nurses bearing down on them and they began searching for a line of retreat when an authoritative command cut through the tension.

"You will stop this fighting immediately."

All eyes turned in the direction of the voice to see the tall, angular frame of Doctor McDowell watching them. Beside her stood a guard, his face an emotionless mask, the rifle in his hands pointed straight at them and they sensed, from the cold look in his eyes, he would not hesitate in using it.

"I told you once before I will not tolerate this type of behaviour," said the Doctor.

Nesta James stepped forward and defended their action saying the Australians did not start the ruckus and suggested the two civilian women be disciplined.

"I am not concerned with who started this, Sister James," replied the doctor, "I am only concerned that it does not happen again because if it does I have been told the Japanese will intervene and you know that their methods can be excessive."

The petite Senior Sister squared her shoulders and gave the doctor a piercing look before telling her that they would try and find a solution to the problem and indeed work toward a harmonious existence with the women. " However," she said in closing," if my Sisters are attacked by these harpies again we will retaliate regardless of Japanese intervention and the consequences that may follow....we will not be bullied."

With these words she turned to the Sisters and instructed them to bring Sister Ashton inside for attention, the rest were to return to their duties.

Vivian, helped by Veronica Clancy, gathered up the still dazed Sister in Charge and took her inside leaving Jessie Simons to recover the suntop while Doctor McDowell remonstrated with the now downcast women who started the affair.

The months passed slowly for the inmates of Irenelaan during which time many of the Australian nurses fell ill as a direct consequence of the inadequate diet forced on them since their incarceration.

Eileen Short, or Shorty as the girls called her, knocked her leg and a gross infection followed. Clancy suffered an attack of myocarditis, Gladys Hughes caught an acute ear infection that would not heal and was subsequently sent to hospital. Wilhelmina Raymont had an abscessed tooth extracted without anaesthetic, Shirley Gardam knocked a leg and it became badly infected, Betty Jeffrey suffered an attack of appendicitis and both Vivian and Wilma returned to Palembang with a secondary attack of tinea.

As Christmas approached, morale amongst the prisoners slumped badly for the Japanese told of many victories in the Pacific, the bombing of Australia and of that country's imminent invasion. Without the means to check these statements they became confused as to the real progress of the war and fearful for their families and friends.

In an attempt to take their minds off these depressing thoughts the Entertainment Committee of the Australian houses planned a series of concerts. Written, produced and performed by the Sisters they included such rollicking extravaganzas as *Who Killed Cock Robin*, *Riding Down From Bangor*, *The Jolly Swagman* and *The Running of the Melbourne Cup*.

The lyrics were written expressly to reflect life under the Japanese and were often cutting, sarcastic and sometimes cruel yet always delivered enthusiastically and boisterously in true Aussie style. These shows became so popular that many Dutch and British women would squeeze into the house for the performance or, if that was impossible, stand at the windows and doors. For a while this form of escapism worked extremely well for both the audience and the performers. Then it was Christmas.

The men and youths were accommodated in a jail well removed from the women's camp.

Each day they would be marched by their captors down a path to the site where they were working on the construction of a new camp. At one point

138

this pathway came within four hundred yards of the women's compound and it was normal for the married women and their children to assemble at the wire each morning and night in the hope of catching a glimpse of a husband or father as they passed.

The men, on reaching this section of the track, would slow down and wave. The women and children would respond hoping it was their loved one they were waving to, for the distance made identification very difficult.

When Christmas Eve arrived the women gathered well before the men were due to pass and stood silently watching the empty track, anxious to see the first man emerge from the sea of green foliage.

"Here they come." cried a woman as a lone figure materialised from out of the jungle to be followed by others until a long line snaked down the hill.

The women, many racked with dysentery, dengue fever or malaria, stood quietly waving as the tears ran down their cheeks until a lone woman's voice began to sing the old Christmas favourite, *Come All Ye Faithful*. Automatically the whole group joined in and their carol reached across to the men who stopped to listen to the beautiful sound of their women and children singing. Spontaneously they too took it up, their deeper tones blending with those of the women. The guards began running up and down the line urging the men forward with the point of their bayonets, the women however continued to sing and long after the last lonely figure had paused to wave before melting back into the jungle. The carol had given the women hope, hope that one day the wire would no longer separate them.

Christmas Day 1942 dawned with an accompanying tropical storm that brought wild winds, driving rain and high humidity.

In the Australian houses the occupants rose and following an exchange of good wishes headed off together for 'The Shed' where a special Christmas service was to be held. 'The Shed' was in fact a garage that had been taken over by a number of missionaries.

Regular services were conducted there for the camp's inmates.

On this day there were hymns, carols and readings from the Bible before a diminutive, middle-aged woman got up and standing before them raised her eyes to the ceiling and proclaimed to a silent and expectant audience in solemn tones "Thirty years ago today the Lord saved me from sin." She then went on to reveal the facts associated with what she called a "former unworthy life."

Pauline Hempstead, the incorrigible Queenslander, leaned over to Vivian and in a loud whisper asked "I wonder what the bloody hell she did for heaven's sake?"

Vivian reddened. "Shoosh Blanche you're in church."

"Come on Bully I know that, I just wish she would get to the point, it could be interesting."

"I was a mere slip of a girl, a hard-working girl in a Lancashire cotton mill' intoned the woman, "when sin came to me."

She paused dramatically and a breathless expectation descended on the now wide-awake congregation as they eagerly awaited the terrible revelation, the tragic story of an innocent young woman's fall from grace and of the cad who perpetrated the crime.

With her eyes closed the confessor crossed her arms over her breast.

"But the Lord did not forsake me Sisters" she said, her voice becoming stronger as she raised her hand in the air, the palm open in an act of supplication, "I was forgiven and He led me to a life of self righteousness and enlightenment. Praise the Lord, Sisters. Now let your voices be raised in joyous song."

With a strong and steady voice the little woman commenced to sing the first strains of *Jerusalem* and the congregation joined in.

"Yeah?" said Blanche to Vivian in a loud voice that could be heard over the swelling chorus, "but what the bloody hell did she do?"

Viv shook her head in amusement, "Well, whatever it was she is not going to tell us."

"Then I think that stinks," said Blanche indignantly, "she could have at least told us about the bloke."

"Perhaps there wasn't one involved."

"Aw come off it Bully, how else is a girl gonna sin if there isn't a bloke involved?"

Vivian burst out laughing but when a number of people around her began to show their annoyance Vivian quickly launched into the chorus of *Jerusalem* with the rest.

Christmas lunch was a special treat, courtesy of the men who reduced their own rations which they sent to the women's camp "so they could have a decent meal."

By bribing the guards they were able to deliver a small quantity of meat, together with a sack full of potatoes and onions, which the women turned in to a baked dinner adding a final touch of their own, a plum pudding.

The pudding was made by grinding brown rice with shelled peanuts and beans to which was added cinnamon and gula java. The mixture was then placed in a piece of cloth and boiled in the normal way. It was a splendid repast and later they gathered around the piano to sing the old favourites and think of home and loved ones.

In the late afternoon the Australian's were invited to visit the Dutch ladies, who had put up a tree and decorated it for the children. Festooned in colourful tinsel and trinkets it bore many toys and dolls, in fact one gift for each child in camp.

Sitting around the tree, in the main room of their house, sipping tea and conversing in English, the Sisters enjoyed the chat with the Dutch women while awaiting the arrival of the children and the distribution of presents.

At first they were uncertain as to what it was they had heard as the sound drifted through the open door and windows. Then the voices became clearer and they could identify it as children singing.

As one, the women rose and went out on to the verandah.

In the half gloom of the late afternoon they could see a long, twisting line of dancing lights wending its way down the hill toward them.

The lights were candles and each child held one, winking like so many fireflies, as their angelic voices sang *Away in a Manger*. Watching the beautiful scene before her unfold, Vivian, for a moment, tried to erase the war from her thoughts and her heart brimmed with love for these little innocents caught up in the savagery of man's greatest folly. Around her the Dutch women were crying, no doubt for their lost husbands and the future of their children, but as much as Vivian felt the emotion of the moment, the tears would not come.

Arriving at the house with flickering candles casting shadows on their upturned faces the children gathered around the adults and finished the last chorus of their carol. One of the ladies then invited them to share the Christmas tree and gifts. There was no need for a second invitation and the excited children flowed through the door and into the main room where their loud gasps of surprise and wonderment reached Vivian and Wilma standing outside.

"Makes me feel like I want to be a kid again," commented Wilma.

"Yes," said Vivian with thoughts of her mother and Broken Hill flitting through her mind, "me too."

Leaving the children to enjoy their presents Vivian and Wilma headed back to the house.

****

The Australian's New Year's Eve party was going at full throttle as the girls tried to forget the tragedies of 1942 and looked to 1943 as the year they would see an Allied victory and their release from prison camp.

The piano player was thumping out the old favourite, *The Quarter Master's Store* and the majority of the revellers were standing around the old battered instrument giving vocal support.

Vivian was feeling tired and she indicated to Wilma that maybe she would not reach midnight.

Looking around the packed house, where there wasn't a square foot of floor space Wilma dryly asked her friend, " Where do you think you are going to put your head down?"

As Vivian began to ponder the problem Blanche wandered over. In her hand was a tobacco tin from which she took a sip, her face twisted in a look of disgust and several drops of purple liquid dribbled down her chin.

"Bloody hell!" she exploded, "that's liquid dynamite."

"What is it?" asked Vivian also screwing up her nose.

"Chris Oxley made it, calls it Chilli Wine. It's like pouring petrol down your throat and setting it alight....want to try some?" Blanche held the tin out to Vivian and Wilma.

Both women refused, Vivian on the grounds that she did not feel like tasting it and Wilma because she was teetotal.

"I'll ask you again in 1944 then," said Blanche with a wide grin and turning she sauntered off to join the crowd around the piano still sipping from the tobacco tin.

As she walked away Vivian had a sudden mental picture of her short-cropped hair bobbing from stretcher to stretcher outside Saint Patrick's School. Oblivious to the shelling, unmindful of the hours that had passed since she had last slept, there was always only one thing on Blanche's mind and that was to look after her boys.

Vivian remembered the tough little Sister, physically exhausted, to the point of collapse, finally being ordered to bed by the medical staff; Collapsing on to her cot crying herself to sleep thinking of the boys who had died that day. 'How could anyone forget Pauline Blanche Hempstead?' she said to herself looking over to the piano as Blanche took a swig of chilli wine then let out a booming chorus of "there were eggs, eggs, nearly growing legs in the Quartermaster's store."

The noise level continued unabated until almost midnight when tea and rice cakes were served and Jenny Ashton gave a short speech in which she expressed all their hopes that 1943 would see an end to the war and their return to Australia.

The pensive expressions on the women's faces as they listened to their Sister in Charge was proof of the extent of their homesickness and the constant yearning to be free.

"Happy New Year!" shouted Jenny and the room erupted with their response followed by a few ragged voices that began to sing *Auld Lang Syne*.

They all joined in, their voices swelling, filling the room, to flow outside and be carried on the night air to all corners of the camp. It was a haunting song of remembrance, of sorrow for those who had died and it was a song of thanksgiving for their lives and of optimism that would see them survive captivity.

Linking arms in the traditional way the women formed a rough circle and swaying from side to side found joy in the closeness of one another. Slowly the tempo increased until they were frantically pumping their arms up and down at a furious rate and the words of the song became a continuous blur as they charged back and forward at one another for this was the way you did it in Australia.

The dancing, if that is what you could call a stampede, came to a halt and as the winded participants stood catching their breath Blanche raised the old tobacco tin to her lips and drained its contents.

"Happy New Year, you mob!" she cried which was the signal for an exuberant bout of hugging and the exchanging of good wishes, the most fervent being they would celebrate next year at home as free women.

The long piercing blast of a whistle was a familiar sound to Vivian and along with the others she quickly put to one side what she had been doing and hurried outside.

Forming up with the rest of the camp for tenko the Australians awaited the counting of their ranks by the House Captains. Some one behind Vivian whispered a warning concerning one of the guards.

Surreptitiously she looked along the line of Japanese and spotted one fellow slightly apart from the rest leaning on his rifle, shoulders hunched and with a truculent look on his face that sent warning signals to those who could read the signs.

The count continued in the oppressive heat and as some of the smaller children began to grizzle, frantic mothers tried to pacify them lest the guards became annoyed.

Vivian watched the sour-faced one whose beady eyes she saw slowly traversing the ranks of the Australian women before shifting to those of the British, then the Dutch.

Then the Jap's eyes stopped, he had seen something and the sullen expression was quickly changed to hatred as his thin lips curled in a snarl and he emitted a low growl that came from deep in his throat.

Shifting his rifle to the trail position he strode over to where a large woman stood in the front line of the Dutch contingent. Stopping before her and with amazing speed he gripped the rifle with both hands and slammed it, butt first, into the astonished woman's mouth.

Propelled backward by the force of the savage blow the unfortunate woman collided with several others in the rank behind her before slamming to the ground, semi-conscious, blood spurting from her broken mouth.

The infuriated Jap screamed something in Japanese which sounded like "Kuchi-beni!" to Vivian, then he turned to his right and drove the rifle butt into the face of the unsuspecting woman next to him. She went down swiftly, without a sound to lay unconscious as the blood from her injury began to pool in the dirt.

Without a glance at his two victims the Jap guard strode angirily back to his former position where he glowered at the women.

"He's sure got his knickers in a knot," Vivian heard one of her lot whisper and suspected the voice belonged to that of Blanche.

Then the word was passed. The Jap had screamed something about lipstick or scarlet mouth and evidently had it in for any woman who wore it.

Furtively those women who were wearing lipstick removed it by wiping their mouths with the back of their hands as the guard in question was distracted by the continuing count.

Finally concluding the odious task both House Captains and those of the British and Dutch reported to the Japanese N.C.O. who rejected them all and demanded another count.

On the third count, all of which had been identical, he accepted the figures.

Dismissed, they were wandering back to the house discussing the unprovoked attacks when Betty Jeffrey suggested they give the guard who had an intense dislike for lipstick a nickname.

"Let's call him Lipstick Larry," she said and they all agreed it was an apt name for the Jap and so this one joined the ranks of the many others who had been given nicknames such as Ah Fat and Moonface.

As they reached the house Mrs. Blake was spotted making her way, rather hurriedly, down the hill heading in their direction. Immediately they warned Sister Ashton and all of the nurses gathered to await the arrival of the kindly British woman.

"Sister Ashton, you must hurry, the guard commander wants to see you," said Mrs. Blake between large intakes of air.

Jenny thanked her for the message and asked if the guard commander had mentioned what he wanted her for. Mrs. Blake replied that she did not, where upon the Acting Sister in Charge took off up the hill leaving instructions for Mrs Blake to be shown inside and given a spot of tea.

Vivian was unable to join them because she had promised Wilma she would fetch a bucket of water so she could wash, following a trip to the latrines. Wilma had contracted dysentery several days before and was getting progressively worse.

Asking Blanche Hempstead for a hand the two went outside and picking up a large pole, to the middle of which was secured a large bucket, they hefted it onto their shoulders and proceeded down a jungle path to the well.

Fetching water was an exhausting task. After the container had been filled it was hand hauled some twenty feet to the surface, then decanted into a bucket, which in turn was attached to the carrying pole. The return journey, with the weight of the water quickly sapping one's strength, had to be negotiated up a steep and winding jungle track.

On their way back Vivian felt the pole biting deeply into her shoulder, as the incline grew steeper. Fearful of stumbling, she mentally overrode the pain in her swollen feet, setting them firmly on the track and maintaining a steady pace.

Standing at the top of the hill watching the two struggle with their load, Jenny Ashton experienced a feeling of both pride and sadness for the two young women forced to endure such physical torture so a friend may bathe. It was at that moment she felt very humble to be one of them.

Calling out to Vivian and Blanche, Jenny began the descent to where they had set down the pole and bucket and collapsed on the ground.

Reaching them she held out a card to each Sister. Approximately five inches wide by three deep, one side was blank while the other carried some Japanese writing at the top and down one side.

"What is it?" Vivian asked.

Jenny explained that it was a prisoner of war service card. They were to use it to write home and the Japanese had given her one for each Sister with a guarantee they would be forwarded to the International Red Cross. They would also send a list of prisoner's names for broadcast to Australia.

Cheered up by this wonderful news the bucket appeared to become lighter and the two completed their task leaving the water for Wilma in the bathroom while they sat down and thought about what they were going to write home about.

Women's Internment Camp
Palembang. Sumatra.
18.3.43

Dear Mother,
   Sorry to cause you so much worry but don't. I have not and never will
regret leaving home. My roving spirit has been somewhat checked. I am
very well in fact I'm close on eleven stone I'm sure. I have let my hair
grow and am now sporting a nob if you please. We do a little nursing
about the camp but the sick cases go to the hospital. We find suntops and
shorts the ideal uniform. Have learnt to play contract bridge you should
learn to play it is by far the superior game and we have a very keen
school of players. How is John my love to him and ask Zelda and Con to
tell all friends that I am well and often think of everyone give them all
my love. I hope it will be possible to hear from you soon. Many happy
returns of last month mum I hope you are well and keep smiling and
don't worry over me. Once again love to all in Melbourne, Perth, Adelaide
and Broken Hill.

   Lots of love. Viv.

Vivian re-read the small and spidery writing on the card given to her by
Jenny. She was pleased with the result for it sounded as if everything was
alright by her and the thought of her mother holding this same card created a
physical link between them.
   "Write a book, Bully?"
Looking up Vivian saw the pert and smiling face of Eileen Short.
   "I squeezed in about a hundred and fifty words I suppose." she answered.
   "Did you keep it light and bright?"
   "Light and bright 'Shorty', light and bright."
The two chatted on about their common desire of telling Australians what
was really happening to them so the government would get a spurt on and
rescue them.
   "Now there's a thought ," said 'Shorty', "I can see a battalion of Aussie
soldiers coming down the street, tall handsome with sunburnt legs all nice
and muscled. I just love those short shorts they wear, don't you, Bully?"
   Shorty had rolled her eyes in such an exaggerated way that Vivian could not
help letting loose a loud burst of laughter causing the other letter writers in
the house to raise their heads inquisitively in her direction, smile, then go
back to their composing.
   As the days merged the need to relieve their boredom led to a flurry of
activity amongst the camp's inmates.
   A library was founded by pooling books, with those who contributed able
to borrow from it and volunteers were called to give informal talks on a varying
range of subjects.

Mrs. Drysborough spoke on *Northumberland Legends* while Shirley Gardam presented a travelogue on Tasmania and Iole Harper spoke about *Life on a Sheep Farm*.

A Choral Society had been formed inspired by an English woman, Norah Chambers, who had graduated from the Royal Academy of Music, London.

Frequently they gave recitals in the garden of house number seven in front of a large audience assembled on the roadway. Without the aid of musical instruments the women of the choir had acquired the skill of blending their voices in such a way as to create beautiful harmonies that enthralled their listeners.

Miss Dryburgh, a pioneer missionary in China and Malaya, assisted Norah Chambers to write the scores and went on to produce a masterpiece, *The Thief of Palembang*, based loosely on the score of *The Thief of Bagdad*, and inspired by the Jap guards stealing habits. Later, this very talented woman wrote the words and music of *The Captives' Hymn* which expressed the thoughts of all who were incarcerated by the Japanese.

Later that month the rumour-mill produced a new piece of information, claiming the men were to be moved and the women would go to a place called Lahat.

Jenny Ashton assembled the girls of her house and told them the rumour was rife in the camp and that this time they were going to be ready even if it proved to be a furphy. She gave instructions for everything they could carry to be marked A.A.N.S. and this was to include cooking utensils, bricks for fireplaces, old tins, scraps of wire, sections of timber, firewood, plants and even curtain pieces. They were to be ready to move at a moment's notice.

Wilma, who had been slotted for movement back to the hospital because of her back, refused to go on the grounds she did not want to be separated from the rest if a move was imminent. It was only when Jenny and Vivian promised they would not leave without her that she agreed to go to hospital for the X-rays.

She need not have worried for it wasn't until she returned from the hospital that the Camp Commandant issued the order for their movement.

CAMP THREE....THE MENS' CAMP

A convoy of ancient lorries trundled into the camp the day after the order to move was promulgated and loading the women and children roared off down the road leaving Irenelaan vacant for the first time in over a year.

Fifteen minutes later and much to the surprise of the women they pulled up at what appeared to be the men's old camp. Built by the male prisoners, the buildings, being very basic included four long barracks with open sides and crumbling attap roofs. These very rough jungle wood structures formed a hollow square around the outside of which ran the inevitable perimeter of barbed wire.

Strewn about on the ground was an appalling collection of rubbish and filth. Later they learnt the men had been given the impression the Japanese were to occupy the camp and so they had gone to great pains to leave it in as bad a condition as possible.

Standing in a group after being ordered to dismount from the lorries the Sisters looked in dismay at the dark, dank and foreboding place they were now to call home and for how long? Well, only God knew that.

The guards began to demand they unload the vehicles and goaded them into action with the points of their bayonets.

The prisoner's spirits crumbled and to make matters worse, it began to rain.

First thing the next day a group discussion was held and the needs of the camp set out and co-ordinated.

With the Japanese taking over the hospital in Palembang for their own use the Dutch nuns had been sent to what the women referred to as the Mens' Camp. A barracks was chosen for the hospital and with the co-operation of its occupants, who agreed to shift their bedding along by six inches, they were able to create a reasonable area of bamboo platform for its patients.

The Dutch nuns accepted the task of running the hospital and the Australians rostered ten Sisters to assist them, the remainder were allocated to District Nursing within the camp.

Using their initiative the two groups obtained a limited quantity of old rice sacks which they stuffed with dried grass and gave to the seriously ill.

The hospital was also without lighting so the enterprising nuns came up with crude lights made from a cigarette tin. A section of wire was wound around the tin and where it stretched across the open top a fibre wick was attached and allowed to trail into a quantity of red palm oil, a local cooking product. Although it could not be compared with a pressure lamp or electricity, it did give a measure of light in which to work by at night.

Drugs on the other hand were non-existent, the Japanese refusing to supply them. This forced the Sisters and nuns to improvise and by pooling their knowledge they were able to manufacture several compounds from resources found both in camp and in the surrounding jungle.

For the treatment of diarrhoea and dysentery they pounded charcoal, obtained from the cooking fires, to a fine powder. They boiled the bark of a tree for its juice which the locals said would cure beri-beri, caused by a deficiency of Vitamin B.

The Sisters and nuns knew these remedies had little effect but gave the patient some measure of reassurance that an effort was being made to treat them.

This absence of drugs, combined with malnutrition, had a dramatic effect on the camp's general health and the death toll rose steadily.

In a number of cases death was a result of mothers' giving their rice ration to the children. Once these women were hospitalised those attending them had to resort to force feeding, however many were too far gone and died within days.

The staff were intimately involved in all deaths that occurred in the hospital. Not only were they constantly at the side of a dying patient, they carried out the necessary preparation for burial, then using a makeshift stretcher, helped carry the body to the cemetery outside the camp.

Their final commitment to the dead was to dig a grave, in sweltering heat and with makeshift implements. Then with bowed heads they listened as a nun intoned a prayer for the soul of the person they had laid to rest.

With an empty stretcher and laboured steps the burial party made their way back to the camp knowing their visits to the cemetery would become more frequent in future.

****

Vivian, rostered for hospital and burial duties, was all in, both mentally and physically at the close of a very tiring day.

Although the light was dimming in the makeshift hospital she could clearly make out the forms of two very sick women lying on the bamboo platform before her. Seated on the dirt floor facing them she looked at their pale and bloodless faces, one, a middle-aged person, was dying. The other, unconscious, could last another day.

Vivian reached for an old milk tin full of water. Taking a piece of cloth she dipped it in the tepid liquid and gently wringing it out sponged the women's brows. Powerless to do more she sat back to await the death of the weaker of the two.

A movement on the matting between the bodies of the sick women caught her eye and she leaned forward.

At first she was puzzled by what she saw in the fading light, then recognising them for what they were she recoiled in horror, revolted by the horde of fat little creatures tumbling off the body of the older woman.

148

Quickly she checked the older woman's pulse and heartbeat. It confirmed what she suspected .... the woman was dead.

Looking back to the moving mass of lice, Vivian assumed they had anticipated the extinction of life in the body and left it in search of another which happened to be close by

She watched the lice as they moved towards the living body of the younger woman, the flesh creeping horror of it sickening her. A flood of self-pity and grief overwhelmed her and as Vivian's great inner strength gave way she folded her arms on the bamboo platform in front of her and lowered her head.

Closing her eyes she willed the tears to come to release the pent-up misery within her... but there were no tears, only a deep despair

Vivian was at the lowest point in her life.

****

Apart from McDowell there were several other medical doctors in camp including Smith, whom the Australians immediately nicknamed 'Smithy', and a German Jewess by the name of Goldberg. The latter's background was both vague and doubtful as was the question of her loyalty to the Allied cause.

It was known that Goldberg was interned in Singapore following the outbreak of war and after eluding the authorities during the capitulation she boarded the ill-fated *Vyner Brooke* on a British passport.

Captured by the Japanese when she reached shore from the sinking, Goldberg posed as a German citizen to avoid imprisonment. Some time later the Japanese swept through the country picking up all Europeans and Goldberg was caught in their net. Ignoring her protestations that she was German they informed her that good relations with Germany were at an end because of the way the war was being waged by her countrymen. As a result she became a prisoner of war.

Sent to the mens' camp following the closure of the Palembang hospital to prisoners, the doctor always appeared to have had a ready supply of money. This meant she ate well, with food purchased on the black market, a point that did not escape the notice of the other prisoners.

For the Australian Sisters, it was a case of existing on the rice ration, supplemented from time to time with a little food purchased from outside. The money was obtained by doing manual chores for prisoners who could afford to pay for their services. These tasks included hauling water, cutting firewood, making grass hats and clothes from old material as well as sifting through a rice ration. The latter was a tiresome job and entailed separating the rat droppings, small stones and twigs from the rice which was swept from the floors of the godowns and sheds.

Even Norah Chambers was forced to sift rice to gain a little money for extra food. As a result the choir lapsed and with the Australians not having the time or energy to produce their musical plays the entertainment aspect of camp life collapsed.

It was not until the approach of Christmas 1943 that Nora Chambers sought out her fellow countrywoman, Margaret Dryburgh, to discuss the possibility of forming a choir.

Dryburgh, who was an accomplished pianist, organist and choir director, readily agreed and combining her skills with those of Chambers they soon had a number of arrangements.

Written in four parts for women's voices the scores were condensed to a five-minute choral work from a fifteen minute movement without losing the flow or a sense of balance.

The parts, faithful to the original keys, were copied onto small scraps of precious paper and included such classical masterpieces as, *Largo* from *Dvorak's New World Symphony, Bolero, Poet & Peasant, Andante Cantabile* and the first movement from *Moonlight Sonata.*

A choir of 30 voices was selected from camp volunteers and rehearsals began within weeks of the arrangements being completed.

Choir practice, lasting up to an hour, was held behind the kitchens at the far end of the camp so their fellow prisoners could not preview what was in store for them.

The women soon learned to use their voices as instruments and within weeks reached a level of proficiency that convinced Chambers and Dryburgh that the time had come for the choir's debut. Their first public performance was to be 27 December 1943.

Christmas Day was celebrated with only a fraction of the enthusiasm of the previous year and the singing of several carols was followed by, in the Australian houses, a *Chinese Christmas Dinner.*

The dinner comprised mainly of rice scraps. Apart from the religious significance of the day there was nothing exciting to eat, drink or give.

The event they were all looking forward to was the forthcoming recital by the choir on the night of the 27th and by all reports the entire camp was going to attend.

****

The women began filing into the quadrangle in groups of three and four. It was late afternoon on the 27 December, those arriving felt excited in anticipation.

The Japanese guards were confused by the unannounced assembling of the women and they ran into the compound aggressively waving their rifles and shouting, " Iku Kotai Suru!"

("Go back!")

Ignoring them the women flowed into the quadrangle and sat on the ground facing one of the barracks.

Seeing the women were content to sit and be orderly the perspiring guards ceased their exertions and withdrew to the shade of the surrounding trees where they could observe them in comparative comfort.

The heat was going out of the declining sun and a light breeze encouraged by the damp of the monsoon season wafted across the quadrangle as the diminutive Mrs Dryburgh, her greying hair swept back and tied in a knob, led the choir onto the ground.

With her back to the audience she waited while the nervous performers arranged themselves in several rows before her. Looking to their director with faces that showed the intenseness of their concentration they awaited her signal.

The chatter in the audience dwindled then stopped and a deep stillness descended on the camp as they waited for the first sounds to reach out and touch them.

Mrs Dryburgh slowly raised her arms, paused momentarily, then with a sweeping movement gently stroked the air which caused a soft, distant note to rise and fall. So faint and delicate was the far away sound that it was barely audible to the audience straining to capture it.

Then it broadened and grew, increasing in volume and they felt the soulful tones of *Largo* from the *New World Symphony* as it enclosed them in a capsule of sound that carried them away from the physical bondage of the camp.

Vivian sat entranced and totally involved in the magic that swirled around her. The voices were so heavenly, the notes so sad, yet they were uplifting. Closing her eyes she experienced an intense feeling within her as the camp with its dilapidated shacks seemed to melt away and the hospital of human suffering and the cemetery began to dissolve leaving her mind clean and clear. The music carried her upward and she soared upon the waves of glorious sound, higher and higher, over the razor-sharp wire, above the tallest tree and into the sunlight of the brightest day she had ever seen and the voice within her said "I am free...I am free."

The voices gradually receded then faded to nothing leaving a deep stillness to settle over the camp and its occupants.

The cries and shouts of heartfelt appreciation for their comrades, who had carried each of them on a journey of joy, came from their hearts and the tears tumbled down the cheeks of the audience and those of the performers.

It was a night of consummate beauty, a beauty they thought had died long ago with the loss of their freedom, their enforced separation from loved ones and the ravages of malnutrition and disease. Yet, in the space of a few minutes, it had been revealed that true beauty still existed, even in a squalid prison camp, for it existed in the spirit of the women.

****

New Year's Eve slipped by without celebration and the opening months of 1944 blended into a numbing sameness varied only by the choir and their brilliant performances.

Finally even this was denied the prisoners for rations became leaner and more inmates began to die of malnutrition. The choir lost 19 of its members and was forced to disband.

Vivian, during this time, found it difficult to spare time from her hospital duties to see Betty. When an opportunity did arise she went in search of her young friend and was shocked at the girl's appearance.

She had deteriorated during the weeks since she had last seen her. Her emaciated body was draped in scraps of ragged cloth. Her feet were wrapped in leaves bound with jungle vines and her little face was drawn and pale.

The infectious grin, she was happy to see, was still there and they greeted one another warmly before setting off for a walk around the perimeter of the camp with Betty's thin little hand slipping easily into Vivian's.

After grumbles from Betty about lazy women in camp who wanted the older children to do everything for them, the conversation, guided by Vivian, turned to food and she asked Betty if she was getting enough to eat.

Although she said she was it was obvious to Vivian that she wasn't.

In her efforts to convince Vivian she was not hungry Betty spoke of the pumpkin she had grown and how every night she tied it to her leg so it wouldn't be stolen. When it was just about ready to be eaten it had disappeared one night while she slept. "I think it was the woman next door," she said, "because she was always looking at it."

"But what do you get to eat?" Vivian asked.

"The rice ration", came the reply, "and the extra bits."

"What extra bits?" said Vivian pressing her.

It seemed the children gathered each night under the guard's hut around the time the Japs sat down for their evening meal.

As the men scooped the rice from their bowls with chopsticks some of the rice granules would fall through the cracks in the bamboo floor and land in the dirt below. The children would pick this up and share it around grain by grain.

"But I think they know we are there," said Bet in a conspiratorial whisper.

"How come?" asked Viv.

"Because at the end of each meal they scrape what's left over onto the floor then flick it through the gaps with their chopsticks."

Vivian thought about this. Was it out of sympathy for the children or was it a part of their standard cleaning process? If it was done out of consideration for the children's suffering then it was contrary to their normal behaviour, 'But then again,' she told herself, 'the Japanese are totally unpredictable.'

Before leaving to return to the hospital Vivian made Betty promise she would be careful, just in case the guards did not know of their presence beneath the floor.

On the 1st of April 1944, Captain Siki assumed command of the camp and called for all inmates to be assembled.

A small, far from handsome man, Siki had one fixed brown eye while the other, bloodshot and rheumy, stared malevolently at them from out of a pudgy face.

He sat at a table placed in the quadrangle facing the ranks of prisoners with two N.C.O.'s and a private soldier flanking him. One, a senior sergeant, nicknamed 'Ah Fat', for obvious reasons, stood glaring at the line of women while the other, a middle-aged Warrant Officer with a softer face, looked bored by the proceedings. The private soldier, Vivian guessed, was the interpreter for it was understood the new commander did not speak English.

All the women and children stood in a long snaking line, under a boiling sun to wait their turn in which to pass Siki's table. As each person came abreast of the commander they would bow and announce their name before moving on.

The ceremony had taken most of the morning and when he had acknowledged the last in line Siki stood and addressed the rows of prisoners. It was a long rambling speech, delivered in Japanese and confined to the glorious victories gained by the Imperial Japanese Forces and the inevitable defeat of the Americans and their Allies. The interpreter translated each sentence as it was spoken.

Concluding, Siki warned of possible air raids on the nearby oil refinery at Pladjou adding that should this happen they would be evacuated to a rubber estate, not far from the camp which was considered to be outside the danger area.

When the interpreter translated this Vivian felt her spirits lift momentarily for air raids on Sumatra meant Allied planes were nearby and that implied the Japs weren't winning the war.

Her theory was given some measure of credibility several days later when they were given injections against typhoid, dysentery and cholera, something the Japs had refused on countless occasions in the past. In fact 'Ah Fat' would look scornfully at the delegation of doctors who regularly pleaded with him to release the necessary drugs and say "Why worry, there is plenty room in the cemetery." He would follow this remark with a high-pitched giggle.

Shortly after receiving the injections an edict from Captain Siki was read out at tenko that all rice rations were to be reduced because of the shortage of food on Sumatra. Further, all women and children would be required to join work parties and plant vegetables.

They would work from five in the morning to six o'clock at night for seven days a week.

The next day they were issued with eleven-pound "chungkals", a type of native hoe made of wood, marched out of camp and under guard directed to clear the jungle in preparation for the planting of sweet potato and tapioca.

Even the hard-baked earth of the padang was dug up and planted with a variety of vegetables.

The heavy work with its long hours, together with a reduced rice intake, had an immediate and adverse effect on the health of the women and children and large numbers began to succumb to a range of illnesses, many of which led to death.

The Australian Sisters, in addition to joining the work parties, were also expected to work on a roster basis, caring for the sick at the now overcrowded hospital.

Vivian was gently bathing the brow of a very ill woman when a loud noise, not unlike an explosion, made her look up. Several other bangs followed and then a shrill, high-pitched shriek told her from experience that it was an air raid. Flinging herself over the woman she had been bathing Vivian heard the bomb burst in the nearby jungle with a thunderous roar, drowning out the now wailing camp air raid siren.

As predicted by Siki, the Allies were bombing the oil refinery and the camp was receiving a few of the strays. This heightened the excitement, for over the din of exploding bombs and the frantic shouting of the Japanese could be heard cheering, which came from the throats of hundreds of women and children who saw freedom in each gigantic flash.

As quickly as it had started the raid stopped and in each barracks the women discussed the implications of this first raid and the possibility of victory over the Japanese until late into the night. The raid had given everyone hope and it was the first morale-booster they had experienced since being captured.

At the next morning's tenko Siki issued an order restricting prisoners to their barracks during air raids and most importantly they were not to look outside. Those who disobeyed the order would be severely punished.

Several days passed before the camp's air raid siren again announced the arrival of Allied bombers and the women and children, restricted to their barracks, could only listen intently to the distant explosions.

In the Australian Sisters barracks there was great excitement as the second raid within days got underway. Sisters Wilhelmina (Ray) Raymont of the 2/4th C.C.S and Valerie Smith of the 2/13th, unable to kerb their curiosity, peeked out of the barracks at the Japanese running around the compound in a state of confusion and terror.

Unfortunately they were observed by Sergeant Ishimara and it was he, in company with an armed soldier, who burst into their barracks and hauled the two Sisters away to face Siki..

Captain Siki ignored the Senior Sister's pleas for mercy and the fact that Raymont had not only malaria but a heart condition. He sentenced the two Australians to stand in the blistering heat of the day, without hats, at his pleasure.

Ray was the first to keel over during the hottest part of the day and despite threats from bayonet-wielding guards the Sisters advanced en masse and picking up their unconscious colleague they bore her off to the hospital.

Val Smith continued to stand in the furnace heat for the remainder of the day surrounded by the other Sisters. At sunset they carried the comatose nurse into the barracks and treated her for sunstroke.

CAMP FOUR....DEAD MAN'S ISLAND

In the dying days of August, rumours predicted a move back to the fever-ridden island of Bangka and an early official confirmation of this gave the prisoners time to prepare for the journey.

They were to leave in groups, the first being the hospital patients and their nurses.

This threw Vivian and Wilma into a flurry of activity as stretchers had to be constructed to transport the seriously ill; those patients who could walk needed assistance with the packing of their belongings. Then came the search for food to carry them over the trip and finally the gathering of their own personal items.

The hospital group moved out the next day and, negotiating the 60 miles down the Musi River, arrived at Sungsang where they were placed on board an antiquated tri-deck ferry to await the arrival of the other groups. When everyone was accounted for the small ships crossed the river and tied up to a wharf adjacent to the Kertapati railway station.

Here they took on board 120 Indonesian and Indo-Dutch internees plus a number of Dutch nuns from surrounding camps, with their worldly possessions which lay strewn across the wharf.

Vivian saw the guards approaching and knew something bad was about to happen.

They headed straight to their group and pushed the nurses down the gangway and onto the wharf. They were then ordered to carry the internees and other prisoners' luggage aboard.

It was an act designed to humiliate the Australian Sisters in front of hundreds of watching Asians lining the decks of the ferries.

Assembling every ounce of dignity that their frail bodies and tattered appearance would allow, the Sisters bent to the task and started loading the luggage which varied from large sacks of corn to heavy stone grinders and cumbersome trunks and boxes.

As they struggled to lift their burdens and carry them up the gangway the guards ran amongst the women smiting them on the legs with the flat of their swords and screaming "Hayaku. Hayaku." (Hurry up. Hurry up.)

They worked like this for several hours until all of the luggage on the wharf was cleared.

Totally spent by their efforts the women staggered up the gangway one more time and collapsed together on the hard deck.

They had barely settled when the guards reappeared to rain blows on their bodies and scream for them to get up. Dragging themselves upright they stood sullenly, eyeing their tormentors, cold anger building within them and the Japanese stared back with undisguised contempt. No one moved. It was as if time had been frozen capturing the two groups at the precise moment before they flung themselves at each other with murderous intent.

The little tubby NCO whom they called 'Ah Fat' broke the hostile silence with a shouted command that galvanised the guards into action. With bayonets levelled they pushed and prodded the surly group of Sisters down the gangway and across the road to a rail-siding and several freight cars.

Sliding open the doors on the freight cars 'Ah Fat' told them to unload the cargo and take it on board the ferry.

The distressed Sisters looked with dismay at what appeared to be hundreds of bags of rice stacked to the roof of the cars.

Too fatigued and depressed to resist, the Australian women moved slowly forward and hefting a sack each staggered toward the ferry and the gangway they knew so well.

Vivian felt the weighty sack bear down on her back and the pain in her side began to surface as wearily she forced her body to climb the ramp to the ferry's deck.

In front of her was Wilma, almost bent double with her load, and she thought of the torment her friend must be going through with her back injury caused by the falling life-rafts.

Then blocking out all thoughts in her mind Vivian became insensitive to the pain in her body. With the other Sisters she became part of a large circle of automatons who picked up a sack, took it to the ferry, dumped it and returned for another.

They endured until the last sack was carried aboard at roughly three o'clock in the morning.

Finding a vacant spot on deck the Sisters settled down and immediately succumbed to an almost death-like slumber.

The little ships got underway at first light and journeyed down the Musi to Cape Carat where they set course for Muntok.

Leaning on the rail later that day the Australian Sisters thought of their comrades as they passed near the spot where the *Vyner Brooke* had gone down. Each had their own thoughts as in solemn silence they gazed down at the heaving sea.

To Vivian Singapore would forever remain the link between those Sisters who had been lost and those destined to live, for it was there, in the balmy days before the Japanese struck, that they shared so many wonderful days and nights together in a city of contrasts and charm.

****

Anchoring off the jetty at Muntok the prisoners were transhipped into junks for the trip to the pier where they commenced the long walk to land. Here they boarded a convoy of trucks and were taken to their new camp on the outskirts of Muntok.

The women's camp was thought a palace compared to the men's camp at Palembang.

There were 6 large huts, each capable of accommodating 140 persons in comfort. The main kitchen was located in the middle of the compound with two smaller ones a short distance away. There were some 50 concrete fireplaces. The Japanese had however disregarded normal health procedures and built the lavatory pits and communal bathrooms alongside the kitchens.

More importantly there was an adequate supply of water with 9 concrete wells scattered around the camp. The water was some 50 feet down and needed a windlass, with a bucket, to haul it to the surface.

The best aspect of the camp was its position. Located on a hill it would capture any sea breeze and the ground was predominantly gravel which would ensure better drainage, eliminating the muddy conditions they previously had to contend with during the monsoon season.

Further, each prisoner was issued a new rush sleeping mat and the men confined in the Coolie Lines sent over a large quantity of salt fish, rice and vegetables as a "welcome" gesture.

These allowances by their captors could only reflect the turn in the tide of war because the Japs were not noted for their humanitarian ways.

By the end of November an alarming number within the camp were coming down with a deadly fever that manifested itself with a bursting headache followed by raging temperatures, skin eruptions and finally unconsciousness which led to death.

Unknown amongst the four doctors in camp, but believed to be mosquito-borne, the illness was labelled 'Bangka Fever'.

Within a week of one another, Betty Jeffrey, Shirley Gardam, Mickey Syer, Jenny Greer and Mitz Mittelheuser had become victims and were hospitalised.

Much larger than the previous hospital, the one at Muntok had a main ward capable of holding 19 patients on one long "bali bali", a form of shelf made by binding rubber tree branches together in one long line.

The children's section accommodated four, with 2 infants in a couple of old cots and the infectious block took 12 in four separate rooms. Fifty yards away was the convalescent hut that could take upwards of 30 people.

Four doctors were responsible for the health of over 700 inmates for which the Japanese would supply 100 quinine tablets every six weeks. No other drugs were issued.

Sister Jenny Ashton and Sister Reynelda, a Dutch nun, were appointed joint Matrons of the hospital and half of the available Australian, British and Dutch nurses were allocated duties at the hospital while the remainder continued District Nursing.

The camp cemetery was outside the wire on a gently sloping hillside set in a clearing which was surrounded by a proliferation of exotic jungle flowers and verdant greenery.

An idyllic setting, it had evidently been there long before the war for the hillside was dotted with old Chinese tomb markers, some leaning drunkenly to one side and showing their age.

To this peaceful place, more frequently now, came the burial parties from the camp.

The grave diggers, following behind a crudely constructed coffin with their weighty "chungkals" slung over aching shoulders, led the missionary and a few friends of the deceased while several paces behind the small cortege came the armed Japanese guard.

The grave-diggers were drawn from the stronger women in camp and the young boys were given the task of building the caskets from any scraps of wood they could either find or scrounge.

The markers took the form of roughly made crosses onto which the name of the person was burnt. Burials soared during December.

Christmas Day went solemnly by with friends mumbling a few good wishes, exchanging a sheaf of jungle flowers or presenting an old re-endorsed Christmas card. For dinner that night they ate a small serve of fried rice topped with half a prawn and the atmosphere was sombre.

Thirty-one out of the thirty-two Australian Sisters had malaria.

Ray Raymont had been very ill for some time, having never fully recovered from the effects of being forced to stand out in the sun as punishment for ignoring Captain Siki's order.

Gradually her condition deteriorated and she was now desperately ill with cerebral malaria.

Vivian and Wilma specialled their colleague frequently during their rostered hours as did the others throughout their shifts with Val Smith, Ray's good friend, spending as much time as she could at her bedside.

Eventually Ray slipped into a state of unconsciousness, yet even in this twilight world she could not escape the massive agony generated by her swollen and infected brain. Her high- pitched screaming, born out of this excruciating pain, at times went on for hours and reached into every corner of the camp. For all that knew and respected the gentle Australian, her cries penetrated to their very soul and they prayed that it would end for her sake.

"Can't you shut her up?"

Vivian looked at Wilma, shock registering on both their faces and together they turned to see Doctor Goldberg standing before them, her face a mixture of frustration and anger.

"She can't stop Doctor", said Vivian stiffly, " she doesn't even know she's doing it."

"Well I'll stop her if you won't." said Goldberg, aggressively brushing Vivian aside to deliver a vicious slap to the face of the unconscious Sister.

Vivian and Wilma shot to their feet, bodies rigid, faces contorted with uncontrollable rage, their eyes boring mercilessly into those of the woman in front of them. When Vivian spoke her words were cold and deeply menacing.

"Don't ever do that again."

"Never," said Wilma her strong jaw thrust forward.

The atmosphere was tense and Goldberg was obviously undecided as to the attitude to adopt given she was not dealing with the average junior nurse.

Evidently she chose not to be confrontational for she hurriedly left the room leaving Vivian and Wilma to turn once more to the needs of Ray.

Sister Wilhelmina Raymont, died on February 8, 1945, at the age of 33.

The day was hot with a high degree of humidity, like the many that had gone before, yet it appeared to be different because the air was heavy with an inexplicable grey gloom and even the children had ceased playing their noisy games.

The inmates were gathering and they stood in hushed groups watching as the small parade of women passed through the camp on its way to the Chinese cemetery bearing the coffin of Wilhelmina Raymont.

That morning the Sisters had taken carefully-folded garments from where they had been hidden amongst their belongings. For the first time since their incarceration they were going to wear the uniform of the A.A.N.S.

To the onlookers it was inconceivable that one of the Australian women had died for they appeared to be indestructible. Their ability to overcome the privations of camp life and the way they went about caring for their fellow inmates had endeared them to almost every woman and child behind the wire. In the survival of the Australians lay the hopes of them all.

Now they watched as the party went by with three Sisters on either side of the coffin gripping the poles that supported it, while the others followed behind at the slow march.

As they reached the gate the camp guards came silently to the attention and removed their garrison caps in mute respect and the little band made its way out of the camp and up the hill to lay to rest one of their own.

The monsoon season broke and Bangka fever, malaria, beri beri and various other tropical diseases were rampant in camp.

Rene Singleton, from Victoria and a member of the 2/10th, was admitted to the hospital with chronic beri beri during the same month. Blessed with a quick wit and a very dry sense of humour Rene had contributed much to the upkeep of morale within the Australian group.

Now her emaciated body lay on the hospital's 'bali-bali', her once clear blue eyes a watery grey as her rasping voice asked her fellow Sisters, "if there was anymore breakfast." Shortly after making this request Sister Rene Singleton died from a disease easily cured by a balanced intake of vitamin B. It was February 20 and Rene was 36 years of age.

Also in hospital at the time was Shirley Gardam who was very weak from malnutrition and Pauline (Blanche) Hempstead who was suffering from beri beri and malnutrition.

Vivian, who loved the larrikin streak in this tough little Queenslander, spent as much time with her as was possible and witnessed the distressing wasting away of a friend who had brought so much laughter into their miserable existence.

Always colourful, Blanche called a spade a spade and often in very colourful language but they all knew that beneath the rough exterior lay a very big heart.

During her last days in early March she kept apologising to the Sisters attending her for "being such a nuisance and taking so long to die."

She died on the 19th of the same month aged 34.

There were twenty-nine of them left.

CAMP FIVE....LUBUKLINGGAU

March had almost gone when Siki announced they were to be moved to a new camp at Lubuklinggau in south western Sumatra and located at the end of the railway line.

The interpreter explained the move would be by way of lorry to Muntok where they would board a boat for Palembang, transferring there to rail cars for the journey into Sumatra.

Feelings amongst the prisoners concerning the move were mixed. For many it meant an escape from the dreaded 'Bangka Fever' and the island the locals called 'Dead Man's Island'. For the remainder it only confirmed what they had been thinking all along. The Japs kept moving them knowing that many would die in the process while the survivors would be seriously weakened. From the description given as to the location of the new camp, deep in a remote sector of the Sumatra jungle, it was an ideal place to bury the rest of their captives and the evidence of Japanese inhumanity to their fellow human beings would die with them.

Four days before the move, on 4 April, Sister Shirley Gardam died.

It happened so quickly that it stunned Vivian who had been feeding her at the time from a small bowl of rice. Shirley was talking about her home state of Tasmania and the training years spent at the Launceston Hospital when suddenly she raised her head, let out a sharp cry then fell back. It was over.

The Australian women went searching for jungle blooms as the gentle 34 year old had held a deep love for flowers and they were determined Shirley would have them for her journey up the hill to the little clearing.

The move began on the 8 April, 1945, with the first group containing half the Australian Sisters. The others were split into several groups and were to follow at intervals.

Vivian, in group one, endured once more the long torturous walk along the Muntok jetty with the added weight of a stretcher on which lay a very sick woman. Watching them were the Japanese crews of the newly installed anti-aircraft guns positioned along the jetty. Lounging against the wood railing they eyed the dishevelled procession, some making remarks in Japanese which brought a laugh from their companions.

Reaching the end they placed the stretchers with their human burden on the decking before making the return journey to pick up the remainder of their patients. During their absence, one of the stretcher cases died and they hurriedly dug a shallow grave in the putrid mud flat under the wharf, recited the Lord's Prayer and returned to carry the rest out to the end of the jetty.

With all of group one assembled at the end of the Muntok Jetty the Japanese loaded them aboard an old coastal vessel which then got underway.

It took the best part of a day to make the crossing during which time several of the sick died and were buried at sea simply by rolling their bodies over the side, a task the Japanese would not help the women do.

Anchoring overnight at the mouth of the Musi River they moved upstream at first light and docked around mid-morning in Palembang.

Here they were transferred to a waiting train. The stretcher cases were put into the cattle trucks while the others crammed into carriages thick with black coal dust. Shortly after, they were given a small portion of soup and rice and told to wait.

The carriages soon became ovens as the temperature rose and the occupants became restless and frustrated at the delay. They were also impatient to commence their journey because of their close proximity to a rather large oil refinery and a lightning Allied air raid could mean near misses.

Adding to their misery was rampant dysentery. This forced the women and children to use a ditch running parallel with the train where they were forced to relieve themselves 'coolie style' in full view of the curious locals.

As darkness settled, the captives welcomed the cooling cloak of night, following some twelve hours of suffocating heat, despite the hordes of mosquitos massing for their nightly assault.

Vivian spent a restless night disturbed by a multitude of stinging bites and the sound of people shuffling in and out of the carriage either on their way to, or coming back from, the ditch beside the train.

A loud sharp impact woke the train's passengers with a start and the hiss of escaping steam told them the engine had arrived. With a jerk they began to move and Vivian looked out at the changing scene as the train gathered speed and rattled through the Sumatran countryside. She was tired to the very core of her bones, her stomach was empty and she really didn't care what fate had in mind for her at the end of the line. She had been existing, a day at a time, for over three years; 'I can't go on for much longer,' she told herself, 'I don't think I have the strength.'

The train sped on past the rising peak of Mount Dempo, north of Lahat, set in an ocean of thick, lush jungle. It crossed an upper tributary of the Musi River and then through a series of hillside tunnels before arriving at their destination. They had been travelling for 34 hours since leaving Bangka Island.

When the guards didn't appear they assumed they were staying overnight.

At dawn the next day they were put into lorries and driven down a dirt road for 15 miles to a rubber plantation.

The place was called Belalau and was located in a disused rubber estate that had been allowed to run-down. Most of its machinery had been destroyed by the fleeing owners.

Some of the camp buildings were on a hill which sloped down to a gully and a shallow creek, straddled by a narrow wooden bridge, while several others were grouped around the communal kitchen and the hospital hut on the other side of the stream.

Most of the Australians were allocated a series of attap roofed huts on the hill. They were of very poor construction. The gaps in the roof of each hut guaranteed that on wet days the dirt floors would turn to quagmires and the sides were totally open to the elements.

The sleeping arrangements consisted of 'bali bali's' made from boards and supported by bamboo legs.

The British, Dutch, Asians and eighteen Charitas nuns, together with ten of the Australian Sisters, were accommodated in similar quarters over the creek.

There were no bathrooms and they would be forced to bathe in the creek in full view of the guards. This was also the case when using the toilet boxes, which luckily had been placed downstream from where water was to be taken for the kitchen.

Rubber trees and a formidable barbed-wire fence bounded the perimeter of the camp and the Sisters voted it as the most primitive camp they had been in.

Experienced at settling into new camps the Australians got busy organising the hospital and District Nursing duties while Jessie Simons dug the first garden bed with a dinner knife and planted several rows of sweet potato. Others formed parties to gather edible ferns and grass growing along the banks of the stream. Despite their efforts to supplement the daily ration of one portion of rice and sweet potato, the average Sister's weight had fallen to between five and six stone.

Malnutrition and disease were taking their toll and Miss Dryburgh, brilliant author and composer of countless songs and intricate vocal arrangements, finally succumbed to both during the last weeks of April.

The entire camp paid homage to this lady, well loved by all, who had devised a corridor of freedom for her fellow prisoners with her music, bringing hope when there was none and creating beauty amidst death.

****

On a day rumbling with thunder and heavy with humidity they brought Betty Kenneison to the hospital.

Desperately ill with fever and dysentery she lay semi-conscious on the "bali bali" as Vivian bathed her emaciated little body.

With nothing to give her by way of drugs, she knew there was very little to be done for her friend and in all possibility they would lose her.

Over the next few days Vivian spent her duty free time with Betty and with careful nursing and extra rations contributed by Vivian and others the little girl began responding to Vivian's treatment and the crisis was over.

Shortly before Betty was due to be reunited with her Step-Grandmother the woman to the right of her died and she watched as her body was picked up from the "bali bali" and placed in a crude coffin made from packing case wood. As the imperfect box was being lifted a bottom plank sprang loose allowing the dead woman's head to flop out. Betty stared at it unemotionally but fascinated by the expression on the face. The eyes were wide open and they appeared to be pleading, 'pleading for life,' thought Betty, 'as if there was something to live for.'

Even in her immaturity Betty was old in the ways of the camp and she had reasoned that this woman must have had children and therefore she didn't want to die.

She continued to watch as a nun gently took hold of the woman's head and tucked it back into the box and securing the slat as best she could helped carry the coffin away.

The next day Betty was discharged from the hospital, her age no doubt an important factor in her recovery.

During the time Betty was in hospital Sister Gladys Hughes, a New Zealander and a member of the 2/13th, was admitted with a combination of beri beri, malaria and malnutrition. A popular personality she was noted for her skill at thinking up different ways in which to present rice. It was a gloomy day on 31 May when the Australians learnt of her death at the age of 36.

By now all of the Sisters except Jessie Blanch had malaria and were running temperatures of 104 and 105 degrees. Wilma was concerned for Vivian who was obviously very sick. Despite a thorough examination by the doctors they were unable to identify the other causes, apart from malaria, that were making her dangerously ill.

Knowing how close Betty Kenneison was to Vivian, Wilma sought out the girl and told her she had taken Viv to hospital.

Alarmed by this news Betty asked if her friend could die to which Wilma replied, "there is every likelihood."

Through her tears the girl wanted to know if there was anything she could do to help her friend and Wilma suggested limes, although she knew there were none in camp and if they were they would cost a fortune.

"I'll get some," said Betty, "I don't want Viv to die, I'll find them."

With that she hurried off as best as her skinny little frame would allow leaving Wilma with the thought that 'if anyone could do it, then it would be little Bet.'

There was a woman trader in camp they called the 'Half-Baked Banker,' dealing in jewellery, money and promissory notes in exchange for goods, which she stored on a special 'bali bali', some eight-foot high, as protection from would-be thieves.

It was to the 'Banker' that Betty was heading knowing that the gold bangle she wore on her arm would fetch a good price. Originally there had been two bangles given to her before the war by her mother, but one had already been sold for food.

The one she now wore had been carefully disguised with tar and mud to hide its value from both the prisoners and guards.

Standing at the base of the tall 'bali bali' she called to the 'Banker' who peered over the side of her perch and asked her what she wanted.

"Limes, have you any limes," asked Betty.

"No," came the reply, "they're very hard to get."

Disappointed she turned away from the 'Banker' and was walking toward the hospital when a thought struck her; 'there was another place she could try,' and immediately she took off for the wire.

Hidden behind a hut close by the perimeter, Betty took off the bangle and cleaned it as best she could on her sun suit then waited for a certain guard to come around on his patrol.

"Hello," she said greeting him in Malay, "I have a gold bangle to trade for limes."

The guard looked furtively about to ensure they were alone before answering her.

"How many do you want?"

"A dozen."

"They are very difficult to get."

"Do you want to look at my bracelet?" she said, holding it up for him to see.

The guard stepped closer to the wire. "Is it gold?"

"Yes, real gold."

"Be here tomorrow," he said quickly and walked off.

Happy with the outcome of her trading little Bet could hardly wait for tomorrow because every hour was important to her.

Standing in the same spot the next day she saw her pinched-faced guard approach.

Satisfying himself no one was looking he motioned for her to pass him the bangle and once he had inspected it he dived into the bushes behind him and returned with a box which he upended sending the contents rolling under the wire.

Betty counted a dozen small limes.

Gathering them up Betty hurried off to the hospital elated that she was able to fulfil her promise and confident that Vivian would not die.

In the weeks that followed Vivian fought for her life, attended to constantly by Wilma and the other Sisters until unexpectedly she pulled through, which many suspected had been a result of the fresh limes and the additional rations they were able to scrounge for her.

Weak and unable to walk it was to be several weeks before Vivian was able to resume her duties at the hospital.

On the day she was due at the hospital Vivian took herself off for a bath in the stream. Ignoring the ogling guards she completed her ablutions and made her way back to the hut where she picked up a mirror and began combing her hair.

All of the hair on the left-hand side of her head came away with the comb.

Impassively she stared at her baldness in the mirror and thought 'if it had happened before the war she would have cried hysterically but now, who cares?'

It was a statement of abject misery, of her declining health and fading hope of ever being rescued from a vast sea of jungle. She had come to the end of her endurance and had accepted the fact that they would all die in Belalau because that was the way the Japanese wanted it.

Sister Win Davis, from New South Wales and the 2/10th, died one week after her thirtieth birthday despite the efforts of her friend Pat Gunther who scrounged eggs and potatoes in a desperate effort to improve her friend's diet.

Sister Dorothy Freeman from Victoria, and also, from the 2/10th , passed away from the effects of beri beri, malaria and malnutrition only minutes after sharing tea with Flo Trotter. She was 32 years of age.

On the 18 August Sister Pearl (Mitz) Mittelheuser from Queensland and House Captain for the 2/10th, slipped away covered in an old rice sack used to keep her warm from the malarial chills that racked her body. She was 41 years of age.

Of the 65 Sisters who left Singapore there were now only 24 alive and several more were admitted to hospital that month.

"THE WAR IS OVER SISTER"

Vivian dragged herself down to the stream to bathe before going on duty.

There were a number of women in the water and as she entered it one of the Asian women greeted her.

"Good morning, Sister the war is over."

Vivian looked at the woman and smiled, "That's nice."

"No, it is true Sister," insisted the woman and her companion verified this.

"Yes, Sister, we were told last night, at a party with some Japanese officers."

A glimmer of hope began to grow in the back of Vivian's mind as she remembered hearing of a party held in the Japs quarters the previous night. 'Could what they are saying be true?' she asked herself.

"Are you sure?"

"Yes Sister," answered the one who had spoken to her initially. " and the interpreter has been crying all night."

'Good,' She thought, wading to the bank where she picked up her faded sun-suit before hobbling up the hill, her excitement mounting, to see if the others had heard the news.

Two days were to pass with life going on as usual in the camp before Siki called for the prisoners to be assembled at three o'clock that day. To make sure everyone attended he sent the guards around the camp with long sticks.

Standing before them dressed as usual in a pair of baggy, badly patched pants and a crumpled tunic, which appeared to be a very tight fit around his well-fed frame, his bloodshot eye flicked malevolently over the ranks before puffing out his chest and announcing that the war was over and consequently they were now all good friends.

The red-eyed interpreter translated Siki's words into English and it was met with stony silence.

The Japanese Commander had anticipated the women would break out into cheering on hearing his news, instead they stood staring at him, their faces slack and expressionless.

A lone voice from the assembly broke the silence.

"Would you repeat that Captain Siki in Malay please?"

Siki complied with the request following which there was silence.

The confusion showed clearly on his face and he abruptly turned and walked up the hill to his house as behind him the women and children broke ranks and drifted away without uttering a sound.

There was a very good reason why there was no celebration on hearing the news. The war might be over but the daily struggle to survive went on as usual. People were still dying from disease and malnutrition and there was little food in camp, certainly not enough to fill their scrawny stomachs. Without food and drugs many were destined to die. How tragic this was for they had fought so hard to see the day when they would be free, only to be cheated by death when it arrived.

On the day following Siki's announcement that the war was over the Japanese released the men and youths from the neighbouring camp and the women and children turned out in force to welcome them.

They arrived in one big mob, matchstick men and boys, their wasted limbs moving slowly, some limping on one leg, the stump of the other supported by a crudely fashioned walking crutch. As they neared the gate the women and children surged forward, their shouts renting the air and the two groups ran together in a confused melee and the search began for loved ones in that sea of smiling faces.

There were cries of joy when husbands and wives were reunited and they flung themselves into each others arms while coy little children clung to their father's legs, fathers they hardly knew or did not know at all.

Not all, however, were to share the euphoria of the moment. They could be seen wandering through the throng of hugging couples searching for a familiar face and wrestling with a growing fear as they realised that person was not there.

Eventually someone would separate from their partner and approach the searcher with the news that their husband or wife had died or was very ill in the hospital.

Standing to one side the small group of Australian Sisters watched the tearful reunions and although they shared their happiness they were also saddened by the fact that it would be a long time before they saw Australia and their loved ones.

****

"There you are, there's Sumatra." yelled the pilot over the roar of the aircraft's motors.

Standing behind him, Major Gideon F. Jacobs, Royal Marines, looked in the direction the Skipper was pointing and through the thick haze made out a long green smudge edged in white.

The sight sent a chill down his spine and he recalled the meeting he had with his chief in Ceylon only a few weeks before. At the time Jacobs was between missions for Naval Intelligence having just completed an exacting and exhausting task. Then came word to report to Headquarters in Trincomalee where he was told to take a small party into Sumatra and pass back intelligence. He was given two weeks to choose his men and be ready to go.

Jacobs chose his men carefully. Tjoeng, for instance, was Chinese and came from the East Coast of Java but at one time had lived in Sumatra. At 25 years of age he was lanky, very fit and a trained wireless operator who hated the Japanese with a fierce intensity.

Sergeant Bates was an Australian from Melbourne. Lean, with a hard square jaw and frank determined eyes, his movements were deft and decisive. His mate, Sergeant Gillam came from Perth and was shorter than Bates but had that typical Aussie look about him that said "take life as it comes."

They always addressed one another as 'Digger' or 'Dig' and appeared to be forever at loggerheads with one another, they were the best of friends. Both Aussies were skilled wireless operators.

The last member of the party was a stocky Dutchman, Sergeant Plesman, who sported a rather savage crew cut. His grey dancing eyes got him the nickname of 'Happy.'

Jacobs, the youngest in the party, was born in South Africa and educated at the University of Pretoria. He attended Military College in 1941 and later the Imperial Officers' College in Palestine. Qualifying as a staff officer he returned to South Africa where he applied for an appointment with the Royal Marines. Accepted, he trained as a parachutist and in commando tactics before service in Europe and then in the Far East following Germany's surrender.

As the Catalina flying boat approached the Sumatran coast the party made their way to the rear of the aircraft to where a small trap door was located. Here they donned parachutes and clipped on canvas jump bags. The latter held most of their equipment and were designed to hang 30 feet below them, on a strap, during their decent. The heavier equipment, such as the wireless transceivers, weapons and food, was stowed in metal containers to be dropped separately. Having given each other the once-over safety check they waited for the signal to go.

The dispatcher's voice could be heard counting down from ten and on reaching "one" a light above them flashed green and Jacobs slid down the chute, through the hatch and into the grey void below.

Landing safely in a clearing the party paused only to pick up the equipment containers before plunging into the jungle.

Later that day Jacobs selected a small clearing as their base camp and they set about laying it out and opening communications with Ceylon.

They were to remain in the camp for several days and while away the dreary hours listening to Radio India. They learnt of the Atomic bombs dropped on Hiroshima and Nagasaki.

The war was over. To corroborate this they made contact with Ceylon Headquarters who confirmed the Japanese surrender and ordered Jacobs to make contact with the Japanese Command Headquarters in Medan.

Building a raft they floated down river and eventually reached a village where the inhabitants knew of a telephone handset in the office of a nearby but deserted rubber plantation. Surprisingly, it worked. Following several frustrating attempts, Jacobs eventually got through to Japanese Headquarters in Medan. The Japanese officer however mistook Jacobs for one of his subordinates whom he thought was trying to impersonate an Allied officer.

Finally convincing the frustrated Jap that this was not the case Jacobs made arrangements for himself and his party to be picked up and transported to Medan.

Colonel Okada, Chief of Staff of the Second Imperial Division, and his Second in Command, Major Inamura, met Jacobs on his arrival. Okada was short and dark with short cropped hair and practically no eyebrows, which contrasted dramatically with that of Inamura who was muscular and powerfully built with three rows of medals that attested to his combat experience.

The Second Imperial Division had fought in China, was responsible for the British defeat in Malaya and overrunning the Dutch garrisons in north-western Sumatra.

Standing before these two officers, Jacobs was aware they had 80,000 armed men at their command, including a strong air force, while he commanded a task-force of four.

Hoping to gain the initiative he imperiously announced that he had come from the Allied High Command and was Admiral Mountbatten's personal representative.

He emphasised that Marshal Terauchi in Saigon had guaranteed his safety as well as the Colonel's full co-operation.

As the two Japanese staff officers wanted to verify this with Saigon they suggested Jacobs and his men could wait, in more comfortable surroundings, at the Hotel de Boer.

Arriving shortly after, Jacobs was about to enter the hotel when three white men approached him identifying themselves as internees from one of the southern camps. One was Doctor Beck, the Acting Governor of Sumatra, the other a Mr Fenton and the third man was Mr Amsler, the Swiss Consul and Chief Red Cross Representative on the island.

After listening to their story concerning conditions in the southern camps and the need for immediate assistance, Jacobs decided to leave for the Rantau Prapat area some 300 kilometres south east of Medan.

Leaving Bates and Gillam to stand wireless watch Jacobs took the rest, together with several Japanese soldiers to ensure a safe passage, and left in two cars for the first camp at Aek Paminki which held 3000 women and children, the majority of them European.

The sight that greeted him sickened the tough Marine Major who wasted no time in gathering the former prisoners around him to explain the dropping of the Atomic bomb. He urged them to stay in the camp so that medical and food supplies could be air-dropped and reassured them an Allied force would be landing in Sumatra soon.

Without undue delay Jacobs left for the men's camp at Ringo Ringo where he was met by the sadistic Chief of Camps, Colonel Sada.

Sada was bull-necked with wild bushy eyebrows set above a pair of dark flashing eyes. His bearing and uncompromising stance indicated to Jacobs that he was an arrogant man.

Bluntly, Jacobs communicated his contempt for the man who would visit such abominable practices on innocent men women and children.

Sada defended himself by saying he had orders from higher command to look after the camps and he had carried out these orders.

"I have seen the camps," stormed Jacobs, "I have seen how you look after people, the lack of food, how sick they are, how they die. You talk of orders, did you have orders to kill and torture? So called heroes! Why, you're only fit to murder defenceless women and children."

Sada drew himself up to his full height and in one lightning movement drew his sword. Anticipating this Jacobs felt the reassuring weight of the pistol on his side and decided he would let Sada take one step forward before he shot him.

"Nippon officer not fail orders," said Sada in broken English and with eyes flashing defiance he turned his back to Jacobs and broke into Japanese. There was a moment of silence as Sada kissed the blade of his sword before guiding the point toward his stomach and falling to his knees impaled himself.

The long blade exited through the back of Sada's tunic and the body toppled forward onto the floor where it lay in a pool of blood.

Calmly stepping over the body Jacobs walked to the door and opening it spoke to the Colonel's interpreter.

"My interview with the Colonel has regrettably terminated!"

In a whirlwind of activity Jacobs and his team visited internment camps in Medan, Buggitt Tingi, Padang, Paken Baroe, Bangkinang, Logas and Palembang at the end of which he was assured by a Colonel Yoshida that he had seen all the prison camps in Sumatra.

Taking Yoshida at his word Jacobs turned to other matters that concerned him appointing a Captain Corrie, the Senior British Officer, and a former inmate of one of the camps, to investigate and report on Japanese atrocities.

In the process of assembling eyewitness accounts Corrie came across a statement by Robert Seddon, Royal Marines, who told of a massacre of nurses.

Seddon's ship had been sunk and he came ashore on Bangka Island where he heard weapons firing. Stumbling up the beach he came upon a party of Japanese soldiers who kicked him in the face before running him through with a bayonet. Thinking him dead the soldiers left.

When he came to he discovered the bodies of some 20 nurses in the water all of whom had been shot and some bayoneted.

Captain Corrie passed on this report to Jacobs.

Not long after, Corrie had another account come to hand which also mentioned the massacre.

It was a statement given by Royal Navy stoker Ernest Lloyd who, having survived the sinking of the *Vyner Brooke,* was able to reach shore together with a number of Australian Army Nursing Sisters.

Landing in a small cove on Bangka Island they decided to give themselves up and a party went off to make contact with the Japanese. Several of the men returned with a Japanese escort and the officer leading them gave orders which resulted in the men being herded up the beach and around a headland. Here they were told to blindfold their eyes with strips torn from the shirts they were wearing. One man refused and when a Jap struck him with his sword the other Japs opened fire. Lloyd dashed into the water and began swimming out to sea but was hit four times and decided to play dead.

On shore he saw the soldiers bayonet the others. When they were satisfied all the men were dead the Japs headed back down the beach to where the nurses had been left.

Lloyd lived in the jungle for three days before giving himself up and later, in a prison camp, heard a rumour that one of the nurses, a Sister Bullwinkel, had survived the massacre of the women and had eventually been brought to Sumatra as a prisoner.

Reading both accounts Jacobs became intrigued by the fact that the ship on which the nurses had been, must have left Singapore during its last days. Therefore it could be assumed they were being evacuated and as a General Hospital. This being the case those nurses who had been murdered would have only been part of a larger party. 'What then,' Jacobs asked himself, 'became of the rest?'

In his search of the camps Jacobs remembered he had not come across one Australian nurse and Yoshida had assured him he had seen all the camps in Sumatra. 'Could this mean,' he pondered, 'that the others had also been murdered? or, perhaps the Japanese had consciously lied to him and there were other camps deep in the jungle, camps they did not want him to see?'

Aware that every day he delayed could mean the death of hundreds of people, Jacobs ordered his men to interrogate every likely person in the camps for news of the Australian women.

Gillam and Bates were assigned the English-speaking ex-prisoners while 'Happy' and Tjoeng were to interview the Chinese and Dutch. Every scrap of information they gathered was to be reported to Jacobs daily.

In only a few days stories surfaced about the Australian nurses being in a camp on Bangka Island before being taken to some remote place in Sumatra where, it was believed, they had all died from malaria.

Armed with this information, although dubious as to its authenticity, Jacobs confronted Yoshida accusing him of being uncooperative and threatening to report him to Admiral Mountbatten if he did not reveal the whereabouts of the secret camps.

Yoshida, his ego badly damaged, promised he would check with the General and report back to Jacobs.

In less than two hours Yoshida returned and feigning anger informed the British Major that a serious mistake had been made and the responsible person would be severely punished.

It would appear there was one camp they had omitted to show him.

Jacobs was not taken in by this cover up and he was certain it was Yoshida who had kept the existence of this camp from him and now that it was out in the open some underling would be shot to protect the Colonel's loss of face.

"Where is the camp?" snapped Jacobs.

"Lubuklinggau," said Yoshida casually, "It's not a big camp and we were going to take them across to Palembang, we thought you wouldn't want to go all the way down there."

"How many?"

"Perhaps a thousand."

"I will fly there immediately." commanded Jacobs.

"But there is no airfield," protested Yoshida.

"Then where is the nearest?" demanded the Major.

Yoshida considered the question for a moment before replying, "Lahat."

"Then we will go to Lahat now."

At Lahat airfield Jacobs and his men transferred to several vehicles and they roared off in their race to Lubuklinggau some ninety miles away. The two Australian sergeants, Gillam and Bates, who were accompanying the party, sat with their faces grim and unforgiving.

As the 11 of September, 1945, dawned there was nothing to suggest it would be different to the previous 1,200 days behind barbed wire and the occupants of the camp at Belalau went about their usual tasks.

Vivian and Wilma had started their District Nursing rounds and hobbled from hut to hut on dreadfully swollen feet.

A high-pitched squeal followed by a chorus of excited voices made them both turn their attention to the source of the disturbance.

Walking through the main gate were three men.

To Vivian they looked powerful, beautifully muscular in their short-sleeved shirts and shorts, and they were tall, not like the skinny little Japanese guards. She saw they were wearing berets and a lump started to develop in her throat as she saw the Australian rising sun badge on two of them. They were Australian soldiers.

In a frenzy of mixed emotions Vivian and Wilma wanted only to tell the other girls and they hobbled as quickly as they could over to their hut where, arriving out of breath they could only manage, "The Australians....the Australians are here!"

The words were hardly out when Gillam and Bates burst into the room both with big beaming smiles.

On entering the compound Major Jacobs asked where the administration hut was and having it pointed out to him moved toward it as Gillam and Bates went looking for the Australian Sisters. Ignoring Siki he demanded the camp committee be called so he could address them and was in the process of doing so when a flustered Sergeant Bates rushed into the room and interrupted him.

"Sir, I found them, the Australian Sisters, they're in a hell of a mess; but it's old 'Dig', he's gone bloody mad says he's gonna shoot all the bastards. You'd better come quick 'cos I tell you he'll do it."

173

Jacobs and Bates ran from the hut for the last thing the Major wanted was for the war to start again, especially when there were only three of them.

Rounding one of the huts he came upon the normally quiet and reserved Sergeant Gillam, his automatic carbine levelled at a dozen petrified Japanese guards whom he had lined up along the barbed wire fence.

"Alright where's the bastard called 'Moonface'," he was shouting, "come on step forward 'cause I'm bloody well gonna give it to yer."

Jacobs could see that Gillam had worked himself up into a murderous rage, no doubt triggered by the sight of the Australian nurses and the stories they had told him. Now he wanted to even the score.

"Gillam," Jacobs kept his voice low and steady but heavy with authority, "now is not the time, believe me, it will come later when they're charged with war crimes."

Purposely he stopped talking and waited for his sergeant's decision.

There was a tense silence as Gillam's jaw muscles worked furiously and the Japs nervously eyed the muzzle of the carbine

Suddenly Gillam lowered the weapon.

"Ah, how I hate their bloody guts!" he exploded and strode away.

That night Jacobs and the two Australian sergeants sat around with the Sisters and listened as they related the events from the time of the first bombing of Singapore. The soldiers recounted how Superfortresses of the United States Air Force had fire-bombed Japanese cities while the Army and Navy had island-hopped their way to Japan's doorstep. On the eve of a land invasion of the Japanese home islands the Atomic bomb had been dropped, ending the war.

The women wanted to know who was Prime Minister of Australia? Was Roosevelt still President of the USA? Was Churchill still Prime Minister? What about the *Queen Mary*, had it been sunk? What were the popular songs? and who was Hollywood's biggest movie star?

The questioning went on for hours. For the Australian women it was as if they were emerging from a cocoon in which they had slept for three and a half years. It was a whole new world.

While the Australian nurses continued to absorb the information fed to them by Gillam and Bates, Jacobs sent a message to Headquarters in Ceylon with a request it be repeated to the Australian Ambassador in India and to Australian Army Headquarters in Melbourne.

'HAVE ENCOUNTERED AMONG 250 REPEAT 250 BRITISH FEMALE INTERNEES IN LUBUKLINGGAU CAMP SISTER NESTA JAMES AND 23 OTHER SURVIVING MEMBERS OF AUSTRALIAN ARMY NURSING SERVICES REMNANTS OF CONTINGENT A.A.N.S. EVACUATED FROM MALAYA IN VYNER BROOKE STOP IN VIEW THEIR PRECARIOUS HEALTH SUGGEST YOU ENDEAVOUR ARRANGE AIR TRANSPORT DIRECT TO AUSTRALIA FROM HERE SOONEST STOP AM COLLECTING

PARTICULARS MASSACRE OF MEMBERS A.A.N.S. ON BANGKA ISLAND FOR LATER TRANSMISSION.

Before the return to Australia there was one more train journey to be made over the 90 odd miles from their camp at the end of the line, down to Lahat and its airfield.

GOING HOME

Flying Officer Ken Brown of the Royal Australian Air Force, an experienced Dakota pilot, had been sent from Singapore to inspect the serviceability of the airfield at Lahat. Having completed his mission and cleared it for aircraft to use he took a vehicle and headed for the camp at Belalau to help supervise the evacuation of the Australian nurses to Lahat.

Also arriving by aircraft at Lahat was Haydon Lennard, the senior war correspondent for both the Australian and British Broadcasting Commissions.

Having heard of the massacre of nurses on Bangka Island from two Australian army officers in Singapore's Changi Goal, his further investigations revealed there had been a possible survivor, a Sister Vivian Bullwinkel.

Lennard was determined to track down Sister Bullwinkel and learn more about this major war crime and with permission from Admiral Mountbatten he left for Sumatra.

When Brown left by car, Lennard chose to go to the camp by train as he did not wish to be delayed having been informed by locals that the road was impassable in places.

Both men, as it happened, arrived within an hour of one another and while Lennard interviewed Vivian, Brown set about making arrangements for the immediate movement of the Australian nurses to the rail terminal.

As Vivian hobbled to the waiting trucks supported by a concerned Lennard, she saw Siki standing by the gate. His cold ruthless eyes watched as the women stumbled through the now drenching rain and as she and several others drew abreast of him he hissed at them in perfect English, " You might have won the war but we will get Australia yet." With that his lips curled in a mocking grin and Vivian gave him a contemptuous look.

Her loathing for this creature knew no bounds for it was he who had caused the deaths of four of her fellow Sisters and when he knew the war was over, and only then, did he open the storeroom packed to the ceiling with American Red Cross food parcels and life-saving drugs.

Pure hatred prevented her from replying, instead she walked on through the gate to freedom in the knowledge that for the rest of her life she would never again have to look at this cruel and compassionless man again.

Flying Officer Brown and Haydon Lennard stood in the rain at the rail siding watching as the women filed on board the train. Both men had lumps in their throats and were close to tears as they looked upon these young Australian women who had survived so much.

Dressed in the remains of their uniforms, most torn, one still showing where a bullet had gone through the material, their legs and knees grossly swollen from beri beri, they shuffled rather than walked to the waiting train. Riddled with malaria and running seriously high temperatures, the women, no more than skeletons with yellowed skin stretched tightly over bulging bones and matchstick arms, waited to climb the steps to the carriages.

The men held back, forcing themselves not to help these proud women, sensing that any intrusion would be resented. They had survived because of an individual determination to live and they were not rabble but Australian Army Nursing Sisters and that was how they wanted to board the train today.

The train journey took four hours and on their arrival in Lahat the Sisters flopped down on the grass at the edge of the air-field under the shade of several large trees to await the arrival of the Dakota aircraft that was to take them to Singapore.

Gazing down the length of the shimmering runway Vivian's mind drifted back to that morning just before they left the camp.

She had sought out little Bet to say goodbye.

It had not been easy and as she looked into the serious little face before her it was difficult to find the words to thank her for saving her life with the purchase of the limes and for the friendship they had shared all these years.

When she broke the news of her return to Australia the soft dark eyes filled with tears and she began to cry.

"Betty, please don't cry, we will see one another again one day," pleaded Vivian, "we have had some great moments together and I want you to keep thinking of them."

"I can think of you in Australia no matter where I am," sobbed the little girl.

"And I will do the same," promised Viv.

The two sat together talking for a while until it was time for Vivian to go and shuffling out of the shack she stopped to wave goodbye.

Betty's skinny little arm was raised in response and in the grey light Vivian saw the tears glistening on her wizened little face. She had to turn and hurry away from another world, another life that she was about to lose.

A soft droning caught Vivian's attention and scanning the horizon she saw a bright flash of sunlight on the wings of a Douglas Dakota approaching the air-field.

The aircraft touched down and rolled toward the watching group. As the propellers died a door in the fuselage opened and a crewman attached a ladder to the lip of the floor.

The first to alight was an Australian Medical Officer who announced that he was Major Windsor and asked "where were all the Australian nurses?"

The Sisters appraised one another and realised how difficult it would have been to identify them dressed as they were in remnants of a uniform, makeshift sandals with grass coolie hats perched on their heads.

Nesta James explained who they were and the Medical officer raised an eyebrow in surprise before joining them.

Following the Major down the steps were two women dressed in the familiar grey of the A.A.N.S. There was an involuntary intake of breath from the waiting women for they wore slacks, something never permitted in 1942!

"What's the army coming to?" asked Flo Trotter as the two approached them.

The taller woman introduced herself. "Hello, I'm your Matron in Chief, Colonel Sage, and I think some of you know Sister Floyd here." she indicated the slightly-built young woman at her side.

Those from the 2/10th immediately recognised 'Floydy' who had been with the unit in Malaya and one of the girls evacuated on the *Empire Star.*

"Since the fall of Singapore," the Colonel was saying, "it has been my ambition to come and get you and thank Goodness that day is here."

The suggestion of a frown crossed the Matron in Chief's face. "Weren't their thirty-two nurses? Where are the rest?"

The solemn expression on the faces of the women and their silence told Matron what she wanted to know.

The Dakota banked then sank towards the island below and a shaft of sunlight burst through the passenger window striking Vivian and rousing her from a fitful slumber.

Blinking, she looked out and down at the silver sea then at the approaching coastline with its strip of beach, tall palms and familiar white buildings.

Singapore, her island of memories, so small yet so beautiful. It was a place that would forever remain with her for she was a captive of its gentle people, its heady aromatic smells and the exciting blend of many cultures. What wonderful happy times she and the other girls had had before the war and now something she thought would never happen was becoming a reality, she was coming back!

The wing dipped lower and Vivian saw a big white building to the right, "St. Andrew's Hospital," she thought, "and there's the East Coast Road running parallel to it." They were approaching Katong and Vivian knew that any minute she should catch a glimpse of St Pat's.

They skimmed across the coastline making for the airfield and for one moment Vivian saw the majestic lines of St. Patrick's Boys' School set amongst a forest of stately palms, exactly the way she remembered it.

For one painful moment a picture of the wounded flashed through her mind and she felt a tinge of guilt. They had left them!

Her thoughts dissolved in a screeching of tyres as the aircraft touched down on Singapore Island, her first stop in the long journey home.

Escorted to a private room at the airport, reserved for the returning nurses, they were greeted by a throng of representatives from the Australian press. As flash-bulbs exploded and journalists pressed around them shouting questions, the women became physically afraid for the first time in over three years. Confused by this alien world and the behaviour of the people around them, they stood in a tight group saying nothing as the press asked incessantly for details of the slaughter on Bangka Island.

It was an Australian Army officer who came to their rescue, telling them it was all right to speak to the press about their experiences for Australia wanted to hear their story. He also told them that tea and biscuits were being served by the Australian Red Cross.

This immediately caught their attention and they sought out the Red Cross ladies helping themselves to handfuls of biscuits and ignoring the tea.

There were a few more minutes allocated to the press for photographs before they were ushered out to the waiting buses for a short trip to St. Patrick's.

To Vivian and the other girls the old school had not changed dramatically apart from an unfamiliar wing, which they learnt, had been added by the Japanese during their occupation.

The first familiar face to greet them was that of Sister Trixie Glover who had been evacuated on the *Empire Star* and behind her came the others with whom they had served in Malaya and Singapore.

The reunion was joyous and boisterous and the survivors were led upstairs to the staff quarters where wardrobes were flung open and they were told to, "help yourselves."

Nighties, house-gowns, slippers, dresses, all the pretty things they had yearned for in prison camp were there and they could wear them. Tonight they would sleep in beds, with mattresses, between crisp, pure white sheets.

Before sleep the girls had other priorities in mind. First a bath, then dress, then food.

In fact they found out that years of sleeping on the floor, or on concrete, had ruined their ability to sleep in a soft bed and many were forced to sleep on the floor beside their beds while others prowled around the building looking for more food.

****

Colonel Cyril Fortune, a well-known doctor from Perth, visited the survivors' ward the next morning and heard their complaints about the lack of food.

Turning to the Sister in Charge, Fortune asked her if there was a hairdresser in the unit, to which the Sister replied there was. "Then get her here to give these girls a shampoo and manicure and get their minds off food," ordered Fortune and the Sister scurried off to do his bidding followed by the good doctor.

"What piffle," exploded Mavis Hannah.

"I don't mind being starved by the enemy," fumed Wilma, "but I don't see why we should be starved by our own people." The indignant women argued the matter until the hairdresser arrived, shortly after which they were laughing about the incident as the washing and setting of their hair worked wonders, exactly the effect Colonel Fortune wanted to create.

179

As the days passed the survivors began to respond favourably to the constant medical treatment and a well-balanced diet prepared for them in the kitchen of St. Patrick's Hospital.

The doctors also permitted visitors. These were the men of the Australian 8th Division who themselves had been incarcerated following the fall of Singapore and had survived the 'Railway of Death' in the steaming jungles of Thailand and the infamous Changi Goal in Singapore. Reduced to virtual skeletons they were on the road to recovery and would soon be on their way to Australia.

They had come to pay their respects to the women who had tendered them at Tampoi and St. Pat's and many blinked away the tears when they saw the condition the Sisters were in.

It was so similar to their own.

The visits were very therapeutic for the surviving Sisters as they confirmed that the boys of the 8th Division held no rancour because of their evacuation in the February of 1942. In fact they stressed it was the opposite. They had understood and strongly supported the decision to evacuate the nurses for they feared what the Japanese would do to them, as in the case of the British nurses in Hong Kong. They were however, saddened by the deaths of so many and the years of suffering by the others.

Around this time Vivian received two letters, her first since the start of 1942, one was from her mother.

25 Blyth Street
Fullarton
Adelaide. South Australia
21st August 1945

My Darling Darling Viv,

I do not know where or how or when you will receive this but I hope it will be soon.

Oh my dear, my dear how lovely it is to know you and the other girls will all soon be free and able to come home. I am hoping and praying that you have come through the long ordeal safe and in good health. I am longing for the news to come through that you have been liberated and for some word from you. I hope it comes very soon. It is needless for me to say how John and I are longing for the day we will be able to welcome you home. May that great day come quickly.

I know my dear how you must be starving for news. We have a comfortable flat and we have been so hoping you would come home while we are here and John is in the Adelaide Bank.

As soon as the war ended Miss Warner sent me a telegram. Miss Warner has kept in touch with me and I have promised to let her know the moment I get news of you. She must be a very nice person and she certainly thinks the world of you.

Zelda sent me a telegram too, she married Alex West and has a little daughter and you Viv are Helen's godmother.

Such a lot of people are sending word how glad they are you will soon be coming home, too many to tell you about now also there are lots of people you do not know.

Mrs Drummond, although she knows Irene is not with you, is anxious about you girls as anyone. John is well and back in the bank but he is a very lucky boy to be alive. It was just a miracle that he is.

His fighter plane was shot down in the Middle East about 8 a.m. on the 26th of October 1942. It was in flames and he had to make a parachute descent. He was severely injured as he left the plane, one leg between the knee and ankle was badly broken, a compound fracture. The other leg was badly gashed and he also had a burnt wrist, three broken ribs and one hip and ankle badly sprained. I guess that happened when he hit the ground. He was numb to the hips whilst he was coming down so he didn't feel the landing. Luckily he came down just inside our own lines manned by South Africans. Seeing he was badly injured some men raced across to him. A doctor was in attendance almost immediately

John was in hospital in Alexandria for a month and then sent to Palestine for two months. He came home on the hospital ship Orangie a cot case and arrived in Australia at the end of February 1943. He was twenty months in hospital and he has made a remarkable recovery and has been back at the bank for thirteen months.

Bill, Bob and Boycie Shegog I hope and pray will come home safely and I wonder what has happened to your friend Jim Austin and Major Hunt?

Well my darling I must close now and I will write again tomorrow. I wonder if you got any of my letters and cards I wrote regularly since you left, if not we will have a lot of talking to do when you get back home.

With all my love as usual, I cannot wait to see you again.

Your loving mother.

The second letter was from England.

"Holmdene"
113 Kingshill Drive
Kenton. Harrow.
Middlesex. England.

Dear Sister Bullwinkel'

On reading of your experiences off Bangka Island I wonder if you can give me any news of my brother who was the Captain of the "Vyner Brooke" – (Richard Edward Borton).

We know he was a prisoner as three cards have been received.

I hope you will not mind me taking the liberty to write to you, but we are so anxious to hear some news.

I trust you are recovering from your terrible experiences.

Yours sincerely.

(Miss) Agnes E. Borton.

The request was one that Vivian knew would be repeated many times as loved ones sought the truth as to the fate of husbands, children, relatives and friends.

So many had died in lonely and often inaccessible places their remains either beneath the waters of the sea or in unmarked jungle graves. For the relatives there would be no marker to weep over, only a memory that would persist until their own passing.

As the news of the Australian Sisters' rescue broke in the international press letters and cards began to pour into the hospital at St. Pat's. Amongst those treasured by the girls were those sent by the boys they had left behind.

On an old scrap of stained paper dated 17th September 1945.

To all Sisters

Following the wishes of the members of the 13th Australian General Hospital, Officers and Other Ranks, we wish to express to you all, individually, our extreme joy when we heard here at Changi of your return to St. Patrick's School.

Our great thought is that you will soon return to health and be able to join us again.

Yours sincerely,

Charles H. Osborne Lt. Col.

Written in pencil on a small piece of note paper torn from a book and attached to a large sheath of flowers.

The Other Ranks of the Battalion regret at this stage they can only offer these flowers, but what we can always do is remember.

God bless you all, good luck and a speedy recovery and return home.

The boys of the 2/18th.

From the men of the 2/29th Battalion a beautiful bouquet of flowers for each surviving Sister with a card wishing them a speedy recovery and a swift return to Australia.

The girls vowed these thoughts and wishes would forever remain with them, such was the unique bond that existed between the Australian Army Nursing Service and the men of the 8th Australian Division.

They were kept busy replying to the many letters sent to Saint Pat's but it didn't stop Vivian from writing constantly to her mother. The letters were always bright and chatty and avoided any mention of what had happened on the beach at Bangka Island. Nor did she mention Matron Drummond for there was the question of the family, Vivian believing it was her duty to tell them in person. Then another letter arrived from her mother that changed the situation.

25 Blyth Street
Fullarton
Adelaide South Australia
18th September 1945

Viv My Darling,

What can I say? I have no words to say what I feel. When Aunty Nell rang me from Mt. Gambier yesterday morning and told me a little of your story, which she had seen in the *Melbourne Sun*," I felt almost stunned. In the afternoon news the full story appeared on the front page with big headlines. Oh my darling, my darling what you have suffered. I cannot write about your ghastly experiences and I certainly do not want to distress you needlessly to say, the whole world is shocked. You are considered the bravest girl in the world. The papers have been devoting their front pages to your story and both the *News* and the *Advertiser* have wanted and printed your photograph also the other South Australian girl's photos. You are being claimed by South Australia.

Everybody in Australia is talking about you, your name is on everyone's lips throughout the country and I believe the whole world. Everybody thinks you are marvellous and a very brave girl. All day yesterday at the bank John didn't do any work for people were ringing him all day saying how glad and thrilled they were that you were now in safe hands and what a marvellously brave girl you are.

We have had telegrams galore and letters and people have been ringing me through the phone next door. Everyone speaks of your heroism. Yesterday I listened in to the radio news and the first thing the announcer said was "Sister Bullwinkel has arrived in Singapore. She stepped off the plane in the uniform she was wearing when she was shot three and a half years ago." and then they went on with your story.

Oh darling to hear your dear name again and to know you are safe, what a load has been taken off my heart and mind but I am sad at heart when I think of all you have gone through, may the rest of your life be sweet and happy my darling.

All day long yesterday your name was the main topic in each news session. I have received telegrams from the James in Perth, Zelda, Con and dozens of others and lots of people have been calling in.

Darling I am waiting for one of the greatest thrills of my life....to hear your dear voice again. I received an urgent telegram from Sydney this afternoon asking me to listen in to 5DN at ten o'clock tonight that Sister Bullwinkel will be sending greetings. I have been terribly excited all the evening at the thought of hearing your dear voice.

John and I have great admiration for Haydon Lennard, we feel we owe him our deepest and heartfelt gratitude for the part he played in rescuing you girls also Squadron Leader Madsen and Flying Officer Brown they did a wonderful job.

Now for your lovely voice it's ten o'clock.

Well darling so many spoke before you I began to fear I wasn't going to hear you. At last you spoke and it was wonderful to listen to you although it was all too short my sweet. Anyway you will be home soon.

Well my sweet I will now kiss you goodnight. John joins me with fondest love to your darling self.

Your loving mother.

Vivian was distressed by her mother's letter and immediately wrote back stressing that the newspapers were notorious for sensationalising the facts and that she was perfectly alright and receiving wonderful medical attention at St. Pat's.

In fact the treatment had been so effective many of the girls had gone from five stone to six stone in a week which they attributed to chicken, bananas and eggs.

Their general health had improved so dramatically that the authorities decided they were ready to make the trip to Australia and arrangements were put in place for them to depart on the hospital ship *Manunda*.

Just prior to Vivian sailing word reached her that Betty Kenneison had been evacuated to Singapore and was accommodated at Raffles Hotel.

Meeting at St. Pat's the two talked for several hours during which time Betty told her she hadn't realised how gaunt and thin she was until she compared herself with the hotel staff.

The Red Cross lady, who had given Betty a nice floral print dress and a pair of blue Joyce shoes, said she would get used to wearing wedge heels to which Betty replied, "It's not the heels that bother me, it's wearing shoes again." The lady burst into tears and Betty apologised for anything she had said to upset her. The Red Cross woman replied that it was she who was sorry that Betty had to go through all those terrible years.

When it was time for Betty to go the two friends promised to meet again soon and the young girl went happily off content that she had seen Vivian once more.

There was frantic activity before their departure including a lecture on how things had changed in the A.A.N.S. and the unfortunate fact that they would have to be issued with second-hand uniforms. The girls didn't object to this because they had been used to wearing rags for years and the prospect of clean hand-me-downs looked perfectly good to them.

Eventually, following goodbyes all round at St. Pat's, the returning Sisters embarked aboard their ship together with several hundred other ex prisoners-of-war and following a three-day delay in Singapore they sailed for Fremantle.

Vivian shifted her weight to relieve the pain in her feet and legs, gripping the railing as the ship plunged into a broad trough before shaking the white water from its prow and rise majestically, lifting her high above the waves.

It was then she caught her first glimpse of Australia in three and a half years.

As the ship passed inside Rottnest Island the ecstatic passengers lining the ship's railing saw the pine trees of Cottesloe, just north of the entrance to the harbour, and knew that within a half-hour they would be home.

As *Manunda* drew alongside the wharf cheering broke out from amongst the mass of people waiting on the dock. It grew in volume and the air was filled with waving arms as the returning men and women yelled "cooee" and tried to pick out relatives from the mass of faces below them.

The first to step on board the ship was Colonel Sage accompanied by Matron Kenny from Perth's Hollywood Hospital. Following a simple but moving welcome the nurses were told they were to be moved to Hollywood, located in Nedlands four miles out of the city. Here they would rest over night before moving on to Melbourne; Sisters Iole Harper and Mickey Syer would remain in their home state of Western Australia.

Arriving at the hospital the girls were greeted by the sight of the entrance, corridors, stairways and wards crammed with freshly-cut garden blooms and wild flowers.

They were told a radio station suggested to its listeners the returning Sisters may like to see some Western Australian flowers in their rooms. The response had been so overwhelming that the staff was able to brighten the entire hospital for them.

That night the girls received a very special visitor, Sister Peggy Farmaner's mother, who presented each of them with a posy of flowers in thankfulness of their safe return home.

She did this having only recently learnt of her daughter's death on the beach at Bangka Island and the Sisters were moved by her strength and thoughtfulness in meeting them at such a time.

The party returned to the *Manunda* the following day and after a sad farewell to Iole and Mickey, whom they had shared so much with, they sailed for Melbourne, arriving on a wet and blustery October 24, 1945. Loaded into buses they were transferred to Heidelberg Military Hospital where relatives and members of the press awaited their arrival.

Pandemonium broke loose as the bus came to a halt and excited relatives rushed forward to surround it as camera flashlights popped and both radio and Movietone News journalists called out for interviews.

Vivian saw her mother standing in the crowd. Getting out of the seat she made her way to the bus door, then, pushing through the enveloping crowd found herself face to face with Eva. They stood looking at one another for what seemed to Vivian an eternity before she began to grin and her mother beamed back. "It's nice to have you home Viv."

"It's great to be here mother, I missed you."

A bright light exploded in Vivian's face. Momentarily blinded she heard a man's voice ask, "Are you Vivian Bullwinkel; would you mind answering a few questions about the massacre on the beach, how did it feel to get shot and be the only survivor?"

"Excuse me," she heard herself say, "not now if you don't mind, I'm seeing my mother for the first time in nearly four years."

"But Australia wants to know." insisted the journalist.

She felt the anger rise within her and rounding on the man her eyes looked steadily into his and her tone was cold and deliberate when she spoke.

"I said not now, can't you understand?" turning her back on the bewildered journalist she took her mother gently by the arm "Let's go home and talk," she whispered and the two women, arm in arm, wended their way through the crowd and headed for the main gates.

Later, in the quiet comfort of her Uncle Harold Harvey's Melbourne home Vivian told her mother what had happened to her and the other girls during the years they were apart.

Astounded, Eva listened in awe as Vivian described the battle for Singapore, their evacuation on the *Vyner Brooke* and its destruction followed by the long struggle to reach Bangka Island. Finally, Vivian spoke of the massacre on the beach, the meeting up with Kinsley and her years in captivity.

As she listened to the unending horrors her sweet child had been forced to endure Eva wept as Vivian talked on into the night, her eyes sad but tearless.

During the weeks following her homecoming the press constantly harassed Vivian for details of the massacre and the over-dramatic and sometimes inaccurate stories that followed frequently distressed her.

The real story was not that she survived the slaughter, but rather the steadfast bravery shown by her fellow Sisters as they waded into the water and where they died with great dignity.

How could the press overlook the courage and compassion shown by the Sisters of the 2/4th, 2/10th and 2/13th as they tended the wounded in and around St. Patrick's while under fire. What of the discipline shown as they stood on the sloping deck of the sinking *Vyner Brooke* waiting for the civilians to leave? Of starving Sisters sharing their rations with hospital patients, of the stubborn and resolute attitude they adopted when faced with forced prostitution or death. They cleaned out sewer pits with half coconut shells for the betterment of others; they nursed the sick although racked with the chills of malaria themselves.

They apologised to their friends for taking too long to die and they dug the graves and buried the dead. Then above all that there was their unflinching loyalty to Australia, the Service and each other.

That was what Vivian wanted them to write about, that was what the people of Australia should know.

The Army allowed Vivian to rest for several months before advising her she had been posted to Heidelberg Military Hospital, just out of Melbourne, Victoria, as a Sister in Charge.

The 1,200 bed hospital set in the middle of gently rolling lawn and neatly tended gardens held the young men who were still recovering from wounds or serious illnesses sustained during the war.

Vivian's first day did not start well. Part of her duties required her to check the kitchen for general cleanliness and walking into the room she came to an abrupt halt, at first not sure that what she was seeing was really happening.

The staff was scraping left-overs off the plates and into a large garbage bin. As she watched she saw mounds of vegetables and meat disappearing into its mouth on top of which was tipped the contents of the cooking pots. Vivian immediately recalled the gaunt faces of the women and children from the camp at Lubuklinggau and unable to stop herself, she heard her voice shouting at the staff who turned to face the new Sister in Charge with looks of surprise on their faces.

With no idea of what she was saying, Vivian tried to stem the tirade and failing, stormed out of the kitchen leaving the staff in complete confusion as to what it had all been about.

After this episode Vivian avoided visiting the kitchen immediately after a meal had been served, instead she would make her inspection between meal times.

Several things still upset her. One was wastefulness when it came to food, even to the point of cleaning her plate when given rice. Another was soft beds.

When she had first arrived home Eva could not get used to her daughter sleeping on the floor beside a perfectly comfortable bed. Gradually Vivian was able to make the change but at the expense of many sleepless nights.

By far the greatest ache in her heart was not being able to see her friends.

This was a common feeling shared by all of the returned Sisters and to maintain a degree of contact with one another there was the regular phone around and later the occasional interstate trip.

In April a letter arrived at Heidelberg Hospital for Lieutenant V. Bullwinkel from the Chief of the General Staff, who congratulated Vivian on the occasion of being awarded an Associate of the Royal Red Cross.

This had been conferred upon her by the King for having *"exhibited outstanding devotion to duty in nursing wounded personnel and as a magnificent example during the period nursing sick personnel and doing manual labour under the threat of molestation and personal violence from brutal Japanese"*

Outwardly Vivian received the news calmly and went about her duties as normal, as letters and cards of congratulations poured in from all over the world thrusting her once more into the limelight.

"This," she thought, "will be the last of it."

187

WAR CRIMES TRIBUNAL

Sitting down to breakfast on a warmish October morning in 1946, millions of Australians picked up their newspaper and learnt that the war was not over, that was, not until such time as justice had been served.

The headline was large and bold.

AUSTRALIAN POW FOR JAPAN
WILL TESTIFY AT WAR CRIMES TRIALS

Melbourne October 1st.

Fifteen former Australian prisoners of war will leave for Japan this month to testify before the International War Crimes Tribunal in Tokyo.

These witnesses will cover atrocities committed against Australian prisoners at Ambon, Borneo, Outram Road Goal at Singapore, the Burma-Siam railway, Changi Camp at Singapore and at other camps at Java, Japan, Formosa, Manchuria and Malaya.

The horror of the Bangka Island massacre of Australian nursing sisters will be retold by its sole survivor Sister Vivian Bullwinkel, a South Australian, who is now at the Heidelberg Military Hospital.

Of these witnesses only Sister Bullwinkel, Major J.K.Lloyd and W.O. Stiepewich still remain in the Army.

NET CLOSES ON JAP MURDERERS OF NURSES
2 LEADERS CAUGHT

The net is closing around the Japanese responsible for the massacre of 21 Australian Army Nurses on Bangka Island, off Sumatra, in February 1942.

Lieut. Masayuki Takeeuchi, commander of one of the Jap companies on Bangka Island, was identified recently in a prisoner-of-war stockade, and is now in Taiping Goal, northern Malaya.

A second suspect, Sgt. Major Taro Kato, was captured in New Guinea.

Officers of the Australian Army Directorate of Prisoners of War and Internees investigating the worst individual crime on Australia's long list against the Japanese, have uncovered these facts:

The nurses and other survivors of an escape ship from Singapore bombed 10 miles from the beach were shot by men of two Jap companies of the 229th Regiment of the 38th Infantry Division.

They were regular army veterans who fought against China, took part in the storming of Hong Kong in December 1941 and followed the Japanese paratroops into Palembang, Sumatra early 1942.

The two companies were detached from the main force for the capture of Bangka Island.

The entire division later went to the Eastern Area and met retribution almost to the last man at the hands of the Australians and Americans.

In November, 1942, a battalion of the regiment sailed for Guadalcanal in 14 ships, 11 of which were sunk with 1,000 men. Most of the 500 survivors died in the fighting around Henderson Airfield. Another battalion of the 229th was almost wiped out by the 7th Division AIF, at Buna, only 11 escaping.

A third battalion tried to land in the New Admiralty Islands in June 1944. Half landed and were subsequently reported missing. The other half failed to land and returned to Rabaul. Twenty-six survivors of the regiment are still being interrogated at Rabaul including Major General Tanaka, who commanded during the Sumatra operations.

RUSSIANS HUNT

Capt. (later Major) Masaru Orita, who commanded the two companies at the time of the massacre, fought on the Manchurian front against the Russians in 1945.

Concerning this badly-wanted man, the Soviet Section of the Allied Council for Japan has just informed Australia that he has not been found so far in the Soviet's prisoner-of-war compounds.

****

Vivian was duly notified of her move to Japan and was subsequently taken on board *HMAS Kanimbla* which sailed for Kure where they arrived around two o'clock on a late October afternoon.

Met by a party of Australians, she was whisked away through the bomb-damaged city to a quayside. Here she boarded a ferry for the twenty-minute crossing to the island of Etajima and the former Japanese Naval Academy which now served as an Allied hospital.

Matron H.E. McMahon greeted Vivian on her arrival and the Sisters of the 115th Australian Military Hospital made her feel more than at home. It was here that she learnt the trials would not begin in Tokyo until the December, this meant she would miss out on Christmas with her mother and relatives which she had been looking forward to.

The delay gave Vivian the opportunity of seeing a lot of the countryside. At first she was a little tremulous about meeting with Japanese but was soon able to bury her feelings and take people as she met them. There followed many trips to scenic places, Australian barbeques and unit parties and as she was beginning to relax and enjoy herself word was received that she was expected in Tokyo immediately.

Matron McMahon duly arranged the transfer by train via the "Atomic City" of Hiroshima which Vivian had expressed a wish to see.

Standing in the centre of a wasteland as the wind sighed gently across the twisted shapes and flattened rubble of what had once been a city, Vivian could not bring herself to applaud what had happened. Conversely she could not mourn the people who had died there for they were of the race who had taken the lives of her friends and condemned her to three and a half years of misery and a lifetime of harrowing memories.

As her gaze wandered over the devastation she tried to imagine the hundred thousand who had died on that morning in August but they were faceless. The faces she saw belonged to the skeletal bodies of the dead and dying in the jungle camps.

'How do you apportion guilt, given the two circumstances?' she asked herself and when there was no ready answer she turned her back on Hiroshima and walked slowly back to the waiting car.

During the weeks leading up to the trials Vivian was kept busy by a very crowded social calendar which took her to 'At Homes' and 'Dinner Dances' at a number of famous English and Australian battalions as well as luncheon with the American units in occupation.

At her side constantly was her conducting officer and chaperone, fellow Australian, Sister Beau Mullins.

The courtroom where the trials were to be conducted was located in the Japanese War Ministry Building.

It had an extremely high ceiling with a series of bench-style tables and seating which rose in tiers from the front of the court to the back wall over which there was a public gallery.

The witness-box faced a raised platform on which was the judge's bench and to either side were the tables allocated to the prosecution, defence council, court reporters and interpreters.

A microphone had been placed on the shelf in the witness box.

To ensure security and military decorum there were a number of American Military Police stationed around the court, in smartly pressed uniforms with white braided lanyards, white steel helmets, pistol belt and side arms.

Attending the court were Allied military and civilian personnel with a smattering of Japanese men dressed in conservative business suits.

The defendants sat in two rows of thirteen to one side of the bench, their uniforms stripped of military rank and insignia.

Accused of war crimes were: Seishiro Itagaki, Teiichi Suzuki, Toshio Shiratori, Shigetaro Shimada, Kenryo Sato, Mamoru Shigemitsu, Shigenori Togo, Kiichiro Hiranuma, Iwane Matsui, Hiro Oshima, Osami Nagano, Kuniaki Koiso, Kingoro Hashimoto, Heitaro Kimura, Koichi Kido, Kuniaki Kaya, Naoki Hoshino, Akira Muto, Sadao Araki, Youshijiro Umezu, Takasumi Oka, Hideki Tojo, Jiro Minami, Koki Hirota, Shunroku Hata and Kenji Doihara.

They sat stiffly at attention with expressionless faces, their seemingly uncaring eyes scanning the judges as they approached the bench.

The nations represented were: India, The Netherlands, Canada, Great Britain, The United States of America, Australia, China, U.S.S.R., France, New Zealand and the Philippines.

After the judges were seated, the court rose as Sir William Webb, an Australian and President of the International Military War Crimes Tribunal for the Far East, entered the room and took his position precisely at 9.30 a.m.

The Marshal of the Court announced in a booming voice that carried to the back of the court that the "tribunal was now in session."

Immediately the Assistant Prosecutor, Lt. Col. Thomas. F. Mornane, rose and called for Warrant Officer First Class William Hector Sticpewich to take the stand.

A tall, thin Australian Warrant Officer came forward and following the administering of the oath began his account of the infamous Sandakan Death March and the murder of thousands of Australian soldiers by the defendants.

It was late afternoon before Vivian was called to testify.

Lt. Colonel Mornane rose from his chair and addressed the bench. "If the tribunal pleases, I now propose to call Sister Bullwinkel."

There was a nod from the President and Vivian, wearing the distinctive grey uniform, came forward and was duly sworn in.

Mornane gave her a reassuring look before starting.

"Your name is Vivian Bullwinkel, you are a Captain in the Australian Army Nursing Service; and you reside at 25 Blyth Street, Fullarton, Adelaide, South Australia?"

"Yes," she replied.

"Early in February of 1942, you were on the staff of the 13th Australian General Hospital at Singapore?"

"Yes."

"What happened on Thursday, the 12th of February, 1942?"

"On Thursday, the 12th of February 1942," she began, "sixty five Australian Army Nursing Sisters, with about two hundred women and children and a few elderly men, were evacuated from Singapore on a small ship, the *Vyner Brooke.*"

"Were you one of the party of Australian Nursing Sisters?" interjected Mornane.

"Yes, I was in that party." answered Vivian.

Mornane pause for a moment as if to gather his thoughts before proceeding.

"Other than the Sisters, were there any service personnel among the passengers on that ship?"

"No." she replied.

"Now, will you tell the tribunal what happened at about two p.m. on Saturday, the 14th of February?"

Vivian took a deep breath to steady herself then in a loud and clear voice began her story.

" On Saturday, the 14th of February, at about two o'clock in the afternoon we were in Bangka Strait when three Japanese aeroplanes flew over and bombed the ship and machine-gunned the lifeboats.........."

For the next hour and a half Vivian told the court of the events leading up to the massacre of the men followed by that of the nurses. Her strong voice, amplified by the microphone in front of her, rang throughout the courtroom as she recounted how, with the full knowledge of their impending deaths, the Sisters had marched calmly into the sea supporting their already wounded companions, Sisters Halligan and Wight. As she spoke the faces on the Allied servicemen became grim and some of the women began to weep, while the prisoners sat stiffly to attention, their apparently disinterested eyes fixed rigidly on the opposite wall.

When she had concluded her evidence there was a moment of complete silence before Sir William Webb turned and spoke to Vivian his rich voice echoing in the stillness of the chamber.

"Well, you are a model witness Sister Bullwinkel. You have given your evidence faultlessly."

Lt.Colonel Mornane rose. "May the witness be excused from further attendance on the usual terms?" he asked the President.

"She is excused on the usual terms." replied Sir William.

With a nod from Mornane Vivian rose, bowed to the bench, and left the witness box. She was trembling.

Before leaving Japan for Australia Vivian was told that Captain Orita had been found in a Russian stockade in Siberia. Removed to Sugamo Prison in Tokyo to await trial for the murder of the Australian nurses he committed suicide in his cell.

Australian Army Nursing Sisters aboard the Hospital Ship Manunda on its arrival at Fremantle in late 1945
The woman in the centre wearing dress uniform is Colonel Annie Sage, Matron in Chief of the A.A.N.S.
Vivian Bullwinkel is second from the right, front row standing. The bouquets of flowers had been sent by relatives.
(Australian War Memorial Negative Number P1701. 003)

Sisters Vivian Bullwinkel, second from the left, with Iole Harper, centre and Wilma Oram, holding flowers, attend a homecoming celebration in late 1945. (Australian War Memorial Negative Number P 431/04/02)

Vivian Bullwinkel and her mother Eva at a reception, given in honour of returning Sisters who had been Prisoner's of War, hosted by the 115th Australian General Hospital at Heidelberg, Victoria, late 1945. (Australian War Memorial Negative Number 119674)

Enjoying a boat ride on Sydney Harbour in late 1945 shortly after their release from a Japanese prison camp are, left to right: Sisters Jenny Greer, Veronica Clancy, Vivian Bullwinkel and Wilma Oram.
(V. Bullwinkel collection)

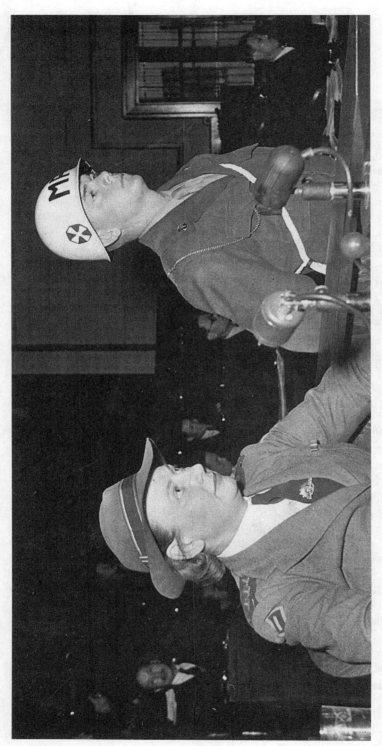

Sole survivor of the massacre of 21 of her fellow Australian Army Nursing Sisters on Radji Beach, Bangka Island, Sister Vivian Bullwinkel gives evidence before the War Crimes Tribunal. Tokyo, December 1946. (U.S. Army Signal Corps Photograph.)

ACCOLADES & MEMORIALS

Returning to Heidelberg Military Hospital, Vivian quickly settled back into the daily routine and put behind her the emotional turmoil of the Tokyo trials.

It was early in May of 1947 that she received a telephone call and an unfamiliar voice advised her she had been awarded the Florence Nightingale Medal and would receive the pertinent documentation in due course.

Vivian had heard of the Florence Nightingale Association and the scholarships they awarded and so naturally assumed that it was one of these she had won. Although pleased with the award she was more than a little reticent concerning the study programme for she found cramming for examinations to be both tedious and time consuming.

The headline in the next morning's paper clarified the matter.

COVETED AWARD
HIGH HONOUR FOR NURSE WHO SURVIVED JAP MASSACRE

Only survivor of the Japanese massacre of 21 Australian Army Nursing Sisters at Bangka Island, off Sumatra, Sister Vivian Bullwinkel, a Victorian, is one of three latest Australian recipients of the Florence Nightingale Medal. One of the highest Red Cross awards, the medal is given for distinguished service in time of war or public disaster. These are the first awards since 1939.

Once more the letters and cards flooded in as warmest congratulations were conveyed to Vivian from Government Ministers and Departments, Military Hospitals, Red Cross branches and the people of Australia.

There were also those messages that she cherished above all others, those from the girls of the 2/4th, 2/10th and 2/13th and the boys of the 8th Division AIF.

One message, written on a blank white card read -

To Sister V. Bullwinkel
With congratulations from H.A.Astill
Malaria patient, Ward A2, Bed 11. Johore Bahru. 1941.

On the 12th of May Vivian, together with Colonel Annie Sage, former Matron-in-Chief of the A.A.N.S. and Mrs Boyd Moriarty, Commandant of the Australian Red Cross, was invested with the award by the Vice President of the Society, Sir John Latham. The ceremony was held at Australian Red Cross National Headquarters, Melbourne.

Vivian, sitting on a stage with the others, listened to the words of Sir John's address, "In recognition....faithful....devoted and distinguished service....no sacrifice was too great....added great lustre to the already proud possessions of their service."

Vivian felt a fluttering in the pit of her stomach as she stood and moved forward to the microphone. She had always feared public speaking and today she was to address both a physical audience and the people of Australia through ABC Radio. Taking a deep breath she expelled it slowly while unfolding her speech and looking out at the sea of faces before her.

Then she began.

"Sir John, esteemed members of the Australian Red Cross, Ladies and Gentlemen.

In having the Florence Nightingale Medal awarded to me I feel it has been awarded not to myself personally but as a tribute to our friends we left behind in other lands.

Our Matrons, Matron Paschke and Matron Drummond, by their ability and level headedness in a time of crisis, were responsible for the calm behaviour of the nurses at the time of the sinking of the *Vyner Brooke*.

The calmness and courage with which my colleagues met their final hour was forever an inspiration to the remainder of us in the following years.

The cheerfulness, the keen sense of humour and the ever-ready helping hand endeared the girls to women and children of all nationalities in the camp and as they left us, one by one, the camp became the poorer.

The comradeship and loyalty I received from the girls who came home with me, enabled me to return safely.

Never did their courage falter and it is for them that I am deeply honoured in receiving the Florence Nightingale Medal. May we never let them down."

Women sniffled as men swallowed hard to regain their composure and the silence seemed never-ending until a solitary hand-clap welled into one rolling sound of applause as they acclaimed a woman who had clearly communicated to them that it was one medal to be shared by many.

Of the thirty- six international awards of this medal, made every two years, only five had previously been awarded to Australian women.

****

Edith Hughes-Jones had never been an army nurse but was a very capable and respected civilian nurse. Born in Tungamah, Victoria in 1905, she had been educated at the Presbyterian Ladies College in Melbourne before choosing nursing as a career. This led her to complete her training at the Alfred Hospital followed by midwifery at The Women's Hospital.

Subsequently appointed Matron of Windarra Private Hospital she carefully saved her money and with a small cash contribution from her father, eventually purchased the hospital in 1938.

It was at this time she met a young nurse by the name of Betty Jeffrey, who, on the outbreak of war applied for the A.A.N.S. and within weeks was accepted and posted to the 2/10th A.G.H.

With the return of the nursing sisters from captivity there was talk of a memorial to commemorate those who had died while on service.

The callous sinking of the Australian Hospital Ship *Centaur* by a Japanese submarine in 1943 had shocked the Australian public. Heading for Port Morseby in New Guinea to pick up Australian wounded and with all lights ablaze, she was struck by a torpedo forward of amidships at 4.10 a.m. and sank within three minutes. With her went the majority of the 332 souls aboard including eleven Nursing Sisters, only Sister Ellen Savage survived.

In the closing months of the war Matron Hughes-Jones gathered around her some of Melbourne's most influential men and women and discussed the possibility of establishing a private club for nurses which would be a fitting memory for those women who had lost their lives with the sinking of *Centaur.*

Supported by Colonel Annie Sage it was agreed that the club should be centralised around all nursing organisations and located in the one building.

A group of nurses which included Jenny Ashton, Betty Jeffrey, Beryl Woodbridge and Vivian Bullwinkel was discussing a similar project while sitting outside their hut at Lubuklinggau.

Motivated with the desire to perpetuate the memory of their fellow Sisters who had died they agreed that a shrine was not what they wanted. Their thinking was more toward something that would be useful, something alive, a place that would be used by people daily.

The returning P.O.W. Sisters stiffened the resolve of the memorial committee and the two groups came to an agreement that the project should centre on a living memorial.

With the assistance of ex-servicemen of the calibre of Sir Albert Coates, who as a surgeon in the Medical Corps chose to stay with the sick and wounded in Sumatra, the committee planned to raise two hundred and fifty thousand pounds for the establishment of a Nurses' Memorial Centre in Victoria. The appeal was to be entitled *Victoria's Tribute to the Nurses* and would be launched by Lady Dugan, wife of the Governor of Victoria, Sir Winston Dugan, at the Melbourne Town Hall on the 1st of December 1947.

The appeal gathered momentum as the nurses of Victoria threw their support behind the campaign. Donations flooded in from performances of *Annie Get Your Gun* at His Majesty's Theatre, the *Alfred Hospital Ball* , *The Ex-Servicemen's Ball* , the *Mooney Valley Racing Club* and from social functions held by ex-servicemen's and women's organisations throughout the state.

The *Queen of Nurses Quest*, which required a nominee from every hospital in Victoria, was organised by Betty Jeffrey who co-opted Vivian to assist her.

Vivian obtained leave of absence from Heidelberg Hospital and the two set off in Betty's Austin car to tour the state and stimulate support for the quest. They had planned to launch it from the Bendigo Base Hospital for it was here that Sister Rosetta Wight had enrolled as a Trainee Nurse and they could not think of a more fitting place.

Where Vivian was shy and retiring Betty was confident and outgoing. There was one thing they both had in common and that was a good old Aussie sense of humour and so the two women complemented one another perfectly.

In all the two completed two tours of the state of Victoria and were enthusiastically received in most towns despite the post-war demands on the community to raise funds for schools and hospitals. During these exhausting tours they took turns in presenting to associations and community groups, honing their presentation and speaking skills to a point that they were no longer nervous about standing up in front of an audience.

The crowning of the *Queen of the Nurses* took place in the Melbourne Town Hall on Tuesday, 6th of April, 1948 before a glittering crowd of formally attired guests.

The lights dimmed leaving the *Cross of Sacrifice and Flame of Hope* glowing in the darkness of the organ loft and flanked by the flags of the Empire. Vivian and Betty, in uniform, walked slowly down the steps to take up their positions beside the memorial emblems as the orchestra, joined by the guests, swelled into a stirring rendition of *Land of Hope and Glory*. Between the two Sisters was a row of vacant seats; one for each Sister who did not return home.

It wasn't until April 1949 that a property at 431 St. Kilda Road, Melbourne was purchased by the Memorial Trust for the sum of 22,500 pounds. Dr. Cairns Lloyd had originally built this most impressive building in 1862. Ideally located, being a short tram ride from the central city, it had adequate facilities for post-graduate training with offices for various nursing bodies and sleeping quarters for nurses awaiting, or recovering from, hospitalisation.

The Nurse's Memorial centre was officially dedicated to the 75 Australian Nurses who lost their lives in World War Two and Betty Jeffrey proudly accepted the position as its first administrator.

It was also time for Vivian to reassess her life and look to the future.

The Australian Government had not formed a Regular Army at that point in time and therefore the Australian Army Nursing Service still remained under the establishment formed to fight W.W. II and now constituted the occupational services following the cessation of hostilities with Japan.

Heidelberg Military Hospital had recently been taken over by the Department of Repatriation and was no longer a military establishment.

This meant that Vivian, with her current rank, would in all probability be posted to Japan if she remained in the service. This she did not want because of her inability to forgive the Japanese for what they had done during the war.

The decision to resign her commission was therefore predetermined by these circumstances and Vivian swapped the grey uniform she loved so much for the stiff whites of a civilian Nursing Sister. Retaining her position under the new administration at Heidelberg Hospital, she was put in charge of Ward 6 and a young bunch of scallywag ex-servicemen who had tuberculosis.

The hospital was full of returned ex-servicemen and Vivian loved every irreverent one of them.

The grounds also held one of her favourite spots, a rose garden.

Running along the fence line near the number one nurse's house was a bed full of beautifully cared for rose bushes. They had been planted in memory of the Sisters lost in the war and so their delicate flowers, when in bloom, held a special meaning for Vivian for in the richness of their colours she saw the remembered smiles.

With Vivian at Heidelberg were ex 8th Division Sisters Kath McMillan, Dallas McNamara and Dottie Burnett, the four shared accommodation and for entertainment indulged in a game of canasta, or visited the local cinema occasionally.

Because of their long working hours and the remoteness of the hospital they were not in a position to meet eligible men. This didn't worry Vivian for she loved her work and was determined to catch up with the three and a half years of her life that had been wasted. 'If her type of man came along,' she reasoned, 'then well and good. If not, why worry about it?'

There was a desire she had been harbouring for some time since her release from prison camp and that was to visit England.

Not only were there relatives to look up but she had always wanted to visit the places of historic importance and, if possible, play in the snow.

Her Sister's wage was two pounds ten shillings a week and she calculated it would take three years to save enough to cover expenses and allow for a period of no income while she looked for work. Naturally Vivian wanted to go with a friend but Wilma had married an Australian soldier, who had been a prisoner of war in Germany, and settled on a farm in Gippsland, Victoria, so that ruled her out. When she mentioned her plan to Betty it was enthusiastically received and the two began their savings campaign with an objective of sailing for London some time in 1950.

THE QUEEN MOTHER

Over the next three years they stuck rigidly to their plan despite many interruptions.

Vivian for example continued with her ex-servicemen and women's work and went back to Broken Hill to unveil a memorial in the hospital's children's playground to Matron Irene Drummond. During the ceremony, which Mr and Mrs Drummond attended, Vivian remembered the day she visited them soon after her return. It had not been easy for her and after briefly relating what had happened she tried to comfort them in the only way she could.

Vivian assured the Drummonds she had seen their daughter hit and fall and that Irene would have died instantly.

There were other relatives she had visited, Wilhelmina Raymont's sister in South Australia, Nancy Harris's parents in Sydney and the others she had either telephoned or written to.

Having to recall these painful pictures on innumerable occasions was difficult but Vivian could see it brought a measure of comfort to the grieving parents because they learnt what really happened from a friend who was with their daughter on that terrible day.

Other events that stood out were brother John's marriage to a pretty ex-Air Force girl, Laura Farrell, and Vivian's transfer to the blood bank at Heidelberg Hospital at the same time that her two years' leave of absence was approved.

Betty, who had contracted tuberculosis in prison camp, was forced to retire from her position at the Nurse's Memorial Centre due to continuing ill health. This occurred not long before their intended departure date. Following a hectic round of farewells to relatives and friends the two travellers sailed out of Melbourne in September of 1950 aboard the *Arawa*, a ship of 14,491 tons.

The *Arawa* called in at Adelaide where John and his new bride whisked Vivian and Betty off to see Eva. Then it was on to Fremantle, and a welcome by Mrs Riches and members of the Western Australia ex Prisoner's-of-War Association whose arms were full of flowers for the two nurses.

Arriving in London, Vivian and Betty settled into the Strand Hotel and while looking for more inexpensive lodgings looked up a number of people, one of who was Air Commodore Modine. The last time they had seen Modine was at the Chinese School in Meulo, just out of Palembang, during the first few months of their capture.

There were also invitations for them to visit with the Marquess of Queensberry, the Duchess of Gloucester, Lieutenant-General Arthur E. Percival, the General Officer Commanding in Malaya at the time of the surrender of Singapore, the Matron-in-Chief and Director of Army Nursing Services and the High Commissioner for Australia.

Then the letter that thrilled the two Australians arrived.

Marlborough House S.W.1
15th November 1950
Dear Madam,

I am commanded by Queen Mary to write and say that Her Majesty is glad to know that you and Miss Jeffrey have arrived from Australia

The Queen would like to see you both but for the moment she is laid up with a particularly tiresome and obstinate cold.

Could you let me know how long you are going to be in London, as Her Majesty does not want to interfere with your plans, but particularly wants to see you at a time convenient to yourself as soon as her cold is really over.

Yours very truly
Cynthia Colville
Lady-in-Waiting

As the two women intended staying in London for some time they advised Lady Colville accordingly and went job-hunting. Friends were called on to help and soon the two had secured nursing positions at St. Mary's Hospital Paddington and at the same time moved into a bed-sitter in Kensington which was conveniently located near a small pub.

In the following February they received word that Queen Mary was rid of her cold and would be pleased to see them at Marlborough House.

When they asked the Charge Sister for a day off to meet the Queen Mother the rather sceptical woman refused to believe the two Australians. When shown the invitation her attitude changed dramatically and Sister became just as excited as Betty and Vivian.

Their meeting and talk with the diminutive eighty-four-year-old Queen Mary was a highlight in their lives. Her Majesty listened attentively to their account of the years spent in Japanese camps interrupting occasionally to put a question or seek clarification of a point. From these the girls deduced that the Queen Mother already knew a great deal about prison camps. The conversation then switched to British nurses in the Far East and finally, to nursing in Australia.

They talked for forty minutes at the end of which the Queen Mother presented them both with a signed portrait of herself and wished them well.

Once more out on the street they were so keyed up that the two went looking for a pub in which to celebrate.

Later that year Vivian applied for and was successful in obtaining a position as Sister-Receptionist in the Medical Section of the Department of Immigration at Australia House, Central London.

During the year, when work permitted, the two friends travelled extensively throughout Great Britain and Europe and it came as a great disappointment to Vivian when Betty decided it was time to return to Australia..

Vivian stayed on in London and Australia House, her spare time taken up with forays into the English countryside, and with visits to the theatre and friend's homes. The draw of Australia however proved too strong for her and in September 1953 Vivian boarded the Orient Line's *Oronsay* for the long voyage home.

*Vivian Bullwinkel, left, with Betty Jeffrey in Nareen Victoria in 1950
at a dedication ceremony to the fallen of World War Two.
(V. Bullwinkel collection)*

Betty Jeffrey pelts Vivian with a snowball during their London visit
and prior to their audience with the Queen Mother. November 1950.
(V. Bullwinkel collection)

Countess Mountbatten of Burma meets Sister Vivian Bullwinkel at the
Repatriation General Hospital, Heidelberg during a visit in April, 1956.
(V. Bullwinkel collection)

*Vivian Bullwinkel places a wreath on the unveiling of the
Australian War Memorial at Kranji, Singapore in March 1957.
(V. Bullwinkel collection)*

FAIRFIELD DAYS

In the years following her return to Australia Vivian was to rise steadily to the pinnacle of her profession.

In 1955 she was appointed Assistant Matron at Heidelberg Hospital. Offered the rank of Lieutenant-Colonel in the Citizen Military Forces in that same year, Vivian accepted and became the Commanding Officer of 3 Royal Australian Army Nursing Corps Southern Command.

Despite her aversion to study Vivian was awarded a Diploma in Nursing Administration at the College of Nursing in 1959. This led to her appointment as Matron of Fairfield Hospital in Victoria with an annual salary of 1,350 pounds 78 pounds for certificates and 100 pounds travelling expenses.

The Queen's Memorial Infectious Diseases Hospital at Fairfield was opened in 1904 to fill a need in the community, for despite immunisation campaigns and antibiotics the management of a great variety of severe and communicable diseases was a rising problem and the demand for beds was increasing.

Initially the hospital was occupied by diphtheria and scarlet fever patients but as more complex diseases began to appear amongst the rising population, Fairfield was expanded to include an isolation and observation block and subsequently three additional wards.

Under Vivian's guidance Fairfield also became a specialised teaching hospital for both Monash and Melbourne Universities.

She encouraged registered nurses to develop their qualifications by pursuing tertiary studies, knowing new medical technologies and procedures needed nurses who could cultivate formal skills.

Using her high profile and credibility within the Australian community, Vivian tried to communicate her thoughts on tertiary education to a public and a media whose harboured image of a nurse was that of 'wife and mother.' This perceived vulnerability, submissiveness and dependence categorised nursing as an occupation and not a profession.

In her battle for the development of higher qualifications for nurses she argued that, " if a nurse was to be recognised and hold a senior position then she must have the appropriate piece of paper." Although supported by the majority of hospital-trained nurses, Vivian had her detractors.

This did not impede her for she had developed during her lifetime a deep understanding of the behavioural pattern of human beings and a trait, common to many, was the fear of change.

To Vivian this was a challenge to be met head on. To convince the minority that higher education for nurses was the path to the future she turned to Fairfield Infectious Diseases Hospital and its nursing staff.

Fairfield Hospital, at that time, was suffering from an acute shortage of nurses who were competent in the treatment of infectious disease.

With the full support of the hospital's Board of Management Vivian established an independent Nurse's Aide School which was officially recognised and accredited by the Victorian Nursing Federation in 1964.

Graduates could then go on to a specialised post-basic course followed by one specifically for fevers. This brought a Nursing Aide to the approximate level of a second-year general nursing student and quickly provided the hospital with a flow of highly trained staff.

The first year's result was highly satisfying for both Vivian and the hospital, overcoming as it did, the shortage of specialised staff and increasing the overall efficiency. It also silenced a lot of her critics.

With her nursing career in full flight and her time totally devoted to her work Vivian was happy with her life and the way it had turned out. Then, in 1966 came the crushing news of the death of her brother John, from a massive heart attack, at the age of 46. The grief of losing her beloved father to a heart attack was now revisited and it seemed unfair that her brother should survive a war to die so young, at work.

Vivian attended John's funeral in Adelaide with her mother Eva.

Infrequently, Vivian would take a weekend off to visit Melbourne for she loved live theatre and would invariably stay at the Naval, Military & Airforces' Club, an establishment for retired and serving officers.

With excellent accommodation and dining facilities and centrally located, it suited her to stay overnight rather than rushing to get the late train.

It was on one of these weekend visits that she was introduced to a former World War Two Lieutenant-Colonel who was at the time serving with the Citizen Military Force's at Divisional Headquarters.

Frank Statham was a tall, well-built man, handsome and with a decisive air that gave Vivian the impression he was used to commanding and leading others. She was immediately attracted to him.

They talked for some time, mainly about the Army and her work at Fairfield, until it was time to leave to catch a show she was going to. Later that night, in the comfort of her room at the Club, she mused about her meeting with Frank Statham. He was such a charming man, with an excellent sense of humour, so very polite and with eyes that always appeared to be smiling at her. 'I wonder,' she asked herself, 'if I will see him again?' Then, with second thoughts, agreed it was most unlikely and her time would be better served thinking about Fairfield.

Vivian was however destined to meet again with Frank Statham.

Granted leave from Fairfield to carry out her 14 days annual training commitment with the C.M.F. Vivian walked in to the Officers' Mess at Puckapunyal and introduced herself to the President of the Mess Committee.

There were a number of officers present and the PMC introduced her to each one including Frank Statham.

"How nice to see you again Colonel." he said extending his hand to her.

"And you Colonel," she replied slightly flustered, " I didn't recognise you at first in your uniform."

They shook hands and he asked if she would like a drink and ordered the whisky and soda from the steward before they sat by the fire.

As he chatted Vivian learnt that Frank was an engineer, originally from Sydney, who worked in the head office of the Department of Works in Melbourne.

As a boy he had grown up in the Solomon Islands where his father ran a plantation. His father died in his early forties of a virulent strain of malaria and young Frank was brought back to Australia to complete his education.

At the outbreak of war in 1939 he enlisted in the AIF, joined the Australian Sixth Division and sailed with the advance party for the Middle East. Later he was transferred to the newly raised Ninth Division as their Commander, Royal Electrical and Mechanical Engineers.

He served with that Division during the Germans' seven-month-long siege of Tobruk, becoming one of the 'Rats.' This was a nickname derived by the Australians from a statement made by the British traitor turned German broadcast commentator, William Joyce, who was referred to as 'Lord Haw Haw' by the British forces.

In one of his broadcasts Joyce claimed that, "the Australians in Tobruk were like rats in a trap," and so was born the name proudly claimed by the men of the Australian Ninth Division, the 'Rats of Tobruk.'

As he spoke, Vivian could not help comparing their situations at the time for while Frank was under siege by Field Marshal Erwin Rommel's all powerful Africa Corps, she was being measured for her A.A.N.S. uniform

By the time she took her leave from the Mess, Vivian had learned a great deal about Frank and her feelings told her that here was a man she could live out her life with in complete contentment. There was one aspect of Frank's life that she did not know about, his marital state, and it was important that this was brought out before she became too involved.

During the two weeks they were in Puckapunyal Frank was able to explain to Vivian that his wife Hazel was desperately ill with tuberculosis. The Department of Works had given him the opportunity to be its Director in Western Australia and the drier climate would be beneficial for Hazel.

Vivian agreed, yet she was bitterly disappointed at losing him at a time when she was beginning to enjoy their friendship.

Frank promised to keep in touch each time he visited Melbourne and it was on that note, at the conclusion of the training camp, Frank moved his family to Perth and Vivian returned to Fairfield.

****

Over the years Frank visited the Department's head office on a number of occasions and always stayed at the Naval Military & Airforces' Club. On his arrival he would ring Vivian at Fairfield and arrange for her to join him for dinner.

It was an easy going friendship based on mutual respect and common interests and both enjoyed the few brief hours they were able to spend together over dinner.

Relaxed, they would bring one another up to date with what had happened in the interim since they last met.

Vivian told Frank of her award of the Army's Efficiency Decoration. This had been for exemplary service spanning more than twenty years and she was very proud to have been recognised. Frank, at that stage, was involved in a mammoth project in the West which was the planning and building of the Royal Australian Naval Base on Garden Island, which he described as, "the highlight of his engineering life."

In 1973 Vivian was made a Member of the Order of the British Empire in the Queen's New Year's Day Honours List in recognition of her long and dedicated service to nursing and the community. Surprised by the appointment, for she felt she had only been doing her job, Vivian was kept busy answering the many phone calls and letters of congratulation.

The messages she cherished most were those sent by the girls of the 2/4th, 2/10th and 2/13th and the one from Frank.

The spotlight on Vivian lasted for several weeks as the press played up her O.B.E. and wartime experiences then it began to wane enabling her to concentrate on the task at hand, the running of a now very large hospital and her commitment to ex-servicemen and women's organisations.

SAIGON RESCUE

It was a cold Sunday night in early April of 1975 and Vivian had settled into her easy chair in front of a large log fire in the Matron's apartment, with the intention of reading before retiring for the night.

It had been a long day as usual with a number of knotty problems to sort out and she just wanted to relax with a good book and her tiny Chihuahua dog "Tao" who was curled up at her feet.

The jangling of the telephone brought a look of resignation to her face and she reached over and picked up the handpiece and spoke into it.

"Matron speaking."

"Good evening Matron," said the voice on the other end of the line, which she immediately recognised as belonging to Doctor Forbes, the Medical Superintendent at Fairfield.

"Good evening Doctor," she replied, "what can I do for you?"

"Matron I want you to get together a nursing team of approximately fifteen nurses for a trip to Vietnam."

"Vietnam?" she queried.

"Yes we are bringing out up to 200 Vietnamese war orphans. They will come here to Fairfield and a lot of them will be very sick children. I'll lead the team with Doctor's Sandlands and Lucas."

Australia's involvement in the Vietnamese war had been going on since the 1960's and although Vivian was well-informed as to the tactical situation she was not aware of the plight of the children caught up in the savage fighting. The prospect of getting 'in country' and bringing out so many children appealed to her immensely and she communicated this to Doctor Forbes.

"When do you want us to be ready by?"

"Tomorrow," was the short reply.

"Then we will be ready."

"By the sound of your voice, Matron I take it you intend going yourself?"

"Why of course, Doctor," she said feeling her excitement grow as she began to plan the staff moves in her mind. "My Deputy Director of Nursing, Sister Lafferty, is more than capable of running things here, besides, I will need a person of her calibre to supervise the opening of additional wards to cope with the influx."

"Yes, very good," said Forbes, "we shall have a conference first thing in the morning. Good night Matron."

"Good night Doctor," she said and put the receiver down. Getting up from her chair Vivian crossed to her desk and pulling out a file started to flip through the hospital's staff records.

It soon became apparent to her that with the day by day requirements of the hospital and the work involved in opening at least three new wards, she would not be able to fill the requirement for 15 nurses. What she would have to do was recruit the balance from other hospitals. Picking up the phone she began dialling.

Several calls later, one of which was to the Matron at Heidelberg Hospital, Vivian had her full compliment of nurses and settled down at her desk to write an instruction covering the evacuation and reception of the children.

Working into the night she covered in detail the duties of those who were to be involved including the opening of Wards 9 & 15 as Admission Areas with two nursing teams responsible for bathing the children and facilitating their transfer to the appropriate Ward.

With the instruction finally finished she re-checked the names of those who were to go with her and noticed Val Seeger's name.

As the Charge Sister happened to be on duty that night Vivian decided to give her the news and went looking for Val anticipating her excitement at being included in the Vietnam party.

The atmosphere at Fairfield Hospital the next morning was feverish given the limitation on time to prepare for the departure and the need to maintain the normal level of patient care.

However by 0930 hours the considerable amount of equipment they were taking with them had been packed and the medical party was ready to go.

Taking aside her Deputy Director of Nursing, Sister Margaret Lafferty, Vivian assured her there was bound to be another evacuation and she would see to it that Margaret would lead the nursing team.

"Thank you Bully," said an appreciative Margaret and with smiles all round the doctors and nurses climbed aboard the bus and settled down for the drive to Heidelberg, where they would pick up the other nurses before proceeding on to Sydney's Kingsford Smith Airport.

Here a charter aircraft would take them to Bangkok where they would transfer to an R.A.A.F. C130 Hercules transport aircraft for the run to Saigon.

It was a travel-weary group that eventually arrived in Sydney late in the afternoon to be told they were to wait. At 7.00p.m. that night they were curtly informed that the airlift was off and they were to return to their hospitals at once and standby for further instructions.

The news was bitterly disappointing for Vivian and her tired nurses who were also beginning to feel a reaction to the cholera shots they had been given before leaving Fairfield. Although they were not given an explanation as to why the flight had been cancelled there was some consolation derived from the official announcement that they would travel back to Melbourne by aircraft and not by road.

Early the next day Vivian received a phone call at Fairfield Hospital informing her that the flight had been aborted because of a breakdown in negotiations with the South Vietnamese Government which the Australian Government was attempting to reopen.

Meanwhile, Vivian and her team were to remain ready to move at a moment's notice.

It would be two weeks before the order came through with an amendment. As only 80 children were to be taken out the staffing level was to be reduced to 22 from Heidelberg and 8 from Fairfield. The latter was to include 2 doctors, Sisters Seeger, Cornish, Piercy, McKrell, De Deug and Vivian.

Embussing for a second time they connected with their charter flight, a Qantas Boeing 707 and they lifted off from Kingsford Smith Airport at 1345 hours on a 8,249 mile, nine hour flight to Bangkok.

Vivian had divided the nursing staff into two teams. Team number two was to stay in Bangkok and convert the returning jet into a miniature hospital. The rear section was allocated to babies and children with serious symptoms, with the centre designated for normal nursing care for those without symptoms. The first class area was put aside for staff meals and rest.

Team number one was to transfer to the C130 Hercules for the two-hour flight to Saigon.

Here they would take the children on board and begin to sort them medically so they would be ready for the appropriate section on board the waiting jet at Bangkok.

There was a misunderstanding with the Thai authorities on landing at Bangkok, which resulted in a long delay until an Australian official could be rushed from the city.

By the time he sorted the problem out it was too late for number one team to proceed and there was a forced overnight stay.

Walking up the ramp into the C130 the next morning Vivian chose the first empty webbed seat and sat down

The noise of the aircraft's turbo engines drowned out all other sounds and made conversation with the other nurses almost impossible. Content to view the activity outside through the open cargo ramp Vivian began to automatically go over the evacuation procedure in her mind until the rising rear ramp cut off both the sunlight and the people outside.

With nothing of interest to look at Vivian let her eyes wander around the dimly lit interior of the huge transporter.

It was obvious to her that the Hercules had not been designed with passenger comfort in mind. The seating consisted of side mounted drop down aluminium seats with webbing back supports. In the central aisle and running the full length of the deck were dozens of packing cases at the end of which was the flight deck where the two Australian pilots sat high above everyone else.

The lack of air-conditioning had turned the interior of the aircraft into an aluminium sauna and because there was no insulation the huge tunnel reverberated to the sound of rumbling thunder as the powerful engines idled.

This changed suddenly and with the high pitched scream of a hundred banshees Vivian felt the Hercules move and they bumped their way toward the designated runway for take off.

215

With its four turbo boosted engines on full throttle the C130 gathered speed and lifted off from Bangkok for the two hour flight to Saigon.

Their approach to Ton Son Nhut airport, the busiest in the world at the time, was low and fast to minimise the risk of ground fire and they literally dropped out of the sky and landed.

Taxiing to the terminal the aircraft came to a halt and with the propeller blades still windmilling the aft ramp was lowered.

The two doctors, accompanied by Vivian, strode down the ramp's incline and headed for a small party of uniformed Australians who were waiting on the tarmac.

"Hello, I'm Forbes," said the doctor addressing the senior officer present, "where are the children?"

"On those two aircraft," replied the tall thin Air Force officer pointing to where two Hercules transports sat with engines running and loading ramps down, "they're ready to go."

Vivian immediately broke away from the group and strode back to where her team was waiting at the rear of their aircraft.

"Come with me," she shouted over the noise generated by multiple engines, " and bring everything with you."

"Excuse me." she heard a male voice shout and turning confronted an Air Force medical officer.

"This one," he shouted pointing to one of the waiting C130's, " contains children and toddlers, the other has all of the babies."

"Thank you." said Vivian and she hurried off to rejoin her nurses.

With cool efficiency she quickly allocated her girls to specific aircraft before boarding her own. No sooner was she seated than the Loadmaster activated the ramp and it began to rise. The lumbering giant trundled along the taxi way, turned into the wind and without hesitating roared off down the runway and lifted off.

As soon as they were airborne Vivian unbuckled her seat belt and began her inspection of the children. What she found distressed her deeply.

The babies were lying in cardboard boxes, two, and sometimes three to a box. Grimy, perspiring and with tear stained eyes these tiny scraps of humanity with pot bellies, spindly limbs and big dark liquid eyes reminded Vivian of the wasted children of the Japanese prison camps.

One child, who Vivian assessed as being 3 years of age, was so undernourished the authorities had mistakenly tagged her as being 18 months old.

As the two Hercules aircraft climbed away from Saigon heading for Bangkok and the waiting hospital jet, the medical team sprang into action.

The doctors moved swiftly amongst the children examining and recording their illness while the nursing staff dispensed liquids and comforted those who found the noise and alien surroundings terrifying.

The diseases identified by the doctors included intestinal infection, salmonella, shigella, intestinal parasitic infection, pediculi skin infection, boils, abscesses, scabies plus a multiplicity of unknown rashes. There were also cases of pneumonia, respiratory infection, varicella, pertussis, tuberculosis and malnutrition.

The team now realised they had a lot of very seriously ill children and that time was the enemy.

The transfer of the 80 orphaned Vietnamese children from the two Hercules aircraft to the Boeing 707 at Bangkok was carried out swiftly and efficiently.

With the enthusiastic assistance of the Thai authorities the way was cleared for their immediate clearance from the country and without delay the Qantas jet departed for Melbourne.

After completing a lightning tour of the jet, Vivian was satisfied that her number two team had done a great job in converting the 707 to a hospital configuration.

The environment within the jet aircraft contrasted dramatically with that of the C130's, being quieter and air-conditioned. The children responded accordingly, some dropping off into a sound sleep while others enthusiastically wolfed down food.

Their lack of table-manners as they shovelled it into their mouths did not appal Vivian, in fact her reaction was quite the opposite for it reminded her of the bitter humiliation and wretchedness of being constantly hungry and then finding food in abundance. She understood their needs and watched them eat with growing pleasure.

The staff worked throughout the night changing nappies, feeding babies, dispensing medicines, giving oxygen and checking I.V. fluids.

The Qantas flight attendants threw themselves into the programme with enthusiasm and prepared all of the formulas, cleared the countless bags of soiled nappies, cuddled children and prepared the meals for all on board. They became an important and integral part of the team and Vivian felt pride in the fact that here were fellow Australians pitching in to give these little Vietnamese waifs a chance to find a new life away from the terrors of their country's war.

The chartered Qantas Boeing touched down in Melbourne in a shower of spray from its wheels and they rolled up to the terminal building through the early morning fog where a fleet of ambulances awaited them.

The sleepy children were transferred into the vehicles and with Vivian and her staff aboard the convoy headed for Fairfield Hospital. They were all feeling a little flat for they had lost one of the babies in flight despite their efforts.

The staff at Fairfield was well prepared for their arrival and with seemingly little effort the tired, sick and very bewildered children were processed through to their wards. Their confusion was clearly reflected in their eyes and Vivian could only assume that not only did they not know what country they were in, they were also surrounded by uniforms.

Uniforms, to those children old enough to know, represented war, violence and death to them and in the weeks that followed this trauma manifested itself in varying forms.

Many over-ate until they realised that food was both plentiful and available to them every day. However, this did not stop them from hoarding what they could not eat under their pillows, mattresses and behind lockers against a day when there may be none.

For some the night held a different type of terror than those of spirits and monsters.

It was a fear of sleeping adjacent to a door or window, for even in their tender years they knew that these were the entry points for rocket-propelled grenades, small arms fire and soldiers.

These children would sleep on the floor beneath their beds and so the staff began moving their cots and beds into the middle of the room each night and left the lights burning.

With excellent medical treatment, good food and constant attention from a caring hospital staff the children began to improve dramatically in health. They became more content and relaxed and formed very close attachments with their favourite nurse, a feeling that was reciprocated by the women.

During the period of the orphan's convalescence the Australian Government had been screening the many Australian families who had applied for their adoption. Anxious to get them out into the community so they could begin to associate with children of their own age and start on an education, the authorities advised Vivian it was time to begin the adoption programme.

The first to leave were the older children.

Dressed in new clothes provided by the Australian Red Cross the first bus load was driven to the airport where two were to fly to Adelaide, two to Perth and three to Sydney. The remaining 6 were to be adopted out to Melbourne families.

The bus ride was a happy one, the children singing the simple songs they had been taught by the staff while at the hospital and they were still giggling when taken aboard the aircraft and buckled into their seats. Suddenly the laughter stopped as the children realised their favourite nurse was not going with them. With looks of disbelief on their tiny faces and tears welling in their eyes, the children's cries of anguish expressed their feelings for the only person who had been kind and loving towards them.

One by one the nurses, unable to control their emotions, were forced to flee from the aircraft with tears streaming down their cheeks.

They had all grown to love these un-named orphan children who came to them as so many numbers. In nursing them back to health many of the staff gave up their days off to be with them and with tenderness and understanding they slowly saw the terror in their eyes diminish, the nightmares stop and the laughter start. There was trust and a genuine love between the nursing staff and the children and the thought of never seeing their special child again was emotionally devastating for those nurses who had formed a close relationship with a little one. This same scene was to be repeated many times until all of the children were gone and the special wards at Fairfield Hospital were empty.

Several weeks' later letters began to flow into the hospital from the children's adoptive parents. Vivian and the staff read them with a deep feeling of satisfaction for they told of the progress of Mai Lee or Nguyon Nong, who were now Kristian and Tim and of many others who had adopted Australian names and lived in suburbs all over the country. Every letter expressed the parent's gratitude for the love and attention given to their adopted child, explaining that they never would have been so emotionally stable without the all-embracing care given to them by the nursing staff at Fairfield Hospital.

The letters continued to arrive over the years keeping Vivian informed as to the progress of the children and how happy they were to be in Australia.

The success of the Vietnam rescue mission reaffirmed Vivian's long held belief in the importance of nursing. She strongly believed in the one on one application of care and understanding which bound both nurse and patient in a common objective; the nurturing of the human spirit, the strengthening of the will to overcome mental defeat and so, stimulating a patient's resolve to recover. In Vivian's opinion there was no greater reward for a nurse than to see a fellow human being survive an illness and know that you had shared in that recovery.

****

On April 24 1977, the day before ANZAC Day, Roger Climpson, the host of the Australian national television series *This is Your Life* lured an unsuspecting Vivian onto the studio set.

During the next hour she heard the voices of life long friends and greeted many who the station had flown in to be with her that night.

Betty Jeffrey, whose daily account of camp life had been published under the title of *White Coolies* attended as did Mickey Syer, Silvia Muir and Nesta James. There was also surprise appearances of Dame Margo Turner, her nephew John Bullwinkel and his wife Libby, June Salter, the eminent Australian actor and Ken Brown who flew in to rescue the Australian Sisters. A special treat for Vivian however was the arrival of her close friend Wilma Young (nee Oram) with whom she had shared so much during the three and a half years of their imprisonment. Her mother Eva was unable to attend but sent a video clip saying how proud she was of her daughter.

It was toward the conclusion of the show when host, Roger Climpson, asked Vivian if she would tell her story for the benefit of the Australian viewing audience.

She spoke briefly of some experiences, glossing over others because she found the cold eye of the camera unnerving. There was also reluctance within her to share some of the emotionally disturbing details, such as the mass murder on the beach at Bangka with the large studio audience, for it smacked of sensationalism and her memories would not permit this. Simple as her account was it struck a responsive chord amongst the viewers and their letters flowed into the television station. The feeling expressed by the writers was one of admiration for a fellow Australian and a renewed pride in having been born in this great country.

Vivian was now 61 years of age and with the workload at Fairfield far from diminishing, was feeling the strain of the long hours she was forced to put in.

The latter stemmed from the wider use of drugs in the community which resulted in a higher incidence of hepatitis.

Earlier she had resigned from the Citizen Military Forces believing this would lighten the load. The demand placed on her by ex-service organisations to travel in support of their branches and requests from others to be a keynote speaker, or to dedicate a plaque, involved a considerable amount of time away from the hospital, which of course had to be made up.

Not wishing to compromise her responsibility to the ex-service organisations, which she considered her duty to support and recognising the danger in pushing herself too hard, Vivian thought of retiring from nursing.

It was also around this time that she heard from Frank Statham and the news that his wife Hazel had passed away following a protracted battle with cancer. Life was crushing in upon her and she had a need to change the pace, to slow down and spend time enjoying those things that pleased her. Meanwhile Vivian promised to complete the projects she had initiated at Fairfield before resigning and in the interim give serious thought to what she wanted to do with the rest of her life.

Some months later, Frank, who was the Chairman of the Inter-Departmental Co-Ordinating Committee of the Department of Works, rang and said he was coming to Melbourne and he would like to have dinner with her at the Naval, Military & Airforces' Club.

Vivian readily agreed thankful of the opportunity in which to share her thoughts of retirement with Frank and seek his opinion as to her future, which at this stage she was unsure of.

The conversation over dinner was relaxed as Frank described to Vivian aspects of the Stirling project which called for the construction of a causeway extending from the Western Australian mainland to Garden Island and the need to calculate the impact it may have on the ecology of the area

Vivian listened attentively for she was genuinely interested in his work as he was in hers. When he had finished with the subject and paused for a sip of coffee Vivian quietly said,

"Frank, I've been feeling a little tired lately and so I'm thinking of retiring."

She waited for him to comment, noting the solemn look that had appeared on his handsome face.

"You want to retire?" he said softly.

"Yes."

"Are you sure?"

"Yes I'm sure." she replied, wondering why he was so emphatic about confirming her decision.

"Then you had better retire in Western Australia."

A wry smile creased his mouth and Vivian caught her breath as she heard the words. Frank was asking her to marry him and it was the first time in her life she had received such a proposal.

Momentarily she reflected on the friendship they had shared over the years and concluded there was no reason why they couldn't productively share whatever life span awaited them given this mutual respect and affection they had for each another.

Her mouth widened in a warm and joyful smile.

"Alright," she said simply, "when?"

"When do you think?" asked Frank.

She considered his question for a moment before replying, "September, it's springtime in Perth."

"Then September it is," said Frank as he raised his hand to attract the steward's attention, "and I think this calls for a Port, don't you?"

Vivian could feel the weight of her worry and fatigue sliding away as the thought of her move to Perth and a future with the man she respected more than any other. Her feelings were similar to those she had experienced that day in the Headmaster's office when told she could play basketball with the Catholic School team. 'Life has once more been kind to me.' she thought then beaming back at Frank she answered his question. "I do too."

They were married on the 16th of September of that year in Perth at St. Margaret's Church, Nedlands, followed by a reception held in the Swan Barracks Officers' Mess.

Vivian then returned to Melbourne and Fairfield Hospital where she tendered her resignation and at the completion of her commitment there packed and with her 91 year-old mother headed for Western Australia and a new life as Mrs Vivian Statham.

A PROMISE FULFILLED

Settling into Frank's home in the leafy riverside suburb of Nedlands Vivian was in demand and found it difficult to refuse invitations involving ex-service associations and the community at large.

She became involved, at executive level, with the Army Wives' Association, Returned Sisters, Military Museum, Red Cross, Royal Humane Society, State War Memorial and the Naval, Military & Airforces' Club Of W.A.

She spoke to schools, prior to each ANZAC Day, of the true meaning of the ANZAC spirit and marched in the commemoration parade until such time as her feet would not permit her.

Vivian travelled to Canberra to deliver the Sir James Harrison Memorial Lecture to the graduating class of the Australian Defence Academy and to Townsville, Queensland, to give the Sister Elizabeth Kenny Oration.

It was in the course of these civic duties that she and Frank attended a Mayoral reception in 1992 for the Indonesian Ambassador to Australia.

Mingling with the guests, the conversation as usual at these types of functions was confined to light topics of interest which were reserved for such occasions.

Joining one group Vivian and Frank were introduced to several Indonesian officials one of whom, during the course of their conversation, mentioned Bangka Island.

Immediately Vivian was focused on the gentleman in question and she asked him if he knew the island, which he said he did and that he was very interested in promoting it as a tourist destination.

"Will you develop Muntok," she asked.

"Not initially," he replied, "we wish to develop Parai Beach Hotel as a resort and convention centre, it is on the opposite side of the island to Muntok."

"If you're going to promote Bangka," said Vivian, "I would like to see a memorial built there."

It was a spontaneous statement that had tumbled out of Vivian's mouth and for a moment she was amazed at what she had said. The Indonesian gentleman also appeared to be slightly confused and Frank, summing up the situation, stepped in and carefully explained Vivian's association with Bangka and the purpose of such a memorial.

He seemed to understand Frank's explanation and before excusing himself he turned to Vivian and smiling broadly at her thanked her for her company and the suggestion.

Casting the conversation from her mind as a little bit of serendipity Vivian concentrated on the next group of people Frank was leading her towards.

Shortly after their encounter with the Indonesian official Frank and Vivian were invited to attend that country's consulate to meet a visiting businessman.

Intrigued, they attended as requested and learned that the visitor had been born on Bangka and subsequently had become very successful in a number of fields including a Directorship of the Rolex watch company. A philanthropist, he had provided the money to build a school on Bangka to service the needs of a thousand pupils and had created a fund to support promising students through to tertiary level.

The reason why he requested a meeting was to reassure Vivian that he fully understood her motives for wanting a memorial built on Bangka and that he would assist in any way he could.

Vivian was taken by his charm and obvious sincerity and expressed her appreciation for his offer of support, to which he replied that it was his intention to pursue the matter on his return to Bangka Island.

Events moved very quickly after that meeting and a phone call from the Department of Veterans' Affairs advised Vivian of the whole-hearted support for her plan by the Minister, the Hon. Ben Humphreys MP and that of the Indonesian Government.

Several days later the Australian Army's Attache in Jakarta, Colonel A.J. Molan AM, phoned to say that the project had received the approval of the Central and Provincial governments as well as the Indonesian Army and Police. Molan went on to ask when it would be convenient for Vivian and Frank to fly to Bangka for a reconnaissance of the island and to select a suitable location for the memorial.

"You name it and we will be there." she said laughing.

"Right," said the Colonel, "we'll make all the arrangements and let you know."

Replacing the telephone handset Vivian looked at Frank, "It's really going to happen."

His gentle grin appeared, "Yes my dear, it's really going to happen."

It was a hot stifling day and the small party made its way down a jungle track to finally burst out of the green dankness of the jungle and into the relative coolness of an ocean beach.

Vivian gazed across the expanse of coarse yellow sand to the pastel blue sea beyond. There was a gentle swell with small curling waves rushing in to make a "plopping" sound as they flopped on the beach.

Lifting her eyes even higher to the blue sky above she traced the soft blue void down to the horizon where several wisps of cloud hung motionless on the stillness of the day.

It was so quiet, so unearthly quiet as if nature knew why she was there.

The stilled palm trees stood like silent sentinels and the jungle creatures withheld their calls as the people behind her began to fade from her sight and she was once more alone on the beach.

Clutching a posy of jungle flowers she had picked, Vivian hobbled towards the seashore, her silver hair glistening in the sun.

"Such a beautiful bay," she whispered as she paused to slip out of her shoes, "so beautiful."

She felt the coolness of the water and the roughness of the sand and as she waded deeper into the sea 51 years in time drifted away. Once more she was with her friends, once more she was fighting to understand why it had to happen?

Slowly, as if in a dream, her arm moved out towards the distant horizon and the posy arched into the air to tumble back and float on the peaceful surface.

It was the end of a long journey, one she had to make so Australians and the world would remember what had happened in this beautiful bay 51 years ago.

Vivian had fulfilled her promise....now she could cry.

On March 2 1993, a memorial was unveiled at Muntok on the island of Bangka and dedicated to the Australian Army Nursing Sisters who lost their lives in the Bangka Strait, on Radji Beach and in the prison camps of Bangka Island and Sumatra. Located on the beach near the lighthouse, which guided many survivors to the shore on that fateful night, it overlooks the waters where, some 10 miles out, the *Vyner Brooke* was sunk.

Vivian Statham and 6 surviving Sisters attended and took part in the ceremony.

The memorial was constructed through the generosity of P.T. Koba, and the land on which it stands was kindly made available by the Governor of South Sumatra.

The plaque on the simple but moving memorial reads:

8th AUSTRALIAN DIVISION
2ND AUSTRALIAN IMPERIAL FORCE

This memorial honours the heroism and sacrifice of members of the Australian Army Nursing Service who served in the Bangka area in the second world war during the years 1942-1945.

Lost at sea off Bangka Island when S.S. Vyner Brooke was bombed and sunk by Japanese aircraft on 14th February 1942.

Matron *O.D.Paschke*
Sisters:

L.M.Bates	M.H.M.Dorsch	G.M.McDonald	A.M.Trenerry
E.Calnan	C.M.Ennis	L.J.Russell	M.M.Wilton
M.D.Clarke	K.Kinsella	M.Schuman	

Shot and killed on Radji Beach by Japanese soldiers on 16th February, 1942.

Matron *I.M.Drummond*
Sisters:

E.L.Balfour-Ogilvy	D.G.H. Elmes	M.I.Hodgson	F.A.Salmon
A.M.Beard	L.F.Fairweather	K.L.Keates	E.S.J. Stewart
A.J.Bridge	P.E. Farmaner	J. Kerr	M.M.A. Tait
F.R. Casson	C.I. Halligan	M.E. McGlade	R.J. Wight
M.E. Cuthbertson	N. Harris	K.M. Neuss	B.Wilmott

Died in Japanese Prisoner-of-War Camps

Sisters:

D.S. Gardam	P.B. Hempsted	W.R. Raymont	L.A.Singleton

On Sumatra
Sisters:

W.M. Davis	*R.D. Freeman*	*G.L. Hughes*	*P.B. Mittelheuser*

Returned to Australia after being Prisoner-of-War 1942-1945
Sisters:

C.J.Ashton	*J.G.Doyle*	*A.B.Jeffrey*	*J.E.Simons*
K.C.Blake	*J.K.Greer*	*V.I.McElnea*	*V.E.Smith*
J.J.Blanch	*J.P.Gunther*	*S.J.M.Muir*	*A.C.Syer*
V.Bullwinkel	*E.M.Hannah*	*W.E.F.Oram*	*F.E.Trotter*
V.A.Clancy	*I.Harper*	*C.S.M.Oxley*	*J.Tweddell*
C.M.Delforce	*N.G.James*	*E.M.Short B.*	*B. Woodbridge*

Dedicated 2 March, 1993 in the presence of seven of the above ex-Prisoners-of-War including Matron Vivian Statham, AO ,MBE ,ARRC ,ED, (Sister V. Bullwinkel), sole survivor of the massacre at Radji Beach.

Vivian welcomes 'Jake' Jacobs to her home in Perth.
Jacobs, as a Royal Marines Major, headed the rescue party that released
Australian Army Nursing Sisters from the Japanese prison camp at
Lubuklinggau, Sumatra in 1945. (V. Bullwinkel collection)

Survivors from amongst the Australian Nursing Sisters revisit
Muntok Camp in 1993 and inspect the water well they used.
Left to Right: Pat Gunther (Darling), Kath McMillan (2/10th),
Jean Ashton, (part hidden) and Wilma Oram (Young)
(Author)

The memorial dedicated to the Australian Army Nursing Sisters who perished in the region during World War Two. Sited at Muntok, on Bangka Island, it is near where survivors of the Vyner Brooke *came ashore. Partly unfinished it was dedicated on the 2ⁿᵈ March, 1993. (Author)*

Colonel Coralie Gerrard, representing the Royal Australian Army Nursing Corps, escorts Vivian Statham (Bullwinkel) from the memorial where she layed a wreath following the dedication ceremony. (Author)

Frank and Vivian Statham at their home in Nedlands, Perth.
April 1996
(V. Bulwinkel collection)

POSTSCRIPT

In the years that followed the fall of Singapore in February of 1942, doubt has been cast upon the bravery and conduct of the men of the 8th Australian Division during the British retreat down the Malayan Peninsular and during the fighting on Singapore Island. The accusations have ranged from the Australians being an undisciplined and untrained mob, to running from the enemy.

Lt.Col. Denis Russell-Roberts, who was a young British Officer with the 5/11th Sikh Regiment at Ipoh, Malaya in 1941 stated in his book *Spotlight On Singapore,*

> "Some ugly things, I believe, have been said about the Australians. This no doubt is because of the few who put up terrible blacks along the sea-front of Singapore town when the evacuation of women and children was in train. Many of these may well have been from the untrained and undisciplined reinforcements which were thrown into Singapore at the last minute. But such stories should never have been allowed to detract from the fighting qualities of most of the 8th Division in Malaya.."

Russell-Roberts goes on to cite a number of heavy engagements involving battalions of the 8th Division concluding with. *"All these actions were worthy of the best Australian traditions."*

Proof of the Australian 8th Division's fighting ability is well recorded in a number of publications including "Ghosts in Khaki" and a "History of the 2/29th Battalion"

In the action at Germas the Australian 2/30th Battalion set an ambush for the Japanese which resulted in hundreds of enemy dead. This action also gave the British forces north of Yong Peng time in which to effect a successful withdrawal to Johore. The Battle of the Muar Road followed and the Australian 2/29th Battalion, with a troop of the 2/4th Anti-Tank Regiment, held a road block beating off countless attacks, inflicting heavy casualties and destroying ten Japanese tanks. This action again bought time for friendly forces moving south to new positions.

In the heavy fighting that followed the landing on Singapore Island by the 5 th & 18th Japanese Divisions together with 9 battalions of the Imperial Japanese Guards, the 8th Australian Division, with only three battalions, held the beach until overwhelmed. Falling back to the Jurong Line they continued to fight doggedly with bullet and bayonet, street by street, until the guns fell silent on the surrender of the island by Lieutenant-General Percival.

The battle deaths of the 8th Division bear stark testament to their bravery.

In five short weeks of fighting nearly 2,500 men were killed, representing approximately one third of all Australian Army battle deaths in the three and a half years of the Pacific War.

As Prisoners-of-War of the Japanese, combined with their killed in action, the 8th Australian Division lost over 10,000 men or, 66% of the total Australian Army deaths in the war against Japan.

What more could the 8th give to prove their valour?

Surviving Australian Army Sisters continue to keep in touch.

Vivian also enjoys visits from Betty Kenneison, now Mrs Edith Leembruggen, who moved to Perth to live not far from her friend.

Vivian, in the late nineties, suffered a stroke and was rushed to Perth's Hollywood Hospital, where she and the other Sisters stayed in 1945.

She survived the stroke mainly due to the wonderful effort on the part of the medical and nursing staff at Hollywood Hospital and following intensive treatment eventually she returned to her home and Frank.

Vivian faced a long period of therapy, however, with the support of the Department of Veterans' Affairs and her determination she went on to both walk and talk again.

Vivian and Frank now live in a Claremont village estate not far from their old home in Nedlands.

Vivian still attends the ANZAC Day parade where she watches from her vantage point next to the official dais and saluting base.

Her many friends and well wishers throughout Australia and other countries will feel happy in the knowledge that Frank's devoted care and understanding coupled with their mutual affection for one another has brought Vivian contentment in the closing chapters of a courageous life.

Norman G. Manners, Perth. 1999

The following inscription appears on the window of the Chapel of the Queen Elizabeth Hospital, South Australia and is dedicated to those nurses who served Australia in time of war.

When you go home
Tell them of us and say
For your tomorrow
We gave our today

VIVIAN STATHAM (BULLWINKEL)

EDUCATION:
Born Kapunda, South Australia, 18th December, 1915.
Morgan Street Kindergarten, North Primary, Broken Hill High School.
Captain of basketball, tennis and vigaro teams.
Captain Burke House 1932.
Captain of Broken Hill High School 1933.

NURSING
1934 Probationer-in-Training, Broken Hill & Districts Hospital
1938 Graduated at Broken Hill & Districts Hospital.
1939 Completed Midwifery.
1939 - 40 Staff nurse, Kiaora Private Hospital, Hamilton, Victoria.
1940 - 41 Jessie McPherson Hospital Melbourne.
1940 Enlisted in the Australian Army Nursing Service, Australian Imperial
      Force.
1941 - 45 Overseas service and Prisoner-of-War Bangka Island and Sumatra.
1950 - 55 St. Mary's Hospital & Australia House, London
1959 Diploma in Nursing Administration.
1947 - 61 Charge Sister & Assistant Matron Heidleberg Repatriation Hospital,
      Melbourne.
1961 - 77 Director of Nursing, Fairfield Infectious Diseases Hospital, Victoria.

POST WAR MILITARY SERVICE
1955 – 70 Lieutenant-Colonel, 3 Royal Australian Nursing Corps Training
      Unit (C.M.F.) Southern Command.

THE RED CROSS
1964-69 Deputy Commandant and Nursing Adviser Australian Red Cross
1980 – 95 Chairperson, Women's Auxiliary Group, Hollywood
      Repatriation General Hospital, Perth.

NURSING ORGANISATIONS
1969 – 78 Vice President, Nurses Memorial Centre, Victoria.
1970 Council Member of the College of Nursing Australia.
1973 – 74 President of the College.
      Member and later Vice President, Victorian State Committee,
      C. of N.A.
Member of the Executive Committee of the Association of Directors of
      Nursing, Victoria.
Nurses Representative on the Nurses Wages Board, Victoria.

GENERAL

1964 – 69 First woman Trustee of the Australian National War Memorial, Canberra.

1972 – 74 Founder, Member and later President Soroptimists Club of Deakin.

1970 – 71 Chairperson, Liaison Committee for Victoria Outward Bound.

1976 Appointed to the Court of Directors of the Royal Humane Society.

1976 Honorary member for Western Australia, R.H.S.

Member of the Executive Committee Naval, Military & Airforces' Club of W.A.

Member of the Executive Committee of the Army Museum of Western Australia.

HONOURS & AWARDS

AO The Order of Australia. Part of the citation reads:

"Her heroism, courage and humanitarian achievements are unique."

MBE Member of the Most Excellent Order of the British Empire.

ARRC Associate of the Royal Red Cross.

ED The Efficiency Decoration. (Australian Military)

FRCNA Diplo'me De La Med'aille Florence Nightingale.

(The Florence Nightingale Medal)

Honorary Life Membership of the Australian Red Cross Society of W.A.

Selected by the National Heritage 200 Committee for inclusion in the Bi-Centennial publication *The People Who Made Australia.*

LAST POST

On the 3 December 1999 Frank Statham passed away, at the age of 83, following a short and unexpected illness. Vivian was by his side.

Although they were married for some 23 years, for Vivian the time appeared to fly as the two pursued an active life encompassing ex-servicemen & women's committee meetings and functions, memorial dedications, ship launchings and civic receptions together with regular trips overseas. The latter were mainly made to Vivian's favourite places Penang and Singapore.

Both Frank and Vivian were military Colonels in their own right and when this author enquired one day as to who was the senior officer of the two Frank replied without hesitation "Why Viv of course, she has one more gong than me." Then with a sly wink he added " And there's no way I am going to get the Florence Nightingale Medal!"

A devoted husband Frank took over as carer following Vivian's first stroke and continued as such up until the time he himself was forced to enter hospital with an unknown but debilitating illness. Following his death Vivian continued to fulfill her engagements as best she could, including the launch of this book in March of 2000, while harbouring a deep sense of loss and a lack of enthusiasm for life without her husband.

Six months later she was admitted to Hollywood Private Hospital and passed away, peacefully, on the 3 July at the age of 84.

The nation mourned the death of one of its favourite daughters and tributes to her life were carried in the news media of Australia and the United Kingdom. At a State Service, held in Saint George's Cathedral Perth on the 10 July, attended by Federal and State politicians, service chiefs and dignitaries, Veterans Affairs Minister Bruce Scott, in his eulogy, said "She was a unique Australian and extraordinary woman." Bishop Brian Kyme in his homily spoke of her as "A much-loved World War II army Sister who made a monumental contribution to easing the suffering of the sick and dying during and after the war." Fellow prisoners-of-war Wilma Young (Oram), Florence Syer (Trotter), Pat Darling (Gunther) and Jessie Hookway (Simons), who had flown in to Perth for the service, placed poppies on the flag-draped casket which carried Vivian's white veil, scarlet cape, medals and decorations. As the cathedral's bells peeled a farewell to this remarkable woman, members of the Australian Defence Force and service organizations bore her casket out into brilliant sunshine which momentarily had broken through the rain and overcast. Monday morning's traffic came to a halt as police guided the cortege along Saint George's Terrace with its buildings flying the Australian flag at half mast and sombre office staff silently looked down on the motorcade making its way to Karrakatta Crematorium and a private committal.

It was then Melbourne's turn to salute the lady they claimed as their own and in that city's cathedral on the 2 August the Victorian Governor, flanked by members of the Bullwinkel and Statham families with some 800 guests, joined in a service celebrating her life. It was, like that in Perth, a day to remember.

The final chapter in the life of Vivian Statham has been written yet her sparkling smile and spontaneous laughter will linger in the memories of all whose lives were touched by this warm and caring woman. Her life was nursing, her two great loves were Frank and her country.

Vale my Colonels.

Norman G Manners Perth, WA September 2000.

BIBLIOGRAPHY

I assembled a substantial amount of the facts used in this book from Vivian Statham during the course of some forty interviews extending over a period of six months fifteen hours of which was recorded. In addition I had complete access to Vivian's voluminous library which included writings, records, newspaper clippings and letters, some of the latter having been written to, and received from, her mother Eva during the period 1941 to 1947. These have been reproduced without editing.

Additional research material was obtained from interviews with surviving Sisters and relatives during the pilgrimage to Bangka Island in March of 1993.

Wilma Young (nee Oram) was particularly helpful.

Written recollections of daily life in the camps were obtained from Jenny Ashton and an account of the escape of the *Empire Star* from Singapore was recorded by Nell Dollman.

Other sources included Lex Arthurson's dairy of "The 13th A.G.H. 1941-1945" and Betty Leembruggen's (nee Kenneison) recollections as a child.

LIST OF PUBLISHED SOURCES

Jeffrey, Betty, *White Coolies* (Angus & Robertson. 1954)

History of the 2/29th Battalion 8th Australian Division. A.I.F.
(2/29th Battalion Association. 1983)

Simons, Jessie, Elizabeth *While History Passed*
(William Heinemann Ltd. 1954)

Glover, E.M. *In Seventy Days-The Story Of Malaya*
(Frederick Muller Ltd 1949)

Jacobs, Gideon Francois, *Prelude to the Monsoon*
(Purnell & Sons. S.A. Pty. Ltd. 1965)

Cooper, Leo, *Singapore's Dunkirk*
(Octopus Publishing Group1989)

Russell-Roberts Denis *Spotlight On Singapore*
(Times Press & Anthony Gibbs & Phillips 1965.)

Cody, Les, *Ghosts in Khaki*
(Hesperian Press 1997.)

INDEX